Education Policy Unravelled

Second Edition

Gillian Forrester and Dean Garratt

Bloomsbury Academic
An imprint of Bloomsbury Publishing Plc

B L O O M S B U R Y
LONDON · OXFORD · NEW YORK · NEW DELHI · SYDNEY

Bloomsbury Academic

An imprint of Bloomsbury Publishing Plc

50 Bedford Square	1385 Broadway
London	New York
WC1B 3DP	NY 10018
UK	USA

www.bloomsbury.com

BLOOMSBURY and the Diana logo are trademarks of Bloomsbury Publishing Plc

First edition published 2012
Second edition published 2016

British Library Cataloguing-in-Publication Data
A catalogue record for this book is available from the British Library.

ISBN: HB: 978-1-4742-7005-2
PB: 978-1-4742-7006-9
ePDF: 978-1-4742-7007-6
ePub: 978-1-4742-7008-3

Library of Congress Cataloging-in-Publication Data
A catalog record for this book is available from the Library of Congress.

Cover design by Catherine Wood
Cover image © Manuela Schewe-Behnisch / EyeEm / Getty Images

Typeset by Integra Software Services Pvt. Ltd.
Printed and bound in India

Education Policy Unravelled

Second Edition

ALSO AVAILABLE FROM BLOOMSBURY

An Introduction to Education Studies
Edited by Sue Warren

Education Policy, Practice and the Professional
Jane Bates, Sue Lewis and Andy Pickard

Education Policy Research
Edited by Helen M. Gunter, David Hall and Colin Mills

The Study of Education: An Introduction
Jane Bates and Sue Lewis

From Gill, for Paul, Stacie and Natalie.

From Dean, for William and Alex.

Contents

List of Tables

Preface

This book is written for those who are interested in education policy, which we find most intriguing. We recognize that many readers will be students and, we assume, are planning to work in the education sector or may be already doing so. With this in mind, our aim is to help and guide these students in their search for understanding. The book offers much more than 'acts and facts', and, as such, we hope our critical gaze on education policy will enable readers to make better sense of developments in education, as well as the education contexts in which they may find themselves, in order to form their own opinions and philosophies.

Note on the second edition

The first edition of *Education Policy Unravelled* provided a wide-ranging analysis of education policy from the late-nineteenth century up until the beginnings of the Coalition government, when many policies were still in their embryonic stages. Reviews of the first edition in 2012, as given in its text, noted:

> Education policy is a subject of constant praise and condemnation. Especially when, as at present, radical changes are being made in England … But such praise or condemnation would benefit from a deeper and more philosophical understanding of what we mean by policymaking. This book provides, in a most accessible style, that understanding … A most valuable additional to educational books at a time when this kind of analysis is much needed.

An accelerated pace of change in education occurred under the Coalition government (2010–2015), a trend which continues into the current Conservative administration. The second edition encapsulates and analyses the most recent educational reforms and restructuring. This new edition scrutinizes the duration of the Coalition's term in government and takes an informed and retrospective critical gaze of the period in question. We build upon the first edition's historical and contemporary analyses, and explore, make sense of and integrate the former Coalition and present Conservative governments' approaches to education policy.

Acknowledgements

We would like to acknowledge and thank the following people:

Rachel Shillington of Bloomsbury Publishing, for her support in providing the opportunity for this second edition.

Maria Giovanna Brauzzi of Bloomsbury Publishing, for her timely assistance during the process.

The anonymous referees whose feedback in the early stages helped shape the book.

Abbreviations

ALI	Adult Learning Inspectorate
AST	Advanced Skills Teacher
CBI	Confederation of British Industry
CPR	Cambridge Primary Review
CPRT	Cambridge Primary Review Trust
CTC	City Technology College
DCSF	Department for Children, Schools and Families
DENI	Department of Education in Northern Ireland
DES	Department of Education and Science
DFE	Department for Education
DfE	Department for Education
DfEE	Department for Education and Employment
DfES	Department for Education and Skills
DH	Department of Health
DTI	Department of Trade and Industry
ECM	Every Child Matters
EHC	Education, Health and Care
EMA	Education Maintenance Allowance
EPPE	Effective Provision of Pre-School Education
ERA	Education Reform Act
EYFS	Early Years Foundation Stage
FE	Further education
FEU	Further Education Unit
GCSE	General Certificate of Secondary Education
HE	Higher education
HEFCE	Higher Education Funding Council for England
HEI	Higher education institutions
HMI	Her Majesty's Inspectorate
KNWS	Keynesian National Welfare State
LA	Local authority
LEA	Local Education Authority
LMS	Local Management of Schools
LSC	Learning and Skills Council

MP	Member of Parliament
NCC	National Curriculum Council
NCSL	National College for School Leadership
NCVQ	National Council for Vocational Qualifications
NSP	National Scholarship Programme
NSS	National Student Survey
NVQ	National Vocational Qualification
OECD	Organization for Economic Cooperation and Development
Ofsted	Office for Standards in Education/Office for Standards in Education, Children's Services and Skills
PGCE	Post-Graduate Certificate of Education
QCA	Qualifications and Curriculum Authority
QTS	Qualified Teacher Status
SCAA	School Curriculum and Assessment Authority
SEAC	School Examinations and Assessment Council
SEN	Special educational needs
SSLP	Sure Start Local Programmes
TA	Teaching Assistant
TTA	Teacher Training Agency
TEC	Training and Enterprise Council
TVEI	Technical and Vocational Education Initiative
UK	United Kingdom
UNESCO	United Nations Educational, Scientific and Cultural Organization
UNICEF	United Nations Children's Fund
USA	United States of America
UTC	University Technical College

1

Introduction:
The Development of Education
Policy in the Modern Era

The nature of education policy

This book explores the nature of education policy, attempting to 'unravel' its meaning in the broadest and narrowest senses. The purpose of the book is to disaggregate education policy so that significant features and characteristics of policy-making and a number of related issues can be dismantled, separated out and examined in depth in order to illuminate particular and important enduring themes and trends as well as encourage the reader to engage in deeper exploration. It is never possible to examine education policy purely on its own as a single, discrete entity. Education policy-making does not 'happen' in a vacuum or bubble, but is subject to a range of competing influences, which can be broadly categorized under the umbrella of social, political, economic, technological, religious and cultural factors. The book therefore examines education policy in the context of a range of constituting factors which have all influenced and continue to impact education in a variety of ways. Education policy is constantly changing, and, over time, different factors have had different levels of prominence; so education systems, organizations, educational activities, learners and those working in education have been shaped in a variety of ways at different points in time. Adding to this complexity is an assortment of different individuals, groups, events, movements, ideologies and perspectives, which may in some way contribute to and shape policy 'problems' and 'solutions' at different historical moments. Our overriding aim in writing the book therefore rests upon conceptually 'undoing' and critically analysing the threads which together constitute the intricately woven tapestry of education and policy-making. Using concrete examples and pertinent illustrations from a variety of sources, we aim to facilitate readers' understanding of key policy issues, facilitate an appreciation of the 'contested terrain' (Ozga, 2000) of education policy research and bring life to the field of education policy. The book combines a broadly chronological approach to developments in education policy with extended analysis on specific issues, as appropriate. The tables given here contain political parties in UK government (Table 1.1), the title of the department responsible for education (Table 1.2), secretaries of state in office (Table 1.3) along with relevant dates. They are intended to provide readers with a quick reference in order to help facilitate their understanding of the political contexts of education reform and change.

The term 'policy' could be regarded as 'obvious' and fairly comprehensible in its own right. However, 'policy' is an often quite loosely used term and therefore can be defined and understood in different ways. In its narrowest form, policy can be considered as a statement of intent – something which is written down in a policy

Table 1.1 British governments since 1970

Political Party (Prime Ministers)	Period of Administration
Conservative Edward Heath (1970–1974)	1970–1974
Labour Harold Wilson (1974–1976) James Callaghan (1976–1979)	1976–1979
Conservative Margaret Thatcher (1979–1990) John Major (1990–1997)	1979–1997
(New) Labour Tony Blair (1997–2007) Gordon Brown (2007–2010)	1997–2010
Conservative–Liberal Democrats Coalition David Cameron (2010–2015)	2010–2015
Conservative David Cameron (2015–)	2015–

Table 1.2 Government departments responsible for education

Name	Duration
Committee of the Privy Council on Education	1839–1899
Education Department	1856–1899
Board of Education	1899–1944
Ministry of Education	1944–1964
Department of Education and Science (DES)	1964–1992
Department for Education (DFE)	1992–1995
Department for Education and Employment (DfEE),	1995–2001
Department for Education and Skills (DfES)	2001–2007
Department for Children, Schools and Families (DCSF)	2007–2010
Department for Education (DfE)	2010–

Table 1.3 Secretaries of state since 1970

Name	Political Party	Period of Office	Appointment
Margaret Thatcher	Conservative	June 1970–March 1974	Secretary of state for education and science
Reginald Prentice	Labour	March 1974–June 1975	
Fred Mulley	Labour	June 1975–September 1976	
Shirley Williams	Labour	September 1976–May 1979	
Mark Carlisle	Conservative	May 1979–September 1981	
Sir Keith Joseph	Conservative	September 1981–May 1986	
Kenneth Baker	Conservative	May 1986–July 1989	
John MacGregor	Conservative	July 1989–November 1990	
Kenneth Clarke	Conservative	November 1990–April 1992	
John Patten	Conservative	April 1992–July 1994	Secretary of state for education
Gillian Shephard	Conservative	July 1994–July 1995	Secretary of state for education
		July 1995–May 1997	Secretary of state for education and employment
David Blunkett	Labour	May 1997–June 2001	Secretary of state for education and employment
Estelle Morris	Labour	June 2001–October 2002	Secretary of state for education and skills
Charles Clarke	Labour	October 2002–December 2004	
Ruth Kelly	Labour	December 2004–May 2006	
Alan Johnson	Labour	May 2006–June 2007	

Name	Political Party	Period of Office	Appointment
Ed Balls	Labour	June 2007–May 2010	Secretary of state for children, schools and families
Michael Gove	Conservative	May 2010–July 2014	Secretary of state for education
Nicky Morgan	Conservative	July 2014–	

document, for example, and an expression of policy-makers' plans, objectives or policy descriptions of practice. In this sense, policy can be regarded as static and fixed. Trowler (2003: 95), referring specifically to education, offers the following lucid explanation of policy as 'a specification of principles and actions, related to educational issues, which are followed or which should be followed and which are designed to bring about desired goals'.

In his conceptualization of policy, Ball (1993) makes a clear distinction between policy as 'text' and policy as 'discourse'. Regarding policy as text, Ball (1993) suggests this is concrete and exists as a written representation of policy; it is 'read'. However, Ball (1993) recognizes that while policies are officially put forward in policy documentation, it is important to comprehend that policies are unlikely to stay fixed since they are typically reworked through speeches, media interviews, 'spin', reports, the agendas of particular individuals and so on. It is highly unlikely that policy unfolds straightforwardly from formulation to implementation and operates at the ground exactly as policy-makers originally intended. Ball (1993) thus acknowledges the contested, changing and negotiated character of policy which is usually an outcome of struggles and compromises between different individuals, groups and interests involved in policy-making. A broader, more encompassing view, therefore, is not just to think of policy as a product or an outcome (such as a policy document), but rather as a *process* which is ongoing, interactional and unstable (Ozga, 2000). So in this sense policy can be considered dynamic. Accordingly, Considine (1994: 3) provides the following definition of policy:

> In a sense everything in the policy world is really just process, the movement of people and programs around common problems such as education, transport and employment. None of these initiatives in these fields stays fixed for very long because the problems themselves keep moving and changing.

We will explore the view of policy as a process further, but first we give consideration to a common-sense concept of public policy as something constructed within the 'machinery' of government, which we can regard as 'big-P' policy. Big-P policy comprises two key features: formal policy and informal policy. In its 'formal' sense, big-P policy is sanctioned by the government and usually legislated. In its 'informal' sense, big-P policy may constitute government-approved policy initiatives which are not legislated and may reflect certain pressures from the ground level or public expectations. One example of formal 'big-P' policy is the decision in 2010 by the UK's Conservative–Liberal Democrat Coalition government to introduce variable tuition fees of up to £9,000 in England, following a review of higher education (HE) funding and student finance (Browne, 2010). This policy aimed to reduce public expenditure and overhaul student funding arrangements. It resulted in transferring the cost of undergraduate tuition fees from the state to the student (see Chapter 7); the devolved nations[1] followed suit, albeit offering different kinds of financial support to home students (of which, more below).

Staying with the notion of big-P policy and discerning policy as a process, we draw on Trowler (2003), who suggests the dynamism of policy is due to a number of sources. First, there is usually conflict of some sort between policy-makers' intentions and those people who implement policies; so there will typically be differences between the rhetoric of policy and the reality of the enactment of policy on the ground. Second, it is important to appreciate that policy can be subject to many different interpretations, which are influenced by different standpoints and interests. In this sense the interpretation of policy can be considered as an active process. Third, the implementation of policy in practice often means the outcomes differ from policy-makers' intentions. Policy intentions, as described, are as a rule usually numerous and often of a contradictory nature. As Ball (1994: 10 cited in Trowler 2003: 96) succinctly captures this form of dynamism, 'Policy is both text and action, words and deeds, it is what is enacted as well as what is intended. Policies are always incomplete insofar as they relate to or map on to the "wild profusion" of local practice.'

The example provided above regarding HE demonstrates the convolution of a policy decision and its impact at ground level. Due to the devolved nature of the government in the UK what subsequently transpired in HE is a situation where from 2012 students living in England are required to pay up to the full £9,000 tuition costs in whatever UK university they attend. In contrast, students living Scotland can study at Scottish universities for free; yet, if they study at a university in England, they are required to pay up to £9,000 tuition fees. For Welsh students, however, fees are subsidized by the Welsh government and they are only required to pay partial tuition fees (£3,810 in 2015) wherever they study in the UK. Students living in Northern Ireland are required to pay £3,805 (in 2015) if they study in Northern Ireland, but up to £9,000 elsewhere in the UK. This particular big-P policy demonstrates how the decision of a government to raise the cap on tuition fees and cut most ongoing direct public funding for tuition (in England), brought about largely as a result of a set of economic factors, will have multiple repercussions. Leaving aside the impact on universities, the consequences for the individual student are tremendous and for many students this policy results in greater levels of personal debt. Others may consider that going to university is not financially feasible and are thus deprived of HE as a vehicle for improving one's opportunities for social mobility. The fee regime also affects students' expectations of HE (Bates and Kaye, 2014).

At another level, we acknowledge there are policies which are formed and enacted within localities and institutions; these could be thought of as 'little-p' policies. 'Little-p' policies might be, for example, in a secondary school or college of further education where there is a policy on homework which has been specifically designed within and for that particular institution. This book is primarily concerned with big-P policy, however, and it is to this policy process that we now turn.

The policy process

The practice of policy-making at the national level is complicated and complex. Policy-making is not necessarily a linear or logical process, but often the reconciliation of competing ideas and interests, compromises and trade-offs. Initial ideas can emerge from pieces of commissioned or non-commissioned research, different government departments, the civil service, political 'think tanks' and/or pressure groups keen to exert themselves in order to effect change. As Apple (1990) suggests in relation to the nature of competing ideologies, political tensions in policy-making are inevitable as groups with different vested interests compete for power in the struggle to make their voice heard. The formalization and formation of policy is often a convoluted process, where initially around fifteen to twenty ideas are given parliamentary time each session. From here such ideas are considered and debated, and a small number will later be selected by the Cabinet of the presiding government to become Green Papers containing big questions about policy direction and what is to be achieved.

Essentially, Green Papers are an exploratory consultative exercise, presenting a preliminary report of government proposals to stimulate public discussion and further debate around particular salient issues and themes. Often they will contain questions that the government would like the public to consider and answer, and this is where resistance is most likely to arise as different stakeholders begin to query and question aspects of the proposal under consideration. In practice, Green Papers are often commissioned by the relevant government department under circumstances in which its administration feels there is an area where new legislation is needed, or indeed where existing legislation requires some modification or amendment. Significantly, however, Green Papers make no formal commitment to action, but rather provide an opportunity for open debate and represent perhaps the first stage in the process to changing a law. Some proposals, particularly controversial ones, can take a great deal of time at this stage, before entering the report stage where Members of Parliament (MPs) are later able to introduce their thoughts and feelings (of which, more below).

Subsequently, the feedback provided from wider public consultation and research carried out by government departments in relation to the Green Paper is used to inform the production of a White Paper. White Papers are issued by the government as a statement of policy, setting out more detailed proposals for legislative change or the introduction of a new law(s). Again, there are usually opportunities for the public to comment on White Papers although such papers represent a much bolder statement of intent or precursor to a Bill, which is a draft law. In some cases, a single White Paper will transform into a Bill; in others, there may be several White Papers combined in one Bill or, alternatively, several Bills emerging from a single White Paper.

Bills are debated by MPs and members of the House of Lords and cannot usually be influenced, at this stage, by the public. Sometimes it is possible, however, to lobby individual Lords or encourage an MP to table an amendment to a Bill, or possibly influence how they might vote. The formalization of policy occurs through a series of readings after the Bill is first introduced to the House of Commons; this is the first reading. The second reading is an open debate of the Bill by members of the House, which can sometimes be followed by a vote, although Bills introduced by the government tend to be accepted by their own MPs. The Committee Stage follows, in which a cross-party committee has the role of debating, amending and agreeing each clause of the proposed Bill before it is put to a vote in both Houses of Parliament (Commons and Lords), where its content is formally agreed and passed. A Bill does not officially become an Act (i.e. law) until it has been granted royal assent, which requires the Queen to agree with the Act and is usually a formality.

Ideology and discourse

The purposes of education are contested; different assumptions can be made about what education should be doing, who should be doing what and how it should be done. We deal with the aims of education elsewhere (see Chapters 2 and 7). The point we intend to make here is that education cannot be regarded as a neutral concept; it is paramount, when exploring education, to examine the relationship between policy and ideology. 'Ideology' is a widely used term with several meanings, each of which has different implications for the process of policy formation. Historically, the term was first coined by a group of French intellectuals called 'ideologues', operating at the heart of the French Enlightenment. For them, ideology was simply an expression for the 'science of ideas', the basis for establishing authentic knowledge and truth about the social world. In the aftermath of the French revolution and following Napoleon Bonaparte's defeat at the hands of the Russian army in 1812, ideology was denounced for its 'false ideas' and so took on a more pejorative meaning. Later on, Marx and Engels adopted it in *German Ideology* to describe the distorted social and economic relationship between the ruling class (bourgeoisie) and proletariat (working class), where ideology had the effect of creating an 'illusion' or type of 'false consciousness', both of which pointed to a political environment producing distortions through doctrinaire thinking. As Apple (1990) suggests, ideology 'works' precisely because its persuasive rhetoric serves to disguise the vague quality of its underlying assumptions. Such disguised assumptions render ideology legitimate since there are always aspects of the concept that remain partly hidden, with the effect that if it appears 'real' it becomes so through its consequences.

Different doctrines or 'belief systems' about what counts as knowledge are shaped politically by dominant ideas, structures and historical patterns that in turn shape social and economic behaviour. Such ideological patterns do not represent 'objective' reality 'out-there', but rather reflect the views influenced by social and historical structures. The notion that ideology produces a scenario in which a minority *dominate* while the vast majority are *dominated* is based on a conflict theory of capital and production. This takes us well beyond the argument of simple abstract theoretical distortions to directly acknowledge the effect of ideology emerging from actual capitalist practices (Freeden, 2003). In this context, it is the 'propertied' class, the class of industrial capitalists (bourgeoisie/middle class), who control the means of production, distribution and exchange and the 'property-less', or large 'working class' (proletariat), who sell their labour for a wage, but unwittingly accept exploitation in the capitalist process. For Marx, the solution to the problem of ideology was revolution, where the proletariat (working classes) would eventually identify the hidden motives of the capitalists, rise against them and thus change the social order.

In contrast with ideology's pejorative meaning, it has also bequeathed a more positive one in the history of ideas. As Freeden (2003: 12–13) explains:

> while Marx condemned the social conditions under capitalism as the source of ideology illusion, Mannheim realized that it was a feature of any social environment to influence the thought processes of human beings and, moreover that knowledge was a 'co-operative process of group life'.

In this respect, ideology is not a 'falsehood' to be demystified but a manifestation of thinking or system of beliefs. Ideology thus represents a set of ideas and concepts about the social world in addition to the influence of important social and historical structures. This has resonance with the work of the French social theorist Michel

Foucault (1980: 118), who argued vigorously against the concept of ideology conceived as 'false consciousness': 'the notion of ideology appears to me to be difficult to make use of … like it or not, it always stands in virtual opposition to something else which is supposed to count as truth'. Indeed for Foucault, like Mannheim, there is no escaping the influence of different systems of ideas which can be only properly understood through historical analysis. In Foucault's (1980:131) idiom, ideology is 'truth' not a 'falsehood' or mere pernicious myth. It is

> a thing of the world: it is produced only by virtue of multiple forms of constraint. And it induces regular effects of power. Each society has its regime of truth, its 'general politics' of truth – that is, the types of discourse it accepts and makes function as true; the mechanisms and instances that enable one to distinguish true and false statements; the means by which each is sanctioned; the techniques and procedures accorded value in the acquisition of truth; the status of those who are charged with saying what counts as true.

Education policy is therefore influenced by different ideologies (political and educational), values, attitudes and beliefs. The period between 1945 and 1979 was fuelled by a social-democratic/one-nation, conservative perspective, whereby there was largely a political consensus about the purpose of education in reducing social inequalities, improving social mobility and creating a more meritocratic society. State intervention was deemed necessary to support educational provision and facilitate equality of opportunity. There was, however, a change in emphasis in the 1980s and 1990s and a shift away from the social-democratic consensus towards neo-liberalism and the market as the main source of resource distribution. Many initiatives were introduced to establish the conditions for a competitive market as part of the wider New Right agenda of change across the public sector. However, these were not true markets in the sense of the free market, but rather internal or 'quasi-markets' (Le Grand and Bartlett, 1997) that were highly structured with indicators to measure performance and regulated through inspection.

The political New Right represents a coalition of neo-liberal and neo-conservative thinking. The former promotes the virtue of a free-market economy as a more effective mechanism for the distribution of social resources, competition, privatization and individual liberty, while the latter privileges tradition, hierarchy, authority and social order. Neo-conservatism is committed to the regeneration of traditional moral values, authority, the virtues of a strong state and intervention of government to achieve these. Under neo-conservatism, individual liberty remains important but ultimately defers to the authority of established government and the concept of 'nation' (Scruton, 1980). Paradoxically, these strands came together under New Right ideology. Educational ideologies also inform and influence teaching and learning and comprise traditionalism (transmission of heritage, subject-centred), progressivism (child-centredness) and enterprise (emphasis on core skills, the workplace) (Trowler, 2003). Political ideologies can crudely be married up with educational ideologies as follows: social democracy – progressive; neo-conservatism – traditionalism; and neo-liberalism – enterprise. All of these ideological forces are competing, have different emphases at different times and work towards different goals.

The New Labour government, in office between 1997 and 1997, pledged to move beyond ideological boundaries espousing a 'what works' agenda based on research evidence and went to some lengths to present policies as distinct from previous administrations through the discourse (rhetorical device) of modernization. Discourse, by definition, is concerned with communication and refers to talk, conversation and dissertation. In the social sciences, its meaning is extended to incorporate statements, knowledge and ideas (Jupp, 2006) that are dominant at a particular time, place and amid certain sets of people (in this case policy-makers) and which are held in relation to other groups of people (e.g. teachers). Such statements, knowledge and ideas provide authoritative explanations of what is problematic and why and the proposed course of action. However, and as Jupp (2006) maintains, the provision of some explanations inevitably excludes other alternatives and so the application of power is implicit in the use of such knowledge.

Discourse and discourse analysis are often associated with the work of Michel Foucault. According to Foucault discourse or discursive practices determine how certain acts become accepted or self-evident (taken as known) at particular times and how these become established as being 'natural'. Legge's (1995: 326, 2) definition of the concept of discourse is both succinct and explanatory and so is quoted here in full.

> 'Discourse' refers to the way in which things are discussed and the argumentation and rhetoric used to support what is said. It also refers to 'reading between the lines' – what remains unspoken or taken-for granted, such as assumptions or evasions. Crucially, discourse analysis deals with issues of representation. That is, it starts with the premise that words do not merely reflect what is being talked about, but they actually construct and even constitute what is being talked about.

What Legge (1995) is claiming here is the way people talk and think about the world reflects the dominance of particular discourses. Ball (1990: 18) puts this in another way asserting that 'discourses construct certain possibilities for thought ... We do not speak the discourse. The discourse speaks us'. Discourses are more than just words or language; they constitute a way of acting in the social world as well as describing it. What is thought and what can be said is not some objective truth about that world, though these ways of thinking and talking tend to become invisible because they are simply accepted as the truth. In this way people's thought processes can themselves come to embody and make stronger particular regimes of power and coercion. The discourses of the more powerful groups in society are more likely to be influential and gain legitimacy often by gaining support in the form of legislation, while the perspectives of subordinate groups are marginalized. In this way the dominance of certain discourses affects how an issue is understood and also helps to establish certain boundaries on the possibilities and limits of debate, how individuals should act and, in some instances, how the state should intervene. Some discourses are thus more influential than others or considered more legitimate and natural. Ball (1993) refers to 'policy as discourse' and Levitas (1998: 3) discusses the 'language of politics as a discourse'. These ideas are drawn upon in this book for making sense of the tensions around 'official' discourses.

Policy developments in the modern era: An historical overview

It is a fact of the modern era that rarely a week goes by without an education-related 'story' being reported in the media or an education-related initiative mooted or officially announced by policy-makers. Policy-makers, commentators, educational 'experts', educational practitioners and professionals, students and pupils, along with the everyday person in the street typically contribute to educational debates, which are frequently given high profile by the media. As such, it is difficult to imagine earlier times when education was not so prominent and not even thought of as particularly newsworthy. Education has become a growing political issue since the mid-1970s (Simon, 1991), and successive governments have attempted to 'reform' education for the better, alleviate perceived inadequacies and improve what currently exists. Since the 1980s education has been in a perpetual state of reform, the nature of reforms reflecting the ideological positions of respective governments. In order to comprehend education policy and policy-making in the present, modern day, however, it is imperative to look back and examine the position education has held in the past; to view changes in education policy and educational provision retrospectively; and to consider the political ideologies, educational ideologies and the discourses at play. This approach provides an explanatory framework for the book as it emphasizes key themes, which are underpinned by the social, political and economic context. Key moments that are especially significant in education policy are outlined below, although more details surrounding some of these particular 'landmarks' are found in the subsequent chapters.

We begin with the landmark legislation of the Elementary Education Act of 1870 (also known as the Forster Act, after William Edward Forster, then vice-president of the Committee of the Council on Education). This highly significant 'event' in the history of education essentially signalled the beginning of the present state-maintained system of education in England. The introduction ten years later of compulsory school attendance was followed in 1891 by legislation that led to the provision of most elementary education free of charge. These pieces of legislation marked a change in perspectives about education, moving it from a purely private concern of families or individuals towards being the public concern of the state. Indeed, many held the view that the principle of 'universality' in the provision of education for the masses would be a dangerous undertaking; an educated population would potentially upset the existing status quo of social stratification (Chitty, 2009). Elementary education was deliberately kept a low level and comprised a basic 3R's curriculum, which was transmitted via didactic methods. In many ways this rudimentary education encouraged the docility, obedience and passivity of pupils and also their teachers. Initiative was discouraged so as not to 'overeducate' the working classes whereby they could learn to improve beyond their station in life. The Codes of Regulations (see Chapter 4) represented the state's attempt to exert some control over education for the lower classes of the population and also have some bearing on generating social consensus at a time of industrialization, social upheaval and change (David, 1980). While there was a building programme and board schools[2] were constructed, the nature of elementary education in providing a basic level of education for working-class children remained relatively unchanged until 1944.

The post-war era of optimism, reconstruction and potential economic growth led to a more interventionist approach by the state in most areas of social life and it was perceived that education could address society's inequalities and problems. A political consensus about the purpose of education in a social democracy ensued with the social-democratic ideology of 'equality of opportunity' as its driving force. Thus it was deemed that every child should have educational opportunities regardless of his or her background, and there was a massive investment in education in the post-war years. The Education Act of 1944 (also known as the Butler Act, after R. A. Butler, then Minister of Education) is, like the 1870 Act, a highly significant legislation as it established a unified system of free, compulsory schooling for children aged five to fifteen. Free secondary educational provision for all resulted in the division of grammar, secondary modern and technical schools which became known as the tripartite system. Although not specified as such in the 1944 Act, a tripartite structure of secondary education was legitimized. Due to the lack of technical schools, however, the reality was a bipartite system. Children were allocated to one of these schools according to their ability, which was ascertained through the 11 plus examination. The separate tripartite schools were supposed to have 'parity of esteem' albeit with different curricula and for different ability students. Problems were identified with the 11 plus (Chitty, 2009), and it became evident through the 1950s that the success or failure of children at eleven years and their attendance in separate schools (i.e. grammar, technical or secondary modern) was effectively reinforcing social class differences and reproducing the existing social order (Jones, 2003). By the 1960s the Labour government was moving towards a system of comprehensive education. Comprehensivization was not universal as selective education continued in some areas because grammar schools remained in the system in England, despite many being closed down by Local Education Authorities (LEAs) in the early 1970s.

From 1944 to the mid-1970s teachers enjoyed relative autonomy and effective control over curricula content and pedagogic methods. They drew on public and political support, as knowledgeable, trustworthy professionals and worked in partnership with LEAs and the Ministry of Education (later Department of Education and Science (DES)). The emerging progressive curriculum and methods transformed primary education and pedagogy from its previous traditional emphasis towards a more child-centred approach. By the late 1960s economic conditions were changing in Britain as a consequence of dwindling world economies. This inevitably impacted funding for education, which was increasingly regarded as expensive, while there was mounting public concern over education and educational standards. However, regardless of the evidence for these assertions (Pring, 1992), the economic crises of the 1970s, along with increasing levels of unemployment, fuelled discontent; education was not delivering its promises. The mid- to late 1970s were marked by mounting anxiety, public and political concern over standards resulting in demands for educational reform and greater accountability of schools and teachers.

The *Black Papers* (Cox and Dyson, 1969a,b, 1970; Cox and Boyson, 1975, 1977) were a series of publications by right-wing academics and policy groups who condemned child-centred, progressive education and advocated a return to traditional teaching methods and disciplines. What became known as the 'William Tyndale affair' (which involved a junior school in Islingtion, London, which utilized radical progressive methods against the wishes of parents) added to the perceived 'crisis' in education and resulted in sensational media headlines. This was the beginning of the scrutiny of education by the media, which we are so familiar with today. In 1976, the 'Great Debate' in education came about following an unprecedented speech by Prime Minister James Callaghan. His speech at Ruskin College, Oxford, focused on public concerns about falling standards, pupil dissatisfaction, the economic relevance of education and social failure; it brought education into the spotlight as an area for public debate. The speech is highly significant as it set the agenda for education policy that would ensue in the following years. Critics of education were concerned about the influence of child-centred approaches, progressive teaching methods and the monopoly of teachers over curricula content and pedagogy. From the mid-1970s it was deemed that school leavers had inadequate skills and knowledge for the workplace. Throughout the 1980s the blame for the decline in British industry and commerce and the high levels of unemployed youth rested with ineffective teachers. There were calls for the DES to have greater involvement in the shaping of the curriculum and more control over the LEAs and teachers. Essentially, there was a call for a more disciplined structure of learning at all stages in the system, a 'core curriculum' of basic knowledge, more vocational training and there was mounting pressure for accountability. Education became more instrumentally focused from the mid-1970s along with a discourse relating to the view that the role of schools was to prepare pupils for the workplace.

The 1988 Education Reform Act (ERA) is another landmark piece of legislation; it brought a tidal wave of reforms, the effects of which were unprecedented and far-reaching. The ERA, introduced by the Conservative administration under Prime Minister Margaret Thatcher, empowered the secretary of state for education to prescribe a National Curriculum for state-maintained schools, creating greater central control over educational content and dramatically changing teachers' ways of working. A mandatory national system of pupil testing, in the form of Standard Assessment Tasks (SATs), was established; SATs were located in four discrete Key Stages for children aged five to sixteen. Children were assessed against the expected 'standard' for their age to ascertain their level of achievement. The introduction of league tables encouraged schools to compete by exposure to market forces and performance indicators and provided comparative information for parents. It also ensured accountability. This period of time saw huge swathes of directives from government to schools (Webb and Vulliamy, 1996) along with rafts of 'non-statutory' advice from the National Curriculum Council (NCC) and the School Examinations and Assessment Council (SEAC). Up until this point there had been largely reluctance by policy-makers to determine methods or the 'how' of teaching in schools. Increasingly, however, the secretary of state for education intervened both in curricula content and pedagogy. Teachers' work intensified and resulted for some in stress and burnout because of the pressure to implement directives and maximize pupil outcomes.

In 1992, the Office for Standards in Education (Ofsted)[3] was established by John Major's government (Conservative) to monitor activities in schools, ensure the 'proper' delivery of the curriculum and enhance the work of the Her Majesty's Inspectorate (HMI). This level of external surveillance was to ascertain that schools were complying with the government's agenda. 'Failing schools', those falling short of the required standards and located towards the bottom of league tables, were thus readily identifiable and could be 'named and shamed'. Through the decentralizing processes of Local Management of Schools (LMS), head teachers were empowered to manage their own budget, set their own expenditure, appoint, promote and dismiss their own staff as required, and assume responsibility for the marketing of their school. The market model of schooling also demanded different types of schools so that 'consumers of education', that is parents, had more choice. In accordance, City Technology Colleges (CTCs) and Grant-Maintained Schools were established through the ERA providing diversity in the system while reintroducing a system of selective education. Conservative policies for education between 1979 and 1997 ensured greater centralization and control. When the New Labour government took up office in 1997, the expectation was the incoming government would be different. What transpired, however, over the next eleven years was essentially tighter governmental control.

New Labour explicitly stated that education would be its number one priority. New Labour's early educational reforms largely consolidated those of the previous Conservative administration; there were few policy reversals. The most notable difference was the reluctance by New Labour to rely merely on market forces to raise standards in schools, but to intervene more directly in education (Ball, 2013). Centralization increased through the setting of national targets and government intervention was proclaimed necessary in order to ensure the government's ultimate aspirations of 'raising standards' in schools were met. Education was given greater prominence for economic purposes, teachers once again found themselves under attack from policy-makers and there was public criticism (Phillips and Furlong, 2001). 'Modernization' was the mantra of New Labour, but at the same time prescriptive strategies in primary schools detailed content and methods for the daily teaching of literacy and numeracy. This level of intervention and prescription was, arguably, far from modern and resonated more with the elementary school Code of the late nineteenth century. Teaching materials were devised for teachers who 'delivered' the curriculum. A revised programme for trainee teachers focused on the standards and strategies. The top down, 'standards agenda' with intervention and prescription was enforced by Ofsted.

Fairclough (2000) is just one commentator who has critiqued the language and rhetoric of New Labour in order to analyse and understand the practices of the party's approach to government and politics. The analysis of language is particularly important in New Labour's political approach because of its 'promotional way of governing' and 'the management of perception through "media spin" – constant monitoring and manipulating how issues are presented in the media' (2000: 157). Fairclough (2000) distinguishes between three different aspects of political language namely, style, discourse and genre, though he notes that these operate concurrently. From his detailed examination of an assortment of texts, including political speeches and official documents, he argues the logic of New Labour was constructed in its political discourse. Fairclough maintains (2000: 158):

> Texts are processes in which political work is done – work on elaborating political discourses, as well as the rhetorical work of mobilising people behind political discourses … text analysis adds to … discourse analysis … it shows how the work of

politics or government is partly done in the material of texts – it gets into the texture of texts, so the political and governmental processes which are going on there can be unpicked. Without text analysis we simply miss the important aspect of political and governmental work.

Fairclough (2000) suggests New Labour successfully positioned itself through the construction of a new political discourse, which incorporated elements of both old left and new right politics and located its ideological thinking as 'the Third Way' (see Giddens, 1998, 2000). Le Grand (1998: 27), in a discussion of the Third Way, suggests there was a commitment to 'robust pragmatism' and the idea that 'what's best is what works'. He argues New Labour appeared to take a broad-minded or eclectic approach in policy-making rather than the set of neo-liberal ideas that essentially underpinned the approach to reform the preceding Conservative administration. According to Flynn (1999: 586) this included 'elements from neo-liberalism, communitarianism, and social democracy', or for Gewirtz (2002: 166) it was a 'contradictory and complex mix of neo-liberal, authoritarianism and humanistic policies for social justice'. For Hodgson and Spours (1999: 8) New Labour's Third Way was positioned between European values of social democracy, social justice and inclusion and the employment-orientated, flexible labour markets of the United States of America. However, whatever the ideological or political origins, there existed a resolve by New Labour to contemplate 'the use of techniques tried elsewhere' (Cabinet Office, 1999: 38) and adopt them in practice if they were considered feasible, were likely to produce the desired outcomes and meet the government's modernization goals.

Fairclough (2000) asserts the political discourse of New Labour was not stable but in a state of constant flux and adaptation because of the condition of shifting relations within the political environment at home and abroad and also other environments, for example, the world of business. Fairclough (2000) maintains the New Labour government articulated its policies in a particular shrewd manner in order to control public perception. Jones (1999), taking a similar line, exposes what he regarded as the 'manipulation' of the news agenda by New Labour, the 'hyping up [of] government initiatives' and 'engineering the right 'build-up' to a big political announcement' (1999: 71). This, Jones argues, was evident by the doubling in number of special advisers (from 38 to 73), whose prime function he noted, quoting the *Guardian* journalist Hugo Young, was 'explaining what the minister wants to get across: the guardians of access and the messengers of perception' (1999: 73). New Labour, he maintains, placed a great amount of energy into ensuring the presentation of policy was executed 'positively and attractively' (1999: 102). The reading of policy documents in this era of policy-making and onwards needs, therefore, to be assessed against the political backdrop of the time and also bearing in mind the trappings of 'media spin'.

The outcome of the UK general election of 2010 was a coalition, the first to have governed since 1945. A Coalition government was thus new terrain for recent UK politics and policy-making. David Cameron of the Conservative Party became the new prime minister; Nick Clegg of the Liberal Democrats was his deputy; and the Cabinet comprised Conservative and Liberal Democrat MPs. Both parties had given prominence to education in their respective election manifestos, and between 2010 and 2015 education policy was uniquely carved out as both parties championed their respective proposals; inevitably there were contestations and compromises. Smithers (2015) acknowledges an accelerated pace of change as both parties had ambitions for education. The Liberal Democrats' 2010 election programme, for example, was based on the principle of fairness influencing the Pupil Premium to improve educational outcomes for children from disadvantaged families, as well as realizing the provision of free school meals for primary children in England up to the end of Key Stage One. It was the Secretaries of State for Education Michael Gove and after 2014 Nicky Morgan and the Secretaries of State for Universities and Science David Willetts and after 2014 Greg Clark (all Conservative MPs) who steered the rapid reforms although outright Conservative control of education was kept somewhat in check by the Liberal Democrats, the minority Coalition partner, who opposed some reforms and advocated others. The Conservative-led Coalition government harnessed New Labour's policy ideas for addressing poverty and social exclusion, educational inequalities and limited social mobility, but these were couched in the milieu of economic austerity as the only rational course of action to restore economic health and address the national deficit. Other notable features are a discourse of 'freedom' for individuals, families and schools along with amplified accountability through market mechanisms, the diminishing of state responsibility and greater emphasis on privatization. The concepts of 'freedom' and 'responsibility' were central to the political narrative of the Conservative's 'Big Society'.

The policies emerging from the Department for Education (DfE), which immediately replaced New Labour's Department for Children, Schools and Families (DCSF), exhibited similar policy tensions to those that existed under the Thatcher and Major Conservative governments between 1979 and 1997 and can, arguably, be considered as the continuation of the unfinished project begun under earlier Conservative administrations. The emerging Coalition policies had a neo-liberal emphasis: diversity and choice, primacy of markets and a minimal role for the state. Parents (and students in HE) remained conceptualized as 'consumers' in an education marketplace with a mantra of greater choice. Provider diversification to transform the school system was exemplified in the extension of the Academies Programme, via the Academies

Act 2010, which enabled outstanding schools to apply for academy status, and the programme was also extended to the primary sector. New types of provision include Studio Schools, University Technical Colleges (UTCs) and Free Schools. Free Schools enable parents, other groups and private providers to establish and run their own schools; again greater choice and diversity is advocated. Lupton and Thomson (2015a: 14) regard these structural reforms of the school system as 'probably the most substantial element of the Coalition's programme of reform'. This policy trajectory, however, essentially creates greater fragmentation in the education system. The *laissez-faire* ('leave to do') liberalism of the Conservative-led Coalition government policy-making is, however, inextricably coupled with Conservative beliefs in traditional curricula 'subjects' and methods of instruction, discipline and authority, and a strong state that has in place mechanisms of surveillance and accountability measures to ensure compliance with government policy. Coalition education policy can, thus, be best expressed as 'an alliance of libertarian and traditional values, continuing the themes of the 1979–1997 Tory governments' (Allen, 2015: R36). Allen (2015) further elucidates, 'To call it a coalition policy might be a stretch; like no other secretary of state in this government, Michael Gove can lay claim to ownership of the direction and drive for change in the department he ran from 2010 to 2014.'

Gove was keen to restore traditional subjects into schools' curricula along with traditional teaching methods and pursued major reforms to school qualifications and the examination system. He condemned General Certificate of Secondary Education (GCSE) qualifications proposing instead English Baccalaureate Certificates and one examination board, but these were subsequently abandoned following criticism (Gove, 2013). However, Gove pressed ahead with GCSE reforms for rigorous end of course examinations in some subjects to be taken after two years of study and which replaced modularization and coursework assessment. Other indications of policy continuity and change revolved around: the review and rolling out of a new National Curriculum, modifications to league tables to include only grades achieved at the first attempt in order to avoid 'gaming', the standards agenda, inspection (targeting failing and troubled schools) and teachers' pay and pensions; schools having more freedom to make local decisions; greater powers to schools to address bullying and enforce discipline; and the payment to schools of a Pupil Premium for those in receipt of free school meals.

The schools' White Paper (DfE, 2010a), *The Importance of Teaching*, proposed wide-ranging and far-reaching changes. Gove sought to improve teacher quality with a more rigorous application process and by creating different routes into teacher training, notably the introduction of Schools Direct 'as the main vehicle for putting schools in the lead in teacher training and making HEIs [higher education institutions] more responsive to the needs of schools' (Whitty, 2014: 469). Whitty (2014) and Brundrett (2015) question the viability of university education departments following the overhaul of teacher training and the extension of school-based approaches to teacher education. Gove expanded Teach First, which is aimed at getting the highest performing graduates into teaching. Troops to Teachers was established; this programme targeted army professionals and those in other high flying careers who, according to Gove, would bring training, discipline, leadership and inspiration to the teaching role (Gove, 2009). In an early analysis of Coalition government policy-making, Exley and Ball (2011: 105) surmise the 'what works agenda' based on 'evidence', which purportedly informed much of New Labour's policy-making, shifted more towards 'gut instinct', 'non-academic and even anecdotal evidence' which is 'highly selective' in nature. Education policy-making between 2010 and 2015 was extensive and provoked conflict between government, on the one hand, and teachers' professional associations/unions, HE students and academics, on the other.

In the general election of May 2015 the period of Coalition government came to an end as the Conservatives gained an overall parliamentary majority. The new Conservative government is committed to further advancing marketization and entrenching the far-reaching changes and structural reforms sanctioned between 2010 and 2015. The continuation of the restructuring of education, begun under the earlier Conservative administrations of Thatcher and Major and which featured in Coalition polices, is evidenced in current Conservative policy. In addition, the existence of a series of tensions or contradictions is apparent in the education landscape. A new, more rigorous and academic National Curriculum is in place, but from which many schools are exempt; with policy pursuing more Academies and Free Schools, indications are more schools could work independently from it. Higher qualifications are required by those entering teacher training, but schools now have greater freedom to employ unqualified teachers. While school autonomy is advocated, conversely the secretary of state for education has greater control. Education operates in a competitive quasi-market, and, while there is greater centralization through the direct relationship between government and schools, there is more fragmentation of the system through privatization and the outsourcing of provision and services as well as a diminishing role for local authorities and universities. What can be said conclusively is that of late education policy-making has been conducted at great speed. There have been radical changes across all areas of education, yet despite investment and intervention, many of the larger issues that have blighted education for decades, namely equality, access and opportunity, still prevail.

Education encapsulates a range of competing different traditions, ideologies and educational philosophies that have permeated its culture at different historical moments and continue to do so. These may be viewed as complementary or contradictory or a mixture of both. Nevertheless, we have the vantage point of being able to look back and explore the legacies and reoccurring themes, patterns and trends in education.

Purpose and structure of the book

Each subsequent chapter attempts to disentangle particular strands of a broad set of substantive issues as they relate to a variety of education policy areas. We take a critical perspective of policy-making and our analysis, which challenges the status quo, and which is situated within the context of broader social, political and economic movements such as neo-liberalism and globalization. The structure of the book is as follows.

Chapter 2 begins with a provocative question of whether education leads to improvement or social control. It then moves on to examine the aims of education in order to question what our society should be like, and ask what 'good citizenship' might entail. Following this we present a critical analysis of successive policies for citizenship education in the secondary curriculum in England. We focus here specifically on the absence of 'race' and ethnic politics in order to show how citizenship education is formulated in ways that often constrain (as well as enhance) the possibilities for social improvement in and through education, and across the life course. Finally, we review the change in emphasis in policy from New Labour to the current Conservative government, and consider how such planned policies and discourses around citizenship and inclusion, participation and community have evolved with implications for the reconfiguration of education in terms of improvement, regulation and control.

Chapter 3 examines education policies in Britain in relation to social justice giving emphasis to the tensions manifested in the education policies of previous and current governments. The chapter considers three discernible philosophical traditions namely, liberal-humanist, market-individualism and social-democratic in its analysis. We show how policies promoted as providing greater equality of opportunity and access do not necessarily lead to equitable educational outcomes.

The evolving primary curriculum is the focus of Chapter 4 and we provide a genealogical analysis illustrating how it has changed over time. In doing so, we demonstrate how the curriculum has been a site of conflict, whereby, historically, education policy has enabled the shifting of control over curricula content and pedagogy as policy-makers have attempted to address a range of contemporary social, economic and political issues. In doing so, the chapter also explores the 'colonization' of the primary curriculum and the de-professionalization of teachers.

Key policy developments for early years in the English system are examined in Chapter 5. We chart the growing importance of the formal education of young children, the monitoring of their development and the training and professionalization of the children's workforce. We show how the amount of young children's provision, care and education is inextricably linked to government funding for education and also the impact of shifting employment patterns and women's involvement in paid employment. Changing views of children and childhood also play a very significant role in policy goals over time, whereby historical concerns regarding the nurturance and health of young children have been superseded by educational priorities which feed into policy agendas for raising standards and improving pupil attainment. The gradual development of an early year's curriculum, which dovetails with the National Curriculum in England, is a significant feature in contemporary policy-making.

In Chapter 6 we examine the relationship and tensions between the process of education and modern economy. We examine how the notion of what counts as relevant and real in educational terms has tended to become conflated with the changing preferences of modern politicians, while simultaneously evolving alongside more radical, structural change in the political economy within a regime of neo-liberalism. Initially taking an historical perspective, we reflect upon the birth of instrumentalism, in particular, the academic and vocational divide, the resonance of which has created a legacy for the process of policy formation today. We analyse in some detail the formation and development of policy in the modern era, since the Great Debate up to the present, charting important continuities and nuances along the way. Finally, we question whether post-compulsory education may have failed in two senses, both as a means to address the economic imperative and panacea to virtuous social policy.

The 'economics of education' is the theme of Chapter 7, in which we critically examine the increasing role of market solutions in public sector policy. In particular, we focus upon the intrusion of economics in state education, which has produced not only a radical reconfiguration of education policy but more recent alignment of education with human capital theory. Against this backdrop, we present a set of genealogies of policy discourse in HE, tracing the various moves, continuities and changes in policy-making, where, over the last fifteen years, widespread systemic and institutional change has taken place. We analyse how neo-liberal policy imperatives in HE have led to a radical marketization of the sector and an equally radical emphasis on commercial activity, the commodification of knowledge and creation of so-called university 'products'. This, we suggest, has served to produce divisions between the more and less well-off, and created an inequitable system in which the virtue of welfare-capitalism has been seriously compromised.

Inclusive schools, special educational needs (SEN) and disability is the focus of Chapter 8. We take a retrospective view of policy developments which have sought, at different times, to segregate and then include children with particular needs. We select some of the key policy moments, legislation and documents which illustrate societal and political attitudes of their time in order to track developments encapsulating SEN, integration, inclusive education and the notion of educational equity.

In Chapter 9 we examine the nature and meaning of globalization and its impact on education systems. An international, comparative stance is adopted to show that, in spite of the influence of globalization, significant differences remain in the construction of policy between different education systems. The chapter identifies key differences in the overlapping discourses of globalization, policy-learning and policy-borrowing. Particular cases are drawn upon to illuminate instances of policy convergence and divergence and which highlight the tensions and points of resistance that impede the transfer of policy from one context to another.

Finally in Chapter 10 we reflect upon what it means to unravel policy before presenting a 'futures perspective' on education in which we consider a number of possibilities and contrasting visions. In this chapter, we attempt to displace the discourse of neo-liberalism with an alternative philosophy and language for educational change and social justice. Using a variety of radical examples that might usefully inform the development of future policy-making, we invite the reader's critical involvement in policy analysis to create more challenging intellectual conditions and hopefully further realize a more socially just and democratic future.

Notes

1   The complexity of analysing 'national' education policy is reflected in the context of devolution in the UK whereby from the late 1990s a range of powers were transferred to the Scottish parliament, the National Assembly for Northern Ireland and the National Assembly Wales; England remains with the UK Parliament.

2   Board schools were elementary schools that received rate aid and were managed by local elected school boards.

3   The Office for Standards in Education, Children's Services and Skills (Ofsted) came into being in April 2007.

2

Education: Improvement or Control?

Introduction

The title of this chapter, which implies a choice between two contrasting and often conflicting educational outcomes, is a bit misleading. The idea that such concepts of improvement and control are essentially incompatible ignores the possibility of a system in which instrumental aims are actively encouraged. Viewed differently, for example, education for social control can be seen to align directly with a pragmatic notion of social and educational improvement, where better regulation and 'control' implies the prospect of a system of enhanced possibilities for social engineering. Such a system existed, for example, in Victorian Britain, where a key aim in the establishment of compulsory elementary education post-1870, and the emergence of secondary education at the turn of the twentieth century, was to address growing concerns about the rise and role of the 'raggedy' working classes (David, 1980). A similar case can be made from an economic perspective, in which education more explicitly supports the needs of business and industry in a capitalist system, a system which, in turn, serves to reinforce a division of labour (and hence control) along class-based lines (see Chapter 6). However, our purpose here in contrasting the outcomes of 'improvement' and 'control' as binary opposites is merely to draw attention to the philosophical aims of education in such a way that their social and moral purpose amounts to more than functionalist view. Thus, in the broadest sense, we appeal to the idea that education might actually produce an intelligent participatory democracy, in which young people are capable of thinking autonomously and, with this, developing the required forms of knowledge, skills and attitudinal dispositions that allow them to fulfil their individual potential, however so conceived.

The question of what shape or form education should take in order to address such concerns regarding the importance of autonomy and participation in learning is something that all citizens are entitled to deliberate. As White (1982: 1) notes, such difficult questions relating to the wider aims and purposes of education are aligned with broader conceptual, social and political questions like 'what should our society be like?' From this, a variety of perspectives are produced, giving rise to different value positions and often contested ideological visions of the future (Ranson, 1994). Such diversity across a spectrum of national and institutional boundaries and cultural affiliations creates a platform for the constitution and further definition of educational aims, conceived largely as an active and mutually reciprocal process. In this sense, the concept of participation is somewhat akin to Crick's (2000) reading of the Ancients in which the aims of education, and presuppositions of citizenship, rest firmly upon a 'sharing of social power among the citizens of the same … land: this is what they called liberty' (Crick, 2000: 147). From this we can usefully extrapolate that 'good education', and hence education for 'improvement', is explicitly related to 'good citizenship', which relies, in turn, upon a notion of autonomy and participation, as well as equity and social justice (see Chapter 3) to ensure that all citizens are treated with equal dignity and equal respect.

Pause and ponder

Think about the different aims and purposes of education, including the following educational models: liberal democracy, social replication of labour, cultural socialization, cultural transformation and vocationalism.

1 What is your personal philosophy of education?
2 What are the advantages and disadvantages of implementing your philosophy in mainstream education?
3 Which groups within society would benefit most from this approach to education?

Against this political backdrop, we present a critique of citizenship education in England as a means to illustrate the contested terrain of educational aims and purposes through successive policies for citizenship in the secondary curriculum. Throughout, we question the extent to which such policies provide a reputable means for social and educational improvement, or whether, alternatively, they operate more coercively as a form of planned regulation and social control. In this, the analysis concentrates specifically on the absence of 'race' and ethnic politics[1] in order to show how successive policies for citizenship education have been formulated in ways that often constrain (as well as enhance) the possibilities for social improvement in and through education and across the life course. Finally, we review the change in emphasis in policy from New Labour to the Conservative government, and consider how such planned policies and discourses (see Chapter 1) around citizenship and inclusion, participation and community have started to evolve since the last general election with implications for the reconfiguration of education in terms of improvement, regulation and control.

A beginning: *Education for Citizenship*

In providing an historical overview of policy for citizenship education spanning the last two decades, the chapter begins by focusing on three significant documents: *Education for Citizenship* (NCC, 1990), *Education for Citizenship and the Teaching of Democracy in Schools* (QCA, 1998) and the *Curriculum Review: Diversity and Citizenship* (DfES, 2007a). In a sense, it could be argued that such a selection is not strictly comparable, since the first two documents (NCC, 1990; QCA, 1998) were clearly influenced by the Speaker's Commission on Citizenship (1990) – an eclectic assemblage of educationalists, industrialists, two bishops and a politician from each of the three main political parties – which gave considerable political weight to their discursive formation. Moreover, *Education for Citizenship* emerged under a Conservative Government (1979–1997), whose political rationality was to make education more efficient and standardized, and thereby erase all notions of ideology and politics from curriculum policy and discourse (Pykett, 2007).

Later, the Speaker's Commission had political resonance in the discourse of New Labour policy, where *Encouraging Citizenship* became part of a 'social panacea': a discursive landscape of social and educational reform in which the behaviour 'of the whole child as citizen' came under increasing regulation and surveillance (Pykett, 2007: 304). In contrast, *Diversity and Citizenship* (DfES, 2007a), commissioned by the Department for Education and Skills (DfES), was a low-key affair, developed in-house and without cross-party political representation. It emerged from a wave of 'inter-ethnic group violence' (Kiwan, 2008: 18), 'fears about "home grown terrorism"' (Osler, 2009: 86), policy developments around community cohesion (Home Office, 2001a,b, 2002) and, later, the Nationality, Immigration and Asylum Act (TSO, 2002), prompting changes in the process of naturalization (Home Office, 2005; Kiwan, 2008). However, the apparent incommensurability of the selected documents does not negate the fact that the politics of 'race' is consistently present in its absence in the policy discourse of citizenship education. Put simply, it is conspicuous by its absence. Moreover, all three documents act as crucial signifiers of (and critical moments in) recent curriculum developments and the teaching of citizenship in schools: first through non-statutory guidance (NCC, 1990), then statutory provision (QCA, 1999a) and, finally, in providing a fourth strand to citizenship education in England (DfES, 2007a).

Against this political backdrop, the analysis draws upon the historical antecedents of the politics of 'race' and white supremacy in Britain. It examines the relationship between notions of equality and 'difference', and usefully considers how the process of policy formation, to 'include' and 'omit' or, indeed, 'select-in' and 'select-out' particular discourses around citizenship, serves both to enable and/or constrain (Giddens, 1987) notions of equity and social justice. This is especially significant given that schools are regarded as important repositories of social and moral values, where teachers have a duty to raise the level of political literacy among young people, not least as part of the formal requirement of the revised curriculum for citizenship education (in England) (DfES, 2007a), but more especially for moving into the context of the Conservative Party in government with emergent notions of the 'Big Society' (see Chapter 3).

However, we begin by addressing the document *Education for Citizenship* (NCC, 1990), which provides an initial reference point for the absent presence of race within a 'neutral' and de-politicized policy discourse. The articulation of rights and responsibilities presumes a liberal understanding that all individuals *qua* citizens are equal and all communities are unimpeded by structural inequalities. Society is fair and just under the rule of law which operates to ensure that no infringements occur and that equality exists between 'different types of community' within a 'pluralist society' (NCC, 1990: 6). The liberal conception thus assumes a fundamental equality of rights and responsibilities, as a means to counteract the negative consequences of a market-driven economy (Miller, 2000). As such, on the face of things, it may be assumed that such policy promotes a form of education for social 'improvement'.

However, the absence of a discourse on social rights and the welfare state provides further evidence of the politicized nature of the document presented as a largely neutral and de-politicized formation, thereby obscuring the 'politically informed criteria and standards' that the authors' 'own use of the concept [of citizenship] unavoidably incorporates' (Carr, 1991: 374). This suggests two things discursively in terms of citizenship education policy. First, the lack of any serious consideration of social rights means that structural inequalities and social injustice around 'race' are casually overlooked, since, despite appearances, 'neutrality is an impossible goal' (Kymlicka, 1995: 108) in any liberal model of citizenship. Second, this important omission (and tacit condonation) suggests that the relationship between the citizen and state is conceived in terms that are explicitly contractual (Miller, 2000). This parallels with the politics of the New Right and libertarian conception of citizenship, where the dominant discourse translates to a 'naturalized' politics of citizenship education, combining an uncritical and depoliticized knowledge of how the institutions of government work with a passive socialization into the status quo (Carr, 1991). Indeed, this is hardly surprising given the political context of a Conservative administration under which the document emerged, and whose principal purpose was to achieve a muted consideration, if not complete and permanent erasure of more radical forms of social and political engagement. Such statements have greater resonance in the context of their social and political emergence.

The policy discourse of *Education for Citizenship* (NCC, 1990) emerged from a 'general set of Education Reforms designed to create a free market system of education' (Carr, 1991: 382). While bringing improved wealth and prosperity to many of the white majority, it also exacerbated economic and structural inequalities for most minority ethnic communities (Gewirtz et al., 1995). The pervasive influence of markets in education and transformation of the discourse of citizenship education into a depoliticized form of political rhetoric was matched with the appearance of a so-called 'new racism' throughout the 1980s (Barker, 1981). This emerged from a long and chequered history of ill-feeling and discrimination (Rex and Moore, 1967; Mullard, 1973), deficit theorizing (Coard, 1971), hostile immigration policies (Patterson, 1963) and deep structural inequalities. Throughout the 1980s 'the "new racism" served to reinforce Powellite[2] views of who was to be included or excluded within a British national identity and provided a rationale for xenophobia and racism towards minorities'(Tomlinson, 2008: 71). Accordingly, white hegemony (i.e. the ideological dominance of 'whiteness') was allowed to prevail and racism came to be seen as something normal (Taylor, 2009) in a system seeking to control the membership of 'in-groups' and 'out-groups', and thus reinforce a number of potentially damaging hierarchies within education and society.

A radical break with the principles of the welfare state coincided politically with a move towards competitive individualism (Tomlinson, 2005), and a growing belief in the need to safeguard and protect the British national identity (and white majority) from the 'enemy within' (Gilroy, 1987). As Ball (2013: 91) suggests, in this climate 'inner cities are represented as a pathological "other" in relation to certain fixed core values', where, for example, the history curriculum became more traditionally British and 'nationalistic' (of which, more later). Such pronouncements were later reinforced through statements like 'teachers should teach children how to read, not waste their time on the politics of *race*, class and gender' (John Major, cited in Tomlinson, 2008: 110: emphasis added). As Gillborn (1998: 718) notes, 'education reforms of the 1980s and 1990s came increasingly to be characterised by a "de-racialised" discourse that effectively removed ethnic diversity from the agenda and glossed many discriminatory processes'. By the mid-1990s, the non-statutory guidance of *Education for Citizenship* (NCC, 1990) had all but disappeared: eclipsed by the hegemony of neo-liberal reform, which served to produce an 'absent presence' (Apple, 1999) of race and ethnicity in education.

Pause and ponder

Market reforms in education have been relentlessly pursued by different governments since 1979. Obtain as much information as you can from newspapers online, looking at the pros and cons of a marketized education system, and answer the following questions.

1 What are the assumed benefits of the introduction of markets in education?
2 Which groups within society are markets most likely to benefit and disadvantage?
3 What are the implications of such market reforms in education for the development of empathy among citizens living in different social and economic conditions?

Policy reincarnation: *Education for Citizenship and the Teaching of Democracy in Schools* (Crick Report)

This historical analysis usefully maps the descent of citizenship education, reflecting the status of 'race' and multicultural politics within the 'policyscape' (Ball, 1999), leading up to the beginning of the Crick (QCA, 1998) era under New Labour. The change of government in 1997 and installation of 'Third Way' (Giddens, 1998) thinking brought new hope of a radical shift towards the politics of inclusion and social justice, in particular the possibility of 'developing palliatives to mitigate disadvantage' (Tomlinson, 2005: 91). However, the discourse of inclusion was tempered by a contradictory and altogether more performative régime, with more exacting standards and pervasive micro-politics of surveillance, including forms of self-policing (Foucault, 1988). Here, citizens are to assume responsibility for their own social, moral and economic welfare and community involvement, through the new mixed economy of positive welfare (Jerome, 2009) and political technologies of 'civility and decency' (Pykett, 2007: 305). The emphasis on the performative and managerial, as technologies of control, in this process illustrates the constraints under which various members of the hand-picked Advisory Board were apparently operating. Thus, any move perceived to 'rock the boat' and undermine the contrived neutrality of the report and its fixed core values was strictly not an option (Pykett, 2007: 307), especially when a 'political opportunity … had to be seized quickly' and where the absent presence of diversity and anti-racism was acknowledged only many years later (Crick, cited in Kiwan, 2008: xiii–xiv). In this policy context, it is no surprise that the reincarnation of citizenship education through the Crick Report (QCA, 1998) should contain only two paragraphs on multicultural issues (Tomlinson 2008), and, significantly, no mention of racism at all. As Osler (2008: 13) elaborates, 'the Crick report to some degree reflects, rather than challenges, the institutionalised racism of British society: it characterises minorities as having a deficit; it uses patronising language and stereotypes in its depiction of these groups'. Some of these issues of regulation and 'control' can be illustrated through a detailed analysis of the political formation of the document, drawing insights from two earlier critiques (Garratt and Piper, 2008a, 2010).

A useful starting point is the Advisory Group's assertion that with 'the increasingly complex nature of our society, the greater cultural diversity and the apparent loss of a value consensus … Cultural diversity raises the issue of *national identity*' (QCA, 1998: 17: emphasis added). Here, as Garratt and Piper (2010: 45) argue:

> the discursive formation and linkage of the terms nation, value consensus and the need to address cultural diversity in the context of national identity is significant as 'diversity' can be read to imply a 'lack', or otherwise interpreted as a 'persistent anxiety' or 'problem' … to be dealt with through a frame of 'ethno-cultural unity'. (Watson, 2000; Osler and Starkey, 2001)

The political response to 'restore a sense of common citizenship, including national identity that is secure enough to find a place for the plurality of nations, cultural and ethnic identity' (QCA, 1998: 17), is significant as an affirmation of 'naturalized' fixed core values. Thus, while a surface reading points to a rhetorical reintroduction of the politics of 'race' (and hence improvement in education), at the same time it appeals to a 'sanitized (white-washed) version of history' (Gillborn, 2009: 52) and majoritarian conception of 'Britishness', prevalent throughout the 1980s and 1990s. This in turn privileges a public discourse of political community and national identity that is suspect on at least two counts. First, by ignoring the theme of racism, the Crick Report (QCA, 1998) is complicit with the continuation of the absent presence of 'race' in education and 'other structural disadvantages which act as a key barrier to full and equal citizenship' (Osler, 2008: 13). Second, it treats minorities as somewhat 'suspect communities' (Pantazis and Pemberton, 2009) of the 'enemy within' (Gilroy, 1987): to be held apart from the white majority and challenged their right to belong as legitimate members of the political state. The tendency towards deficit theorizing in Crick can be found elsewhere within the report's discursive formation, for example, in the following statement: 'a more plural approach to racial *disadvantage* requires forms of citizenship which are sensitive to ethnic diversity and offer respect both to individuals and to the social groups to which *they* feel *they* belong' (QCA, 1998: 17, emphasis added). This formation can

> be read to convey an implicit pathology of difference, where the locus of the meaning of 'disadvantage' is entwined with the concept of 'race', which itself is a social construct. Then portrayed as requiring … sensitivity or special treatment, ethnic diversity is condemned as the inferior 'other', through the deployment of a notion of belonging that is characterised 'exotic' and which is taken to reside somewhere outside the territory of the authored claim. (Garratt and Piper, 2010: 45)

The persistent 'othering' and implicit condescension and assimilation of minorities within the discourse – against the 'common-sense', invisible perspective of whiteness – is present in the assertion that 'majorities must respect, understand and tolerate minorities … minorities must learn and respect the laws, codes and conventions as much as the majority' (QCA, 1998: 18). As Garratt and Piper (2008a: 11) claim:

> critics of this implicit hierarchy (Osler and Starkey, 2001; Hoffman, 2004; Faulks, 2006) note that its condescending tone can be read to imply that minorities are less law-abiding than the dominant white group … thus, 'it seems that the dominant group is doing all the teaching and the ethnic minorities all the learning!' (Hoffman, 2004: 267)

In this crucial sense, 'toleration' implies a form of regulation and control: a strong disapproval of behaviour endured by the ruling white majority whose assumed sovereignty can be used to suppress such behaviour if necessary (Modood, 2007). Yet, arguably, integration should always be a two-way process or even a 'multilogical' one (Modood, 2007: 65), that is, multidirectional. The rationality and discursive regularity of this 'colour-blind' emphasis is consonant with the 'policyscape' of New Labour and represents something of a continuation with the past (Tomlinson, 2008). However, it can be argued that colour blindness is wholly impotent as a means of promoting social justice, since, by definition, this 'prohibits the recognition of particular group identities so that no citizens are treated in a more or less privileged way or divided from each other' (Modood, 2007: 68).

Thus, ironically, colour-blind policies that form part of the landscape of liberal politics may actually serve to reinforce and perpetuate existing racial inequalities by placing 'race *equity* at the margins ... [and] retaining race *injustice* at the centre' (Gillborn, 2009: 65). Consequently, claims about the pedagogical value of political literacy in Crick, to ameliorate the absence of an anti-racist stance (Olssen, 2004; Osler, 2008), seem mildly optimistic. Like its predecessor, the Crick Report neatly (and perhaps even deliberately – cf. Kiwan, 2008) manages to side-step such issues and offers no clear guidance for teachers on how to resist the enduring problem of widespread racism. Meanwhile societal ignorance around the politics of 'race' and racism continues unabated amid a smokescreen of performative, managerial and choice-oriented political technologies, and neo-liberal social and education policies (Chitty, 2009; Ball, 2013).

The third coming – *Curriculum Review: Diversity and Citizenship* (Ajegbo review) and beyond

At the beginning of the twenty-first century, debates on diversity and citizenship began to increase and intensify in the wake of interethnic disturbances in northern towns in 2001, the 9/11 terrorist attacks in America and London bombings in 2005, with urgent calls for citizenship education to address these issues (Rammell, 2006, cited in Kiwan, 2008). As noted above, the Home Office published a series of reports to address the resulting emergent political themes of community cohesion, diversity and belonging, as well as the need to find a way of reinforcing British values and national identity, while countering the potential threat of terrorist activity (Osler, 2008). As Kiwan (2008: 24) notes, Gordon Brown, then Chancellor of the Exchequer, 'had played a major role in initiating the review ... and particularly in influencing the framing of its terms of reference'. In 2006, for example, in a speech to the Fabian Society on the 'Future of Britishness', Gordon Brown raised the question of what it means to be British in a post-imperial world of plural identities and changing values (Brown, 2006). This followed an earlier appeal in which Brown (2004) questioned the 'core values of Britishness', claiming 'there is a golden thread that runs through British history', comprising 'liberty', 'tolerance' and a 'tradition of fair play'. Going further, in 2007 Jack Straw, then leader of the House of Commons, claimed that 'we have to be clearer about what it means to be British ... a "British story" must be at the heart of this' (Straw, 2007).

Given the terms of reference, it is perhaps not surprising that any critical consideration of the concept of 'Britishness' is conspicuously absent in the report of the Ajegbo panel (DfES, 2007a). For example, just prior to its publication, Alan Johnson (then Secretary of State for Education) is reported to have 'proposed that schools should focus on "core British values of justice and tolerance"' (cited in Kiwan, 2008: 94), despite otherwise significant concerns regarding the complexity and contested nature of 'Britishness' in relation to matters of 'race'. Moreover, some would say that 'race' itself is an invidious naturalizing concept (Miles, 1993; Mason, 2000). So, while, more recently, it has become fashionably interchangeable with notions of ethnicity, it remains a socially and politically corrosive concept, 'reflecting the colonial roots of Britain's immigration experience' (Mason, 2006: 105). Accordingly, 'over time the term Britishness has come to mean … different things to different people … identities are typically constructed as multiple and plural. Throughout our consultations, concerns were expressed, however, about defining "Britishness", about the term's divisiveness and how it can be used to exclude others' (DfES, 2007a: 8). In the context of government ministers' political exhortations, the discourse is revealing for its tendency to 'speak' commonsense (white-sense?) to 'race' through an 'unwillingness to name the contours of racism' (Leonardo, 2000: 32, cited in Gillborn, 2009: 54) embedded in the discourse of 'Britishness'. Thus, while extending beyond the narrow colonialism of Crick, the Ajegbo Report (DfES, 2007a) nevertheless fails to engage with the pervasive problem of colour blindness, beneath a veil of liberal democracy. This irony is further compounded by the assertion that 'issues of identity and diversity are more often than not neglected in Citizenship education' (2007a: 7) and 'tend not to be linked explicitly enough to political understanding' (2007a: 8). In conflating and further sanitizing the discursive relations of raced inequities and common values and goals, the panel can be found guilty of breaking its own injunction. This is most surprising given the key findings of the Maylor et al. (2007) review (intended to support the Diversity and Citizenship Curriculum Review Group), which found that

> in order to effectively acknowledge diversity in Britain, the curriculum needs to provide discursive resources to promote 'collective identities' *and to challenge ideologies that construct the nation and national identity in ways that exclude minority ethnic groups.* (2007: 1: emphasis added)

For example, if it is important that young people are enabled to 'consider issues that have shaped the development of UK society – and to understand them through the lens of history' (DfES, 2007a: 8), this would surely show that the politics of 'race' and histories of racism (Taylor, 2009) have been repeatedly overlooked in the reimagining of 'Britishness' and citizenship education.

This question encourages further critical analysis of the link between Ajegbo (DfES, 2007a) and the wider historical context in which such tensions and regulatory policy discourses have emerged. The appeal to debate around notions of 'Britishness' as a means to resurrect a 'British story' (Straw, 2007), or 'golden thread that runs through British history' (Brown, 2004), is dubiously melancholic (Gilroy, 2004), but also highly pertinent to the development of a fourth strand for citizenship education. To this, there are three components: 'critical thinking about ethnicity, religion and "race"; an explicit link to political issues and values; the use of contemporary history in teachers' pedagogy to illuminate thinking about contemporary issues relating to citizenship' (DfES, 2007a: 12). Politically, the inclusion of 'critical thinking' in the review usefully encourages the possibility of opening up the discourse of citizenship to enable an interrogation of Britishness and nationalism as otherwise conflated concepts. In terms of educational improvement, this might allow an acknowledgement of 'Otherness' and further develop a more cosmopolitan conception of national identity as 'essential difference' (Pykett, 2007: 310), counting beyond the binary of two: majority/minority. Disappointingly, however, the discourse forecloses prematurely on the possibilities for examining ethnicity and 'race', by twice displacing (and subordinating) the concepts: 'issues of ethnicity and "race", whilst often controversial, are more often addressed than issues relating to religion' (DfES, 2007a: 7, 84). Instead, the review runs the risk of trivializing the issues, by suggesting that 'pupils should have the opportunity to celebrate and embrace diversity' (2007a: 106), much in the way that multiculturalism was criticized by anti-racist commentators in the 1980s for its perceived flagrant tokenism (Troyna, 1993). Ironically, elsewhere we are reminded that 'myths and stereotypes are still around' (DfES, 2007a: 26), that 'there is evidence that issues of "race" and diversity are not always high on schools' agendas' (2007a: 34) and, further, that 'there is insufficient training for teachers to feel confident with issues of identity [and] "race"' (2007a: 67). Indeed, if critical thinking on such matters of 'race' and ethnicity is to amount to anything more than mere political rhetoric, then the absence of any articulation of what constitutes criticality in this regulatory context is highly dubious. More so perhaps, given that teachers are widely reported to lack confidence in the area and where such issues have been a low priority in many schools and less so perhaps in the context of 'the revised QCA Programme of Study at KS3 and KS4 [which] does not contain any explicit reference to anti-racism' (Kiwan, 2008: 94).

Pause and ponder

Virtually every major public policy meant to improve race equity has arisen *directly* from resistance and protest by Black and other minoritized communities. Indeed, some of the most significant changes have come about as the result of blood shed. (Gillborn, 2005: 486)

1. What role might education play in the process of changing and thus improving this situation in the future?
2. What needs to be done to improve teachers' confidence in tackling issues of 'race' and ethnicity in the classroom in order to bring about change?

With respect to the improvement and future development of education and society, the tensions of our historical past may be productively employed to develop points of resistance and challenge the absent presence of race in citizenship education. Indeed, this is something which Maylor and others (2007: 1) suggest in their view that it is important that citizenship education 'should allow national identity and historical events to be "retold" in order to demonstrate the contribution of minority ethnic groups to British society'. In the context of the Home Office initiatives noted above, it was disappointing that the idea to 'introduce a fourth "pillar" to the citizenship education curriculum on "British social and cultural history"' (Kiwan, 2008: 70) was ultimately rejected. One might question, for example, why is it that under New Labour, Gordon Brown's (2006) commitment to 'liberty', 'tolerance' and a 'tradition of fair play', as the self-styled trinity of 'white civilizing values' (Gillborn, 2009: 51) underpinning British society, sits at odds with Britain's racist past? Arguably the so-called 'golden thread' running through British history glosses all forms of protest and resistance through a discursive naturalization and reification of majoritarian assumptions. As Kymlicka notes, 'politics is almost always a matter of both identities and interests. The question is always *which* identities and interests are being promoted?' (Kymlicka, 2002: 328), and so there is always a controlling element. In this case it is a form of politics defining a liberal context in which the 'naturalized' discourse of a 'tradition of fair play' (and hence model for social justice) is effectively displaced as the 'state unavoidably promotes certain cultural identities, and thereby disadvantages others' (Kymlicka, 1995: 108). As Osler (2009: 92) suggests:

> The message for educators and the wider public, as reflected in the media, is that Britishness and the British story need to be framed within narrow territorial boundaries. Outsiders need to learn British history in order to integrate into the community of the nation. British history is presented as a single, unproblematic narrative, rather than a complex process, reflecting the various stories and perspectives of Britain as a 'community of communities'.

The importance of such narrow interests and identities can be illustrated through Jack Straw's (2007) tendency towards 'pathological nostalgia' (Gilroy, 2004), in which he argues that within the concept of British nationality

> there is room for multiple and different identities, but there has to be a contract that they will not take precedence over the core democratic values of freedom, fairness, tolerance and plurality that define what it means to be British. It is the bargain and it is nonnegotiable.

In a sense, there is nothing inherently British about such values, which simply represent international human rights principles (Osler, 2009). Yet, ironically, the evolving heritage of multicultural Britain appears to have been erased through the telling of a single 'British story', where 'national identity' under New Labour came to mean 'beyond ethnicity' and/or standing outside 'minority' and 'other' (Mirza, 2007). This served to reinforce the combined effect of the demand for tighter immigration controls (Londinium, 2008) – especially against asylum seekers – and 'more exacting' British citizenship tests, to allow immigrants to demonstrate 'commitment' and 'prove integration into communities' (BBC, 2008). It is also contradictory and at odds with what is known culturally and politically and legalistically, for example, the way in which 'dominant narratives have often rendered aspects of the past (even the recent past) invisible to contemporary eyes' (Osler, 2009: 97). Consider, for example, New Labour's commissioning of the Macpherson Inquiry into institutionalized racism, which, while paving the way for the legal amendment of the Race Relations Act 2000, is still not always fully observed in practice. For example, the Lawrence family could achieve a semblance of justice in the English legal system, through a retrial of the alleged assailants, only in 2011, that is, eighteen years after their son Stephen was brutally murdered. This resulted in two convictions and the subsequent commissioning by Home Secretary Theresa May of an independent review (Ellison, 2014) regarding possible corruption and the role of undercover policing.

From citizenship in schools to the 'Big Society': Old wine in new bottles?

A key change in the development of policy for citizenship education from the latter years of the New Labour administration into the Conservative-Liberal Democrat Coalition government was the recognition that citizenship, delivered as a taught subject in schools, has been largely unsuccessful (Garratt and Piper, 2008a,b, 2010). In many ways, however, this is hardly surprising, for citizenship (beyond any legal entitlement) connotes a notion of 'belonging' (Osler and Starkey, 2005) that challenges the sterile conception of 'civics' and also conceives it as a form of social practice. This can be traced back to the Ancient Greek philosophy of Socrates and Aristotle but is also found in more contemporary writing of the twentieth and twenty-first centuries. John Dewey (2007 [1916]), for example, was fully committed to the idea of participatory democracy and argued that education was not merely preparation for 'life' beyond school, but rather an intrinsic part of life itself. Indeed, education was intended to foster in young people a certain sensitivity towards social and cultural issues through their active engagement and experience, and thus through a process of learning by doing, extending out into the community and across the life course. In this regard, the idea of the 'Big Society' is hardly anything more than very 'old wine' rebottled and rebranded.

In Coalition policy discourses, the 'Big Society' was transported from schools to other institutions within society, for example, through active citizenship in prisons. Ken Clarke, as the Coalition's Justice Secretary (2010–2012), stated:

> currently many people in prison are not encouraged to take responsibility and are compelled to live a life of 'enforced, bored idleness'. The Prison Reform Trust report demonstrates that encouraging active citizenship in prisons should play an important part in achieving the government's aims for a 'rehabilitation revolution' and developing the wider concept of the Big Society. (Ken Clarke cited in Prison Reform Trust, 2011)

Much like the appropriation of policy for citizenship education noted above, the question of whether 'active citizenship' actually serves to 'improve' or 'impair' education is a contested argument. On the one hand, such pronouncements appear to provide opportunities for self-improvement beyond the baseline malaise of 'bored idleness', but on the other there are clear regulatory overtones, in which active citizenship is exploited as a device to achieve the government's aims for a 'rehabilitation revolution', decoded as enhanced social control. Elsewhere, similar ambiguities can be found in the discussion paper *Positive for Youth – Young People's Involvement in Decision Making* (DfE, 2011a). In this, the Coalition government proposed providing funding as a means to enhance young people's participation in decision making:

> [the paper] focuses on the more formal mechanisms through which young people engage with public decision making and democratic processes, and provides 'youth scrutiny', both nationally and locally. Whilst teenagers are the main focus, the paper recognises that the principles that underpin this commitment apply across a much wider age range. Schools also have an important role but it is for them and their governing bodies to decide what arrangements for pupil voice are in place – this funding is primarily intended to support out-of-school participation and decision making. (2011a: 1)

Similar to the way that active citizenship was being promoted in prisons, this chapter conveys a somewhat ambiguous message concerning issues of 'voice', participation and autonomy. The discussion paper connotes both a semblance of participatory democracy through the aim to engage young people 'with public decision making and democratic processes', but then prematurely forecloses on this by determining the regulatory mechanisms through which such opportunities and participation could occur, in this case reinforcing the responsibility of schools and governing bodies 'to decide what arrangements for pupil voice are in place'. In many ways this was strongly characteristic of the way in which the Coalition government articulated its vision of the 'Big Society' (see Chapter 3), so that while it is perfectly acceptable or, indeed, commendable for people to volunteer to assume responsibility for improving their own local communities, it is a notion that nevertheless produces tacit compliance and hence reinforces social control. For example, under the guise of enhanced local governance,

> we want to give citizens, communities and local government the power and information they need to come together, solve the problems they face and build the Britain they want. We want society – the families, networks, neighbourhoods and communities that form the fabric of so much of our everyday lives – to be bigger and stronger than ever before. (Cabinet Office, 2011: n.p.)

Here, the Coalition government was able to establish the 'conduct of good conduct' (Foucault, 2002) by generating a discourse in which people are responsible for both themselves and others through imposed forms of 'voluntarism' (in reality, coercion) and collective action. However, when thousands of people became actively empowered to protest vigorously against budgetary cuts and job losses, or indeed in relation to the inexorable rise in student fees within HE, this was not quite what the Coalition government had in mind. In such circumstances, it would seem that intelligent participatory democracy, which we would regard as education for social improvement, and which is reflected, for the most part, in such radical forms of political protest, was at odds with the Coalition government's view of active participation.

In 2010 the Big Society project was the political mantra of the Conservative-led Coalition, described by the prime minister as his 'mission in politics' in which he pledged 'to fight for it every day, because the Big Society is here to stay' (Cameron cited in House of Commons, 2011: 4). It was against this backdrop of an emerging 'Big Society' that Cameron's political exhortations lay regarding the affirmation of a so-called 'muscular liberalism' in the context of citizenship. Here the concept of 'state multiculturalism' was said to have failed for 'it has stopped us from strengthening our collective identity. Indeed it has deliberately weakened it' (Cameron cited in Sparrow, 2011). Moreover, state multiculturalism has served to entrench the 'idea that we should respect different cultures within Britain to the point of allowing them – indeed encouraging them – to live separate lives, apart from each other and apart from the mainstream'. It has been 'manipulated to entrench the right to difference – which is a divisive concept. What we need is the right to equal treatment despite difference' (2011). This discourse, in turn, generates two thorny problems. First, it serves to manipulate what counts as liberal politics in contemporary British society, so that while 'collective identity' is positively condoned, 'the right to difference' is actively condemned. Indeed, this argument is virtually identical to that of former New Labour Prime Minister Gordon Brown on the issue of 'Britishness', noted above. In reality, 'equal treatment despite difference' actively serves to dismiss the importance of an 'identity-led' politics and politics of recognition (Taylor, 1992), in which equal dignity and equal respect are properly secured. Second, the call to 'strengthen our collective identity' appeals to a form of liberal nationalism, which in turn defines the nature of 'in-groups' and 'out-groups' in a way that serves to reinforce the absence of 'race' and ethnic politics in debates about the future of the 'Big Society' and whether the 'Big Society'. This raises important questions, for example, whether the 'Big Society' is both big enough and sufficiently just to recognize difference and duly respect it?

Such concerns are consonant with research which shows that intending teachers are resistant to 'simple political rhetoric calling for the teaching of Britishness and specific values' (Clemitshaw and Jerome, 2009: 19) and believe that the question of patriotism must 'be classified as rationally unsettled' (Hand and Pearce 2009: 458). Looking outside the frame of the liberal state, the politics of 'race' and 'multiculturalism is Janus faced: it has both a forward-looking or progressive side and backward looking or conservative side' (Kymlicka, 2002: 368). This latter conception, resonant in the rhetoric of British prime ministers past and present, is bound up with the sentiment of nationalism and nation-building, to return to a golden age of 'old fashioned cultural conservatism' (Kymlicka, 2002). However, as Young (2004: 195–199) reminds us in relation to the idea of community, which we can also read 'national identity'/'nation':

> The desire for [national identity] relies on the same desire for social wholeness and identification that underlies racism and ethnic chauvinism on the one hand and political sectarianism on the other ... the project of the ideal [nation] as the radical other of existing society denies difference in the sense of the contradictions and ambiguities of social life ... no telos of the final society exists.

Ultimately, we suggest that unless there is a radical shift in, and reprioritization of, the politics of education policy and practice, it is doubtful any putative system of the future will lead to genuine social improvement. Thus, while we acknowledge that the rights to difference, equal dignity and equal respect within a participatory democratic framework are the essential prerequisites of any 'good' liberal education, and hence education for improvement, we must remind ourselves that 'education cannot compensate for society' (Bernstein, 1968). Indeed, the chances of it doing so seem only remotely possible if education policy and practice is able to become authentically self-critical, democratic and more than a means to instrumental, short-term regulatory aims and purposes.

A revised curriculum for citizenship (the third curriculum) was rolled out in all maintained schools in 2014 following the review of the National Curriculum (see Chapters 1 and 4). The general milieu of the revised curriculum is greater emphasis on 'core knowledge', meaning 'facts, concepts, principles, and fundamental operations children need to be taught in order to progress and develop their understanding in these subjects' (Brundrett, 2015: 50). The schools' White Paper (DfE, 2010a: 42) proposed 'a greater focus on subject content, outlining the essential knowledge and understanding that pupils should be expected to have to enable them to take their place as educated members of society'. The review aimed to reduce the overprescription within the existing curriculum and, by espousing greater freedoms (see Chapter 4), to bestow upon schools greater autonomy 'to decide how to teach [the curriculum] most effectively' (DfE, 2010: 40a). This means there is far less detail provided in 2014 citizenship programmes of study for Key Stages Three and Four (Moorse, 2014). Moorse's (2014: 41) analysis of citizenship in the National Curriculum identifies a shift in the overarching curriculum aims. In 2008 these revolved around developing the '"whole child" and "every child" as "confident individuals, successful learners and responsible citizens"' (2014). This she compares with the revised aims of the latest curriculum 'to provide pupils with "an introduction to the essential knowledge they need to be educated citizens"' (2014). According to Lupton and Thomas (2015b: 13), the Coalition's approach (which is Conservative Party-led):

> relies heavily on an academic-focused school system to rescue low income students and provide them with access to improved life chances, rather than one which invests in the foundations of secure childhoods, putting students in a better position to learn and to make choices. It shifts responsibility, in some respects, from the wider welfare state to schools.

Since 2003 the Citizenship Education Longitudinal Study has tracked the first cohort of pupils (then aged twelve) of statutory citizenship education in England in an attempt to capture the evolving civic attitudes and behaviours from adolescence and into young adulthood. The study's findings show, for example, 80 per cent of the participants (now in their twenties) have 'very low levels of trust in politicians', although 50 per cent are 'very likely to vote'. The researchers suggest, overall, their study shows citizenship education 'can increase positive attitudes towards voting and other political activities' (Keating et al., 2015: 1). Their recommendations for policy in 2015 are to:

> Strengthen citizenship education in schools, and ensure that it is continued in post-16 education and training settings. Continue to support opportunities for learning about citizenship through 'real life' practice and 'active citizenship', including through school councils. (Keating et al., 2015: 1)

Only time will allow us to see the impact of the New Curriculum, the role of citizenship education within it and the capacity of schools to plan provision to address the various sections of the Programmes of Study. We cannot, therefore, yet discern whether the outcome will be the production of an intelligent participatory democracy, and young people possessing the forms of knowledge, skills and attitudinal dispositions that allow them to fulfil their individual potential. We can, however, raise questions about what counts as knowledge and whose 'core knowledge' and 'essential knowledge' are being legitimated? Moreover, we can also question whether this is meant to bring about improvement in education, by igniting the enquiring minds of young people who are capable of thinking autonomously, or ask whether the (inadvertent) intention is more to quell these inherent dispositions and, thus, exert control?

Notes

1   Parts of this analysis have been reproduced with permission from Taylor and Francis publishers from the original article: D. Garratt (2011) 'Equality, Difference and the Absent Presence of "Race" in Citizenship Education in the UK', *London Review of Education*, 9 (1): 27–39.
2   Reference to the 'Rivers of Blood' speech, by Enoch Powell at the meeting of the Conservative Association, 20 April 1968.

Further reading

Hedtke, R. and T. Zimenkova, eds (2013) *Education for Civic and Political Participation: A Critical Approach*, London: Routledge.
Jerome, L. (2012) *England's Citizenship Education Experiment: State, School and Student Perspectives*, London: Bloomsbury Academic.
Race, R. and V. Lander (2014) *Advancing Race and Ethnicity in Education*, Basingstoke, Hampshire: Palgrave Macmillan.
White, J. (1982) *The Aims of Education Restated*, London: Routledge.

3
Policy and Social Justice

Chapter Outline

Introduction

This chapter examines education policies in Britain in relation to social justice. In doing so, the chapter draws attention to the competing aims of education and tensions evident in a number of policy areas. The chapter begins by exploring the different dimensions of the concept of social justice and considers three discernible philosophical traditions that inform political thinking and aspirations in Westernized countries, namely liberal-humanist, market-individualism and social-democratic. Social justice in education necessitates that *access* to the same quality of educational processes should be *equitable,* even if there are unequal outcomes as a consequence. To this endeavour, the chapter explores the tensions which are manifested in specific education policies of the various political parties when in government. First of all, the social-democratic post-war settlement of the mid-1940s with the creation of the welfare state is considered and how this underwent radical reform under the Conservative administration of Margaret Thatcher is also discussed. The education system was just one aspect of the welfare state that was reformed and which further established the foundation for subsequent legislation in successive governments. The introduction of a range of measures and initiatives by the Thatcher government, which culminated in the ERA of 1988, transformed the education system so that it was seen in terms of a market. The producers of education, that is, schools, colleges and universities, have since operated in a competitive environment providing, in theory, greater diversity and choice (see Chapter 7). An analysis of the impact of marketization and privatization of education policy post-1979 to the present reveals tensions between the political discourses of social democracy and the New Right, in relation to the competing aims of equity and inclusion. The chapter examines policy convergences, continuation, overlaps and differences between the policy approaches of successive governments. We suggest the move, by successive governments, to drive up standards and achieve excellence has produced a series of largely unsatisfactory policy composites (Ball, 2013).

The dimensions of social justice

We begin this chapter by exploring the meaning of social justice. Not unlike many other concepts, it has different connotations, is a contested phrase and is politically malleable. The concept typically applies to all aspects of social life and is one where there is social, economic and political (including legal) equity. While a socially just society may be an ideal aspiration, a comparative and international analysis reveals that it is impossible to provide a unified definition because social justice is expressed differently across different nations and cultural traditions (Rizvi, 2009). However, injustice is more readily universally recognizable and has 'material reality': as Rizvi (2009: 91–92) indicates:

> Those who are hungry or poor, or homeless, do not need abstract philosophical discussions in order to realize that they are subjected to marginalization, discrimination and oppression. The idea of justice thus points to something real and tangible, and represents a moral blight on communities that do not attempt to do their best to mitigate its worst effects.

In most Westernized countries over recent decades, social justice aspirations, influenced by the distributive paradigm, have featured in political thinking. While particular local and historical circumstances, cultural traditions, social movement activism and political aspirations impact the nature of social justice, three distinct philosophical traditions informed by the distributive paradigm are apparent: liberal-humanist, market-individualism and social-democratic. These are now discussed in turn.

The 'liberal-humanist' tradition is associated primarily with Rawls' (1999) basic principles, as conceptualized in his *A Theory of Justice* originally published in 1971. Although Rawls (1999) does not utilize the term a great deal in his work, his ideas about social justice have come to dominate contemporary understandings (Wolff, 2008). Rawls (1999: 53) outlines the two principles as follows:

> First: each person is to have an equal right to the most extensive scheme of equal basic liberties compatible with a similar scheme of liberties for others.

> Second: social and economic inequalities are to be arranged so that they are both (a) reasonably expected to be to everyone's advantage, and (b) attached to positions and offices open to all.

The first is the 'liberty principle' and the second actually comprises two parts: (a) the 'difference principle' and (b) the 'fair opportunity principle'. Rawls' (1999) principles encompass notions of fairness and individual freedom in addition to the state's responsibility to create policies and interventions which facilitate access, equity and participation and which eliminate barriers arising from inequitable power relations. It is the difference principle which is closest to traditional notions of social justice and is Rawls' particular contribution to the debate (Wolff, 2008). Chapman and West-Burnham (2010) take this a step further, conceptualizing a socially just society as that which achieves 'well-being' for all its citizens. As such, they offer the following description:

> In very practical terms a society committed to social justice would ensure that every child grows up experiencing the optimum levels of well-being...A socially just society ensures that every child, irrespective of social background, parentage, post code or any variable, has an entitlement in terms of equality and equity to the benefits of growing up in a modem, democratic and affluent society. (2010: 29–30)

It is not the aim here to attempt to provide a definitive conceptualization of social justice, for there are many diverse viewpoints and social justice has varied and disparate uses. Before moving on to consider market-individualism and social-democratic traditions, it is useful at this point to consider what typically lies at the heart of social justice for citizens. Contemporary scholars often consider its focus as egalitarian and entailing citizens having an equal share in terms of access to and distribution of resources, entitlement, representation and also having a 'voice'. Young's (1990) articulation of the 'distributive paradigm' relates to the way in which material and non-material goods and resources are distributed in society; basically, how much people get. It would follow then that a just society constitutes one which distributes its goods and resources (and burdens) fairly. When equity is realized, then justice is achieved. Many contemporary scholars who write about social justice (for example, Miller, 1999) equate social justice with distributional justice (Boyles et al., 2009). In considering the different dimensions of social justice, Gewirtz (1998) raises some important issues, particularly in relation to distributive justice. She explores the different facets of social justice and makes a distinction between its distributional and relational dimensions. Gewirtz

(1998: 472) purports that distributive justice has tended to be conceived in two ways: first, in terms of *equality of opportunity*, noted as the 'traditional "weak" liberal definition of justice' and, second, as *equality of outcome* which is the 'more radical "strong" liberal version of justice'. While equality of opportunity refers to equal formal rights, access and participation, equality of outcome is different in that it seeks to ensure, through interventionist policies, to combat disadvantage and maintain equal rates of success for different societal groups. However, Gewirtz (1998) argues this is a somewhat narrow conception of justice, which needs to be expanded upon. Thus, she suggests a distinction is made between the distributive and the *relational* dimensions of justice. Relational justice constitutes the nature of the relationships which structure society and which Gewirtz (1998) regards as being 'strongly connected' to, though 'separate' from, the distributive dimension. Her explanation of the relational dimensions is, in essence, about issues of power:

> It is about the *nature* and *ordering* of social relations, the formal and informal rules which govern how members of society treat each other both on a macro level and at a micro interpersonal level. Thus it refers to the practices and procedures which govern the organization of political systems, economic and social institutions, families and one-to-one social relationships. These things cannot unproblematically be conceptually reduced to matters of distribution. (1998: 471: original emphasis)

Gerwitz (1998) contends that the distributional dimension is individualistic in nature whereas the relational dimension is holistic and more concerned with 'the nature of inter-connections between individuals in society'. At this point, it is useful to give consideration to what might be considered the antithesis of social justice, namely inequality. Inequalities exist in many forms in society in the UK and are based on, for example, social class, gender, race, ethnicity and physical ability. Inequalities are produced and re-produced in different ways and at different times and, in recent times, often as a result of post-welfarist[1] policies; the restructuring of public services and changes in government; and/or as a result of the global economy impacting on national decision-making. Significantly, however, inequalities are manifested at different times in the range of concerns identified by policy-makers and in the formation of different understandings of what is deemed as 'problematic'. As such, the concept of social justice is not necessarily fixed or static and has seen notable shifts since the creation of the welfare state in the UK in the post-war settlement of the mid-1940s. Phillips (1997: 143), for example, notes a shift in the nature of the language used to talk about social justice issues from the early 1980s onwards noting 'difference in particular seems to have displaced inequality as the central concern of political and social theory'. The focus on 'difference', belonging, for example, to a particular gender or ethnic group, is currently given more attention by policy-makers and, as such, has led to 'politics of difference' (Harvey, 1993; Leonard, 1997).

The social-democratic settlement pursued social justice based on redistribution from the mid-1940s to the late-1970s, when thinking shifted towards individual rights and to market-individualism. This perspective rests on the idea of what people deserve rather than on the notion of fairness per se. It operates on the assumption that the state does not have the right to transfer goods or poverty owned by individuals without their consent. Thus the market is perceived as a neutral mechanism in facilitating social exchange and the exercise of individual choice. In contrast, the social-democratic tradition rejects the notion of individualism while promoting that of community. Also, the idea of the *laissez-faire* market sits uneasily with the social-democratic view and justice, unless markets are controlled to ensure equal treatment, access and participation in decision-making and in power relations. Different governments in the UK since 1945 have emphasized different aspects of these traditions of social justice. These shifts in emphasis are pursued in the next section.

Pause and ponder

1 What is your understanding of social justice?
2 If possible, ask someone else their understanding of social justice. Are your views different? If so, how?
3 Different educational systems address social justice in different ways. In your opinion, how and to what extent should education be structured as an instrument for promoting social justice?

The construction of welfare

In the mid-1940s in the aftermath of the Second World War, the universalist welfare state was created in Britain to provide assistance for all citizens and offered protection from 'the cradle to the grave'. The state directly intervened in what became known as the 'post-war social settlement' or the 'social democratic consensus' to address society's five perceived social 'evils', namely, want, squalor, idleness, ignorance and disease (Williams, 1989). What is evident in this era is a political discourse of social democracy with a positive concern for social justice and various policies, initiatives and interventions that were deemed to be equitable, designed to achieve equality and eliminate poverty. There was a consistent expansion of welfare through social policies from 1945 until the mid-1970s (Jones, 1991; Sullivan, 1992), which was underpinned by a Keynesian approach to the economy (see Chapter 7). Education was regarded as the means by which society's inequalities and problems could be tackled to bring about social change and a socially just society. Educational initiatives were framed by the language (discourse) of 'equality of opportunity' whereby, regardless of social class, family background or location every child was to have educational opportunities via the tripartite system which emanated from the 1944 Education Act (see Chapter 4). Higher education also expanded with the introduction of grants for students and the growth of provision for teacher education. As a means of combating social and economic deprivation, policies such as free school meals came into being for disadvantaged children as well as free milk at school for all children (David, 1980). The prevalence of the post-war social-democratic ideology entailed creating more socially just educational policies and practices.

By the mid- to late 1970s, however, the welfare state was considered inherently inefficient, monopolistically bureaucratic and a tremendous drain on resources, which could not be sustained (Sullivan, 1994). In addition, there was growing disillusionment with education as a mechanism for promoting equality of opportunity. The massive investment in education following the social democratic consensus on education policy was considered very expensive, while standards remained poor (Batho, 1990). Added to this there was teacher unrest between 1968 and 1974 (Grace, 1987). These events were significant in marking a turning point in attitudes towards education and also in the politicization of educational issues. In this climate of economic decline, education, along with all other public services such as health care, housing and social services, came under increasing scrutiny.

The New Right and the reconstruction welfare

The Conservative Party, under the leadership of Margaret Thatcher, came into government in 1979, by which time the welfare state in Britain was thought by policy-makers to be in crisis. Confidence in the system had deteriorated with the onset of economic problems following the world oil crisis of 1973. The rate of economic growth was curtailed as investments and profits fell, the traditional industrial base collapsed, unemployment increased and the economy contracted in the mid-1970s. Advocates of the New Right (see Chapter 1) used the economic problems to challenge the post-war social settlement and the symbolic place of the welfare state within it (Clarke and Newman, 1997). New Right ideology, coalescing neo-liberal and neo-conservative philosophies, challenged the supremacy of the welfare state and became a dominant force in policy. Neo-liberal economics emphasized the primacy of markets, free from state interference, as more effective mechanisms for the distribution of social resources. This philosophy presupposes that the privatization of public services and a reduction in the role of the state would alleviate the burden of public expenditure as the state's bureaucratic structures impeded Britain's economic survival and needed to be dismantled. Competition, it was argued, would increase the efficiency of public sector organizations and offer individuals freedom of choice. Incorporated in New Right politics is a neo-conservative strand committed to the regeneration of traditional moral values, authority, the virtues of a strong state and the intervention of government to achieve these (King, 1987; Gamble, 1988; Tomlinson, 1993). Whether complementary or contradictory, neo-liberal and neo-conservative philosophies came together under Thatcherism.

The New Right philosophy was essentially constructed around three key issues. First, the welfare state was regarded as expensive and a major factor contributing to the country's economic decline. Public expenditure on personal social services, health, housing, social security and education, for example, was viewed as a colossal drain on resources that could not be sustained. There was a very heavy burden on the citizen as taxpayer and this conflicted with the Conservative's commitment to low rates of direct taxation. Second, public services were considered inefficient and bureaucratic, and the citizen, as consumer, was being denied effective choice of service provision. Third, the effects of state welfare encouraged a disincentive to work and undermined individualism and initiative. The citizen being dependent on welfare services in a 'benefits culture' was thus deemed a 'scrounger', receiving public handouts to evade responsibility (Williams, 1989; Sullivan, 1994). New Right ideology perceived the privatization of such services and a reduction in the role of the state would alleviate the burden of public expenditure, increase their efficiency and offer freedom of choice for citizens. These three issues constitute different strands of the New Right ideology: a neo-liberal strand stressing the superiority of markets as more effective mechanisms for the distribution of social resources and the revival of economic individualism; and a neo-conservative strand committed to the revitalization of traditional morality and social authority (Clarke and Newman, 1997).

Margaret Thatcher, as Prime Minister, pursued the ideas and ideology of the New Right, which fundamentally reconstructed the relationship between the state and social welfare. Thatcherite individualism can be summarized as the belief that it is more preferable for people to look after themselves (and their families) than for them to combine as a society to provide for themselves collectively (Rentoul, 1990). This is best illustrated in Margaret Thatcher's classic and widely quoted statement:

> There's no such thing [as society]. There are individual men and women, and there are families and no government can do anything except through people and people look to themselves first. It is our duty to look after ourselves. (Keay, 1987: 8–10)

The ideology of individualism was coupled with the strategy of successive governments from 1979 to transform British society and its values, and to eliminate socialism. Subsequently, competitive markets increasingly became a more prominent feature in the welfare state during the 1980s, with quasi-markets and competition introduced into the public sector. This was most visible in the health and education services. The government's attempt to reduce expenditure was not entirely successful, however, and it actually increased by 11 per cent in real terms between 1979 and 1990 (Johnson, 1990). This was mainly due to increased social security expenditure as a result of rising unemployment and the need to finance the government's tougher policy on law and order and defence. Fundamental changes took place in all aspects of social policy, which led to legislation through major Acts of Parliament. A common factor throughout all areas of social policy was the belief in markets and competition.

The education marketplace: From equality to quality

The adoption of neo-liberal policies and a minimal state resulted in schools, colleges and universities having to operate in a more competitive environment. The chapter concentrates only on policies for schools, however, to illustrate how legislation, notably the ERA and subsequent policies by the New Labour government, encouraged schools to compete for a limited number of pupils in a market environment. The Conservative policies between 1979 and 1997 were deliberate attempts to provide greater diversity and choice by making schools significantly different from each other; new types of institutions emerged after 1988. City Technology Colleges, private schools with a vocational orientation which encouraged pupils to seek future careers in science or technology, were set up (the original intention was they would be sponsored by businesses). Grant-Maintained Schools, which could opt out of LEA control, were also created. These new institutions provided diversity in the system as well as reintroducing selective education. Open enrolment and parental choice became the main determinants of school admissions during the 1980s, and the introduction of a range of measures, such as national assessment and performance/league tables, transformed the education system by introducing market forces. Through the Assisted Places Scheme, the government covered in part or fully tuition fees for 'the most able' pupils to attend schools in the independent rather than the maintained sector.

It is claimed that marketization produces a system more responsive to customer requirements, providing greater diversity between schools and thus greater choice for parents. It is at this juncture that we can see a fundamental shift from the traditional ways of thinking about social justice in education (i.e. the social democratic approach that underpinned post-war policies until the 1980s), with a strong role for the state in realizing greater equality of access, opportunities and outcomes. Hereafter, education is regarded as a commodity, with schools, as rival outlets, competing for parents' custom, and parents henceforth empowered to choose from a range of products. The beginnings of the break-up of state provision and the push for privatization can be seen. Through LMS, schools were empowered, for example, to manage their own budget, set their own expenditure and contract services from outside the LEA. New school types, CTCs, were established which could be taken over and run by business, and the nursery voucher scheme enabled parents to choose from a range of pre-school provision and 'spend' their entitlement in local authority maintained or private nurseries (Ball, 2007).

Proponents of the market ideology argue that all parents should have the right to send their children to the school of their choice (not just the geographically nearest one) as this will enable individual aspirations to be aligned with anticipated school outcomes (Braithwaite, 1992). The state's role and responsibility in such a process is no longer that of provider of a common education service for all children (Pring, 1986), but a role that ensures parents have the right to individual choice of school under free market conditions (Braithwaite, 1992). Advocates of neo-liberalism contend that competition among schools will ultimately raise standards in education, improve quality and provide accountability through the mechanism of market forces. The free market ideology supposes that by encouraging diversity and choice a more competitive environment will be created between producers. The right of choice in education has been given in law to parents, empowering them as consumers of education. Implicit in this process is the assumption that given adequate information parents, as consumers, will make rational choices.

Neo-liberalism presents the market as neutral and all consumers have a viable choice. Parents have been regarded collectively as a homogeneous group of consumers in the education market, with an interest in their child's education. This ideology presupposes that all parents have the resources available to them to facilitate choice: the time to travel in search of the most appropriate school for their child, the availability of cars to transport their child over any distance or the resources to fund public transport and, in the last resort, the capacity to move house. It presupposes that by using indicators of performance such as league tables of national examinations, obtaining prospectuses and visiting schools, the role of parents, as clients or consumers of education, is to make considered and informed choices on behalf of their children (Angus, 1994). However, the lived experience of choice reveals the complexity and injustice of the education market, as Ranson (1993: 337) contends:

> Choice imposes costs which are likely to be prohibitive for many families. As emerging evidence indicates, for many families, certainly in rural areas, the promise of choice is regarded cynically as empty rhetoric. To lack resources is to be disenfranchised from the polity of the market.

The political rhetoric strongly emphasizes increased parental choice. However, largely due to economic or geographical differences, parents do not have available to them, or experience, the same range of choices. In reality, the concept of 'choice' constitutes different meanings to different groups of families and is socially and culturally constructed (Carroll and Walford, 1997). Research conducted on the issue of parental choice suggests that certain types of parent have a greater capacity than others to 'play the market' and are more inclined to make a proactive choice (Gewirtz et al., 1994, 1995; Ball et al., 1995). Parents possessing the appropriate economic, social and 'cultural capital' (Bourdieu and Passeron, 1990) necessary to play the system are more likely to succeed in the education market, making informed choices and securing places for their children in more reputable and advantaged schools. Children from disadvantaged backgrounds, whose parents possess inadequate knowledge of the education system and/or comprehend the choice mechanisms of the education market, are more likely to end up in schools with poorer facilities and whose academic performance is inferior (Gewirtz et al., 1994, 1995; Carroll and Walford, 1997). Researchers have examined the socio-economic inequalities of choice, categorized parents according to the extent to which they participate in the education marketplace and correlated this to their social class. Parents have been labelled as 'choosers' and 'non-choosers' (Adler et al., 1989); 'alert' and 'inert' (Willms and Echols, 1992); 'privileged', 'semi-skilled' and the 'disconnected' (Ball et al., 1995); and 'active' and 'passive' (Carroll and Walford, 1997). These dualisms and categorizations illustrate different responses to choice by middle- and working-class parents. Arguably, this form of school admissions system does not adequately address issues relating to equity and social justice and is a clear departure from the 'earlier implicit consensus commitment to social justice' (Jonathan cited in West, 2006: 15).

Market-individualism is not unique to the UK, however, but emerged due to the global propensity for and convergence towards neo-liberal thinking in education (see Chapters 4, 7 and 9). Nevertheless, the Conservative government (1979–1997) set the stage for a continuation of neo-liberal marketization and greater privatization.

New Labour: An intense phase of educational policy-making

New Labour positioned its ideological thinking as 'the Third Way' (Giddens, 1998; 2000), a perspective which harnesses a social capitalist model (state intervention) and a neo-liberal model (market forces) to create social and economic well-being (see Chapter 1). The New Labour government was committed to the market model and to social justice, but arguably Third Way philosophy is primarily concerned with inclusion rather than equality. Where citizens were 'socially excluded', New Labour saw it was the state's responsibility to step in, albeit to assist in restoring self-sufficiency, rather than creating dependency. Government priorities changed under New Labour with resources targeted towards disadvantaged communities through social security and investment in public services (Driver, 2008). New Labour placed education at the heart of its policies and as a mechanism for change which would alleviate social exclusion and bring about equality of opportunity (Hall and Raffo, 2009). Significantly, New Labour regarded educational qualifications as a route out of poverty and targeted resources at those from socio-economically disadvantaged backgrounds. New Labour thus invested heavily in education to drive government policies via intervention and direction while simultaneously regarding education as 'the best economic policy there is' (Blair, 1996: 66) (see Chapter 7).

According to Exley and Ball (2011: 110), 'New Labour took the Conservative infrastructure and gave it meat and teeth'. Few outright policy reversals were made and were designed 'to benefit the many, not just the few', notably the abolition of the nursery voucher (see Chapter 5) and Grant-Maintained Schools and phasing out the Assisted Places Scheme. The education market remained, as did the mechanism of 'choice'; thus the inevitable reproduction of the inequities of neo-liberalism (as described above) continued. Perhaps the most notable difference of the incoming New Labour government was its reluctance to rely merely on market forces to improve quality and raise standards in schools, but to intervene directly into the curriculum and school organization and by setting challenging targets for pupil and student achievement. New Labour was not averse to the private sector or the involvement of business in providing core educational services and policy delivery. LMS was maintained, which further weakened LEAs, but central control and direction increased. Like its Conservative predecessor, the New Labour government drew attention to failing schools, and pledged there would be 'zero tolerance' of under-performance and 'speedy intervention where necessary'. Prime Minister Blair (1998: 30) stated, 'when schools fail we will intervene promptly to protect the prospects of the pupils'. As such, poor performing schools were 'named and shamed', with arrangements made to close them down and reopen with a new head teacher under 'Fresh Start' or, later on, as an Academy school (of which, more below). Policy-makers proclaimed that 'significant extra resources' would be invested in education; in return 'significant improvements in standards' were expected from school teachers and leaders (DfEE, 1998a: 4). The proposals thus offered 'something for something' (Blunkett, 1998) and investment in education was tied to accountability.

Before considering New Labour's commitment to social justice, we first examine what 'old' Labour represented during its periods in government post-1945 (from 1945 to 1951, from 1964 to 1970 and from 1974 to 1979). Old Labour favoured

Keynesian demand management, whereby the state influenced the direction of the economy (see Chapter 7) underpinned by the philosophy that state planning and investment would maintain full employment. The party also leaned towards state welfarism and a 'tax and spend' approach (Driver and Martell, 1998). Basically, the thinking was that economic growth, as steered by government intervention, would pay for the services of the welfare state, thereby bringing greater equality to society. In addition, there was public ownership (e.g. rail, electricity, gas, telecommunications), controls on private business (e.g. on export of capital) and a strong role for trade unions in the workplace and in the shaping of policy (corporatism). 'New' Labour is significantly different to Old Labour in that in the aftermath of the eighteen years of Conservative governments (1979–1997) it is associated with not re-nationalizing privatized industries, not re-establishing controls on business and not re-establishing a strong role for trade unions. However, when Tony Blair became prime minister in 1997, he contended Labour's old values of community, inclusion, fairness and social justice remained the same (Driver and Martell, 1998). As such, New Labour intervened directly in education to tackle social disadvantage and improve the country's economic performance:

> To overcome economic and social disadvantage and to make opportunity a reality…To compete in the global economy…We must overcome the spiral of disadvantage…I ask of you to join us in making the crusade for higher standards a reality in every classroom and every household in the country. (DfEE, 1997a: 3–4)

New Labour's policies were designed to restore social cohesion and social justice which it perceived as an antidote to the emphasis on the individual and which had emanated through New Right policies. New Labour's development of the concept of 'social exclusion', which it saw as emanating from 'a multiplicity of factors in peoples' lives' (Dyson et al., 2009: 147), led in turn to a multiplicity of initiatives and signified increased awareness of a way in which certain groups of people, for various reasons, live outside mainstream society: those who are socially marginalized and are disempowered. New Labour aimed to combat social exclusion through its policy initiatives, believing the socially excluded are unable to realize their full potential, participate fully in the workings of the institutions that govern peoples' lives or consider themselves full and equal members of the community. In terms of education, New Labour moved away from the notion that educational failure is associated with deprivation and social class position towards the ideas elucidated by the school effectiveness and school improvement research fields and that schools have the potential to make a difference (Reynolds, 1986). Policy-makers, however, have tended to ignore the appeal from school improvement researchers that context-specific improvement strategies are necessary (Harris and Chapman, 2004) and that a 'one-size-fits-all' policy solution is futile. Nevertheless, New Labour invested massively in intervention programmes to support schools in 'challenging circumstances' in order to combat disadvantage. These are too numerous to discuss in detail here (see Chapman and Gunter, 2009) and so we highlight a selection. The *Excellence in Cities* programme (DfEE, 1997b) provided additional funding for schools in deprived areas, aimed to raise achievement among working-class groups and promote social inclusion (Whitty, 2001). Education Action Zones involved business participation and were introduced as part of the School Standards and Frameworks Bill (1998) in areas with low levels of educational attainment and where there were high levels of social exclusion. The Schools in Challenging Circumstances Initiative, introduced in 2001, and the National Challenge in 2008 were initiatives for schools in particularly difficult contexts and those that fail to meet government floor standards.[2] In order to improve standards, they received additional funding and resources, inspection and external support. The focus on urban poverty came with the 2000 City Academies Programme, which built on the Conservative's CTC's legacy. When in opposition, the Labour Party had opposed this policy, considering it unjust and inequitable. Nevertheless, when in government, New Labour created City Academies to arrest the spiral of decline in disadvantaged areas and to improve pupil results. Academies were independent of LEA control and sponsored by private companies, charities or individuals (Beckett, 2007). An investment of £2 million was initially required towards the new school (though this was later dropped) and an Academy was created following the closure of a failing secondary school (or several in a locality). There were changes following the Education Act 2002; the perquisites of urban, failing and city were no longer qualifying attributes; and sponsors included faith or voluntary groups, universities and other schools. There were 203 Academies established under New Labour (Lupton and Thomson, 2015a), representing approximately 6.5 per cent of secondary schools in England.

Early years provision expanded (see Chapter 5), with an increase in places for 3–5-year-olds and greater concentration of resources with the aim of developing high-quality provision to assist the educational development of pre-school children. The *Every Child Matters* (ECM) agenda (DfES, 2004a) gave rise to a package of welfare reforms. Its list of five desirable outcomes (see Chapter 5) led to sweeping changes, including inter-agency collaboration, which were legislated in 2004 through the Children Act. Ambiguities are evident in New Labour's policies as illustrated in ECM: first, for example, the requirement to produce evidence as individual high-performing learning organizations and also engage in inter-agency collaboration as demanded by ECM. Second, two of the five desired ECM outcomes namely 'achieving economic well-being' and 'making a positive contribution' sit outside the remit of the newly integrated children's services. Finally, it is not clear how the five desired outcomes relate to each other, which to prioritize or which services are expected to take the lead. This raises all sorts of questions, especially around accountability and professional boundaries. Which group of professionals are accountable and when? What are the professional territories and boundaries? How can effective collaboration be achieved? These are just some of the ambiguities that those working at the forefront of policy implementation and/or delivery have to reconcile.

Early intervention programmes such as Sure Start (see Chapter 5), Baby Bonds and increasing childcare places attempted to address inequalities at birth, aiming at giving everyone, despite their background, a minimum starting point. Although not equal, this 'asset-based' approach to social justice is one where everyone has 'a fair chance of making the most of their lives given their abilities and effort' (Driver, 2008: 66). However, such policies are problematic as they alone are unlikely to succeed in narrowing the gap in the distribution of wealth and income between rich and poor social groups. While New Labour's policies made some inroads in addressing relative poverty, there are those who may not have had the capacity or resources to participate in the market environment and experience any notion of 'choice'. In that sense, despite radical reform of the public sector and record spending, British society remained unequal in 2010, when New Labour's time in government came to a close.

Pause and ponder

Economic competition, growth and innovation have powerful effects on social structure and processes of inclusion and exclusion. New Labour placed education at the centre of its policies for encouraging economic growth (see also Chapter 7).

1   Can this be achieved without creating social fragmentation?
2   Is the raising of the school-leaving age appropriate, in your opinion, to address youth employment?

Post-2010: Schooling and social justice

While in opposition, and losing the General Elections of 2001 and 2005, the Conservative Party had time to contemplate their pre-1997 policy approach and challenge the propensity for New Right theory. David Cameron adopted the stance of 'compassionate conservatism' with its new focus on social justice:

> We're all in this together ... we have a shared responsibility for our shared future ... *There is such a thing as society*; it's just not the same thing as the state. We will stand up for the victims of state failure and ensure that social justice and economic opportunity are achieved by empowering people and communities. (Cameron cited in Norman and Ganesh, 2006: 1: emphasis added)

According to Exley and Ball (2011), the Conservatives see educational failure, as evidenced in the attainment gap between socio-economic groups, and the lack of social mobility, as issues to be remedied by individuals, families, communities, social enterprise and the market, rather than by state regulation of education.

When the Conservative-Liberal Democrat Coalition entered government in May 2010, there was, almost immediately, a different emphasis in policy which was framed by the rhetoric of the Conservative's 'Big Society'. This had been alluded to in pre-Coalition days and articulated by David Cameron in 2009:

> We believe that a strong society will solve our problems more effectively than big government has or ever will, we want the state to act as an instrument for helping to create that strong society. Our alternative to big government is the big society … The era of big government has run its course. Poverty and inequality have got worse, despite Labour's massive expansion of the state. We need new answers now, and they will only come from a bigger society, not a bigger government. (Cameron cited in Gallagher, 2009: n.p.)

The Big Society embraces the idea that power should reside with individuals, social groups and communities rather than with government and its organizations. Just as 'Thatcherism' and the 'Third Way' evolved as political projects, so the notion of the Big Society was advanced by the Conservatives. There has been much debate among commentators about the Big Society: whether it differs from or is similar to New Labour's policies for reforming welfare/public services and which encouraged democratic participation through involving citizens in decision-making, or to what extent there are differences or similarities with Thatcherite ideas regarding a minimal role for the state. However, those debates aside, the rhetoric of the Big Society, namely 'empowering communities', 'opening up public services' and 'promoting social action' underpinned, in theory at least, the Coalition's policies for schools.

One of the Coalition's first visible changes in education was to scrap the Department for Children, Schools and Families (DCSF), which had overseen the integration of services outlined in the previous section, and replace it with the DfE. With the emphasis in education firmly on 'schools', the Coalition intended to facilitate change by removing some of New Labour's regulatory frameworks, reducing unnecessary bureaucracy, giving schools and head teachers greater freedom, promoting diversity and creating greater choice. The focus on schools is hardly surprising given the indications by the then Shadow Schools' Secretary, Michael Gove, when the Conservatives were in opposition (from 1997 to 2010):

> The central mission of the next Conservative government is the alleviation of poverty and the extension of opportunity. And nowhere is action required more than in our schools. Schools should be engines of social mobility … The sad truth about our schools today is that, far from making opportunity more equal, they only deepen the

divide between the rich and poor, the fortunate and the forgotten … We will break up the bureaucratic monopoly on school provision, which denies parents choice and introduce competition specifically to help drive up standards. (Gove cited in Shepherd, 2009: n.p.)

Tenets of the Big Society emerge in the high-profile 'Free Schools' programme (see Chapter 9), which was heralded in via the 2010 Academies Act and saw 254 opened during the Coalition government. Parents, other groups and private providers are encouraged to set up and run their own Free Schools, which are essentially a new form of Academy. As such, advocates of Free Schools might regard this new policy direction as embracing Big Society ideals by 'exemplifying popular democracy' (Hatcher, 2011: 498). Critics, however, perceive Free Schools as fundamentally violating 'the principles of democratic accountability' (2011: 498) because of the nature of the proposal and approval process (which is not transparent), their governance (the governing body is less democratic than maintained schools) and their lack of local accountability (they are accountable to the secretary of state) (2011). Arguably, beneath the rational presentation of policy, tensions smoulder as independence and self-governance coexist alongside privatization and greater fragmentation in the education system. Higham (2014: 137) identifies 'a critical tension within free school policy' in the Big Society which centres on the 'discourse of openness'. There is an assumption that the market is 'a level playing field', whereby 'new civil society actors' have equal access to 'state resources' (2014: 137). However, some 'actors' or 'proposers' of Free Schools are advantaged as they have greater capacity to play the market as they possess the appropriate 'economic, cultural, social and symbolic capitals' to succeed. The application process seemingly advantages those with 'particular forms of professional expertise and experience', but 'the majority of proposers located in highly disadvantaged areas have aims and expertise that do not fit well with what the government is willing to accept' (Higham, 2014: 137). Ball (2013: 212) observes the tension between 'Big Society and Big Capital' which he elucidates as 'localism and mutualism, on the one hand, and multinational business and large chains on the other'. While these may seem ostensive conflicts within Free Schools' policy, it is nevertheless the intention of the Conservative government to increase their number to 500 by 2020. The secretary of state claims Free Schools are the 'modern engines of social justice' helping 'break the cycle of disadvantage' (Morgan, 2015: n.p.). Announcing the government's intentions, Morgan declared:

Free schools are at the heart of the government's commitment to deliver real social justice by ensuring all pupils have *access* to a world class education. This is at the core of our commitment to govern as one nation – creating a country where everyone, regardless of their background, can achieve their high aspirations. […] Half of all free schools are in the most deprived areas of the country, offering a fresh chance for families to break the cycle of disadvantage by providing a quality of schooling never before seen in many communities. [...] I'm calling on all high performing schools, sponsors, charities, community groups and parents to come forward with their proposals for new schools. (2015: emphasis added)

In order to encourage greater diversity of provision and increase choice in the education marketplace, the Coalition expanded the Academies Programme through the Academies Act of 2010. This enabled outstanding schools, as judged by Ofsted, to seek academy status as well as extend eligibility to primary and special schools, a further deviation from New Labour's original ideas for Academies. Later, 'academization' (the process of changing to an independent state school) was extended via the Education Act of 2011 to all schools. Controversially, schools deemed by Ofsted as poor or failing were forced to become Academies. As with New Labour's approach, academy sponsorship was used to replace failing schools. However, the enforced conversion to academy status is not always wanted by the school and parents; herein lies a notable difference with the former New Labour government whereby consent was gained first from local authorities (Allen, 2015). The rapid academization of schools in England represents a dramatic 'whole system change' (Lupton and Thomson, 2015a: 14). As declared in the schools' White Paper, the ambition is that 'Academy status should be the norm for all state schools' (DfE: 2010a: 52). This aspiration, however, is not that dissimilar to that of Blair, who regarded Academies as an 'integral part' of education that brings 'more choice and higher standards' (BBC, 2006).

The principles of the reforms proposed in the schools' White Paper, and later legislated via the Education Act 2011, purport greater freedom will 'drive innovation', which will 'raise standards' and 'narrow the gap in attainment between rich and poor' (DfE, 2010a). Academies do not have to follow the National Curriculum; they have control of their budget, autonomy over the school year (term times), staff pay and conditions; and they can employ unqualified teachers. Cases of financial malpractice, fraud and mismanagement have received attention in the media (e.g. Stewart, 2012) which suggests some Academies are 'mobilising their new freedoms in improper ways' (Keddie, 2014: 503). Research undertaken in a secondary Academy found greater freedom, and flexibility is curbed, however, by the rigorous monitoring and surveillance mechanisms of the 'audit culture' in schools and the 'tight external strictures holding them to account' (2014: 504). Research within a primary Academy found teachers lack autonomy in the classroom as their work remains 'heavily regulated' and they 'experience greater pressure to deliver the best results' (Chrostowska, 2015). While these are single case studies and their limitations acknowledged, their findings nevertheless provide insight into how Academies experience, mediate and engage their autonomy/freedom and so illustrate the general processes.

Lupton and Thomson's (2015a) findings reveal one in ten primary schools and 57 per cent of secondary schools were Academies by 2014; most belong to chains, although some are stand-alone. Gorard's (2014: 268) research verifies those of previous studies 'in finding no convincing evidence that Academies are any more (or less) effective than the schools they replaced or are in competition with'. Gorard's (2014) analysis reveals that on average Converter Academies take a smaller share of pupils from disadvantaged backgrounds, whereas Sponsor-Led Academies take more. While he suggests Academies are not causing local socio-economic segregation, but reflect the inequitable mix in a local area, he argues 'Academies are not helping reduce segregation (as was one of their original purposes)' (2014: 268). Gorard also contends the Academies Programme is now being 'driven by the purported school improvement agenda, and the social justice element is now largely ignored, meaning that almost any school is eligible to convert. Private fee-paying schools, ex-grammar schools, Foundation schools … have become Academies' (2014: 269). Bhattacharya's (2013: 97) analysis highlights the 'inconclusive nature' of reports about the performance and operation of Academies, noting 'concerns remain about their overall impact on improving the education of children from lower socioeconomic backgrounds'. This public-funded/private provision model of schooling, thus, remains a contested area of policy (Gunter, 2011).

Tackling educational disadvantage and reducing differences in socio-economic attainment were espoused priorities for the Coalition and continue to be so for the Conservative government. The Pupil Premium introduced in 2010 was paid to schools for each pupil eligible for free school meals. This 'extra' funding was targeted on raising the attainment of those pupils and with the onus on schools to determine how they could be best supported. Lupton and Thomson's (2015a: 50) verdict is as follows:

> It may be too early to judge the effect of the Pupil Premium, and certainly too early to say that it has failed. However, the fact that, despite these efforts outcomes seem to be getting worse for some of the most disadvantaged students at the end of secondary schooling, and remain very large throughout the system, should certainly raise questions about whether initiatives of this nature can deliver greater equality and/or social mobility in the context both of increasing family poverty and the broader suite of educational reforms which has been enacted.

The political narrative of the Big Society waned over the course of the Coalition government, featuring very little if at all in policy exhortations five years on. In May 2015 Cameron (2015: 20) articulated the goals of the majority Conservative government:

> Our first aim is to help working people get on … Our second goal is social justice. Educational excellence shouldn't just be the preserve of the wealthy and the leafy suburbs. Free Schools and academies are already putting paid to that notion.

Reforms to schools accelerated post-2010 and there seems little abatement. In October 2015 Nicky Morgan approved the expansion of the Weald of Kent Grammar School in the form of an 'annexe' situated several miles away (Hurst, 2015). This is a highly political decision which has sparked controversy on a number of counts not least because the move portends an expansion of selective education, regarded by some as fostering social mobility and by others as socially divisive and compounding social disadvantage. It will be interesting to see what transpires from the secretary of state's decision and the subsequent impact upon school provision.

The universalism of state education provision was arguably undermined from 1980s onwards and arguably policies have continued to foster social inequalities. The conception of social justice is such that public policies are mostly concerned with issues of distribution and access. So in terms of education, there is an increased emphasis on access to education and raising standards (DfE, 2010a). However, as educational outcomes and research findings have both shown, these measures do not lead to equity and, as has been illustrated in this chapter, the pursuit of equity does not always appear to be the primary objective of some policies.

Over to you …

Understanding the continuities and differences of education policies is an important part of policy analysis. Note down what you think are the key continuities and differences between the education policies of the following governments:

a) Conservative (1979–1997) and New Labour (1997–2010)
b) New Labour (1997–2010) and Conservative-Liberal Democrats Coalition (2010–2015)
c) Conservative (1979–1997) and Conservative (post-2015)

1 How do you account for these differences?
2 Can you identify any particular trends or patterns in policies?

Notes

1   Policies that expect the individual to be economically self-sufficient rather than being dependent on state provision.
2   Expected levels of school and college performance.

Further reading

Gunter, H. M. ed. (2011) *The State and Education Policy: The Academies Programme*, London: Continuum.

Hoskins, K. and B. Barker (2014) *Education and Social Mobility: Dreams of Success*, Stoke-on-Trent: Trentham Books

Smith, E. (2012) *Key Issues in Education and Social Justice*, London: Sage.

The Evolving Primary Curriculum

Introduction

Primary schools in England (local authority maintained) are required to offer a balanced and broadly based curriculum, which comprises as a minimum a statutory[1] National Curriculum and Religious Education (RE). Pupils at the end of Key Stage One are evaluated through teacher-assessed tasks and tests. Pupils at the end of Key Stage Two, their final year of primary education, take national tests. Key Stage Two results are published by the DfE in the form of school performance tables (league tables) in England for public scrutiny, providing 'consumers of education' (i.e. parents, stakeholders and policy-makers) with comparative data. Inevitably, the growing emphasis on output and testing has pressurized teachers, and by default pupils, to focus on performance. Since its introduction in 1988, the National Curriculum has caused much controversy regarding its content and assessment arrangements and there has been increased emphasis on raising standards and the development of standardized indicators of performance through various assessment mechanisms. Inspection and appraisal regimes monitor teaching and learning processes and compliance with government policies and initiatives; schools, leaders and teachers (and also pupils) that are deemed to be 'failing' are subsequently exposed. School leaders and teachers are accountable to the public with much of their time devoted to activities which, arguably, relate to accountability rather than leading and/or teaching. The present situation in primary education and the present primary curriculum are rooted in a long and chequered educational history. Thus, this chapter performs a genealogical analysis illustrating how the curriculum has changed over time and yet has always been a site of conflict because different ideologies or 'traditions' (Blyth, 1965) that dictated curriculum and practice have been emphasized. The more traditionally conservative and classical humanist discourses of education within the primary phase can be 'read' as competing with more liberal-progressive, configuring discourses enshrined in The Plowden Report (CACE, 1967). The idea that a nation's economic success is closely aligned with its levels of literacy and numeracy has invariably influenced the curriculum and remains an enduring trend. The chapter begins by considering the nature of elementary education, which preceded what we now know today as primary education. The analysis examines how, over time, changes in education policy have enabled the shifting of control over curricula content and pedagogy as policy-makers have attempted to address a range of contemporary social, economic and political issues. It is therefore impossible to consider how the primary curriculum has been conceptualized and its nature contested without contemplating and analysing the political, economic, social and historical dimensions in which this change is located. Furthermore, the chapter considers the desire of policy-makers to maintain control over education for the 'masses' and the curriculum and to regulate the work of elementary/primary teachers. As such, the chapter examines the concurrent erosion of teacher professionalism, resulting in what Campbell (2001) regards as the 'colonisation' of the primary curriculum and the de-professionalization of teachers.

Late nineteenth and early twentieth centuries: The early elementary curriculum and 'payment by results'

In order to comprehend the primary curriculum as it stands in 2016, it is necessary to look back to educational provision some 150 years earlier. The Elementary Education Act of 1870 is the landmark piece of legislation which signalled the beginning of the present state-funded system of education in Britain; prior to this, public elementary education for the 'labouring poor' was largely provided by the churches (known as voluntary provision). Provision was patchy and concentrated on basic reading, writing and number skills as well as religious instruction. In 1862, the Liberal government specified the content of the curriculum and divided it into six standards (stages) through 'the Revised Code'[2] (Curtis, 1967). A compulsory syllabus of the rudimentary subjects of reading, writing and arithmetic (commonly known as the 'three Rs' – Reading, wRiting and aRithmetic) – as well as needlework for girls – was prescribed for each standard. The mandated curriculum of the Revised Code fundamentally changed the way teachers worked and how they were remunerated, and imposed a strict regime of regulation and supervision. The 'Revised Code' arguably had a number of functions. It concentrated teaching and children's learning on the basic subjects and made more relevant the content of elementary education to the needs of contemporary society rather than merely those of the churches (Richards, 1999). A grant was paid directly to school managers, the amount of which depended on examinations' outcomes in reading, writing and arithmetic and was undertaken by external HMI inspectors, and also on pupil attendance. Teachers' salaries were then paid by the school managers and linked to the performance of their pupils. Inspectors were empowered to remove teachers' certificates or 'blacklist' those teachers who failed to meet the required standards (Barber, 1992). Inspectors also monitored the effects of the Revised Code in schools and the extent of schools' compliance with it.

Preparations for the examinations entailed a repetitive and mechanical daily drilling by teachers. Elementary teaching viewed the curriculum as a repository of essential subject matter and skills which teachers transmitted and learning by rote was commonplace (Simon, 1967). Elementary education was essentially concerned with product rather than processes, with didactic methods employed so children 'received' the curriculum. Regarding the content of the Code Richards (1999: 55) notes, 'No reference was made to the knowledge, understanding or attitudes to be taught to, or developed within, children; pupils were viewed simply as being able (or unable) to demonstrate a limited number of elementary skills devoid of meaning and context'. Referred to as 'payment by results' this system operated for thirty-five years in schools and had a marked influence on teaching practice. Although its narrowness was later modified to include other subjects, it was nevertheless successful in 'discouraging initiative and developing habits of obedience docility and passivity – in teachers as well as in pupils' (Richards, 1999: 55–56). Commenting on the Revised Code at the time as an inspector Kay-Shuttleworth (1868 cited in Pollard, 1996: 143) stated:

> The inspection has been converted into a mechanical examination of these rudiments. The attention of the Managers and Teachers has, by the conditions of the Capitation Grant, been injuriously concentrated on a daily routine of daily drill in reading, writing

and ciphering. The result has been a larger amount of failures among the scholars when examined in these subjects, and the general neglect of the higher subjects of instruction, and of cultivation of the general intelligence of the children. The schools are lower in their aims, the scholars worse instructed, and there is a tendency to deterioration in the whole machinery of education.

The imposition of the Revised Code is significant in a number of ways. First, it illustrates the state's desire to exert control over education for the lower classes of the population as well as facilitate social consensus at a time of industrialization, social upheaval and change. While it was believed that some basic literacy, numeracy and religious instruction were potentially beneficial for economic reasons, the shortcomings of the Code ensured that the lower orders would not be 'overeducated' above their station in life, moral docility was maintained and the existing social stratification was preserved. Eggleston (1977: 32) maintains 'the elementary school emphasized deference, submission and even servility' through low-status subjects and engendering low-status attitudes. Second, it demonstrates how elementary teachers themselves were controlled by the state through measures that determined what they taught and how they were paid. When 'payment by results' was withdrawn in 1897 although government retained oversight of the elementary curriculum, teaching more detailed content was left to the discretion of individual school boards, schools and teachers. However, the constraining conservative practices instilled by 'payment by results' remained for many years; the emphasis on the 3Rs persisted. Other subjects such as geography, history, nature study, gardening (for boys), art and craft, drama, dramatic play and construction activities (for younger children), physical education and music gradually became more commonplace in the elementary classroom from 1897 to 1944 (Richards, 1999).

Pause and ponder

Periodically the primary curriculum has been criticized for neglecting the 'basics' (i.e. literacy and numeracy).

1 What do you think are the reasons for this criticism and do you think they are justified?
2 Are there any disadvantages with this approach?

The National Curriculum comprises core and foundation subjects:

3 Why are some subjects given more importance than others?
4 Is it appropriate that the status of subjects is not the same?

The interwar years (1918–1939): Educational and economic stagnation

Elementary education remained relatively unchanged, during the interwar years which Simon (1991: 25) describes as 'a period of stagnation, both economically and educationally'. Although schools had greater curricular discretion through a less prescriptive and somewhat vague Elementary Code (1926), any change was slow. The publication of the *Handbook of Suggestions for the Consideration of Teachers and Others Concerned in the Work of Elementary Schools* in 1927[3] provided information and guidance to support the Code and the Board of Education's (the government office) support for teachers to determine their own methods (Richards, 1999). Elementary schools continued to provide education for working-class children, but they were largely excluded from secondary education due to its fees, although there was some limited opportunity through free places and scholarships (David, 1980; Tomlinson, 2005). The widening of post-elementary or secondary education was a key aim of the labour movement and Labour Party. Primary and secondary schools date from the Hadow Report of 1926, which reorganized elementary schools into infant schools for five- to seven-year-olds and junior schools for seven- to eleven-year-olds. (Senior schools were for eleven to fourteen-year-olds.) Primary covered children aged five to eleven as a whole school or in two stages (infant and junior). Re-organization along these lines was gradual and slow, eventually completing in 1972. Streaming of children according to their academic ability was permitted in junior (and senior) schools, regarded at the time as a rational and desirable step and by the 1930s was commonplace (Simon, 1991). While the Hadow Report of 1931 (Board of Education, 1931) acknowledged that primary children required an education suitable to their stage of physical and intellectual development, economic problems impacted educational expenditure in the 1930s and no new policies were instigated. David (1980: 59) describes the school system at this time as 'an administrative muddle', and in terms of curricula appraisal and innovation, no such mechanisms existed.

Post-war consensus (1944–1970s): The pursuit of equality of opportunity

The post-war era was a period of optimism, reconstruction and potential economic growth. The creation of the welfare state to tackle society's five social 'evils' (want, squalor, idleness, ignorance and disease) was concerned with the 'collective' well-being of individuals and of communities (Williams, 1989). There was general agreement among the political parties of a more interventionist approach by the state (Arnot et al., 1999) and education was perceived as the vehicle through which inequalities and problems in society could be addressed and a new society built (Grace, 1987). In terms of education, the notion of 'equality of opportunity' meant every child was to have educational opportunities regardless of their social class, family background or place of residence (Lowe, 1993; Arnot et al., 1999) and policies were pursued accordingly. The 'Butler' Education Act of 1944 set up a unified system of free, compulsory schooling for children aged five to fifteen (later sixteen) and drew a clear distinction between 'primary' and 'secondary' education. The Act represented 'a major step towards the creation of an efficient, cost-effective and "just" education system' (Lowe, 1993: 198) and a political consensus about the purpose of education in a social democracy ensued. Only later was it apparent that the success/failure of children at eleven years, and which effectively determined children's careers and life chances, was linked to social class and was effectively reinforcing social differences and reproducing the existing social order (Tomlinson, 2005).

The status of the Board of Education was raised to that of ministry with the authority to 'control and direct LEAs' (Lowe, 1993: 198). After 1944 there was overwhelming support for extra expenditure on education to provide 'opportunity for all'. Between 1950 and 1960 the expenditure on education system grew faster than any other social service and was the second most expensive, behind social security (Simon, 1991; Lowe, 1993). Demographic changes, the post-war 'baby boom' of mid-1940s and late 1950s, had impact upon schools. Rapid increases in the number of children in primary school, almost one million more in 1954 than in 1944, led to the emergency training of 35,000 extra teachers (Lowe, 1993). The marriage bar was lifted through the 'married women returners' scheme to curtail the shortage of trained teachers as school numbers expanded (Arnot et al., 1999).

Schools were free to determine their own curriculum, which remained under the control of their LEA (the exception was religious instruction, which was centrally prescribed), and the curriculum remained virtually unchanged from the previous period. Primary education post-1944 was dominated, however, by the requirements of the 11 plus selection examination as the provision of free secondary education for all resulted in the tripartite system comprising grammar, technical and secondary modern schools (Simon, 1991). Children were allocated to one of these schools according to their ability, which was ascertained through the 11 plus examination: narrow standardized intelligence tests in English and arithmetic. Selection at age eleven meant primary teachers typically prepared older pupils for the 11 plus by coaching, teaching to tests and practicing tests, with this format sometimes trickling back to the education of younger children. Unlike the days of the Revised Code in the late nineteenth century, there was no national assessment system or the rigorous inspection process. Rather, the Ministry of Education commissioned reading surveys and tests periodically for monitoring purposes and HMI played an advisory role to schools (Richards, 1999).

In 1959 the Ministry of Education published *Primary Education: Suggestions for the Consideration of Teachers and Others Concerned with the Work of Primary Schools*. This replaced the previous handbook and took a broader view of what constituted a good education. It also deliberately sought not to be prescriptive but to 'describe the arrangements and practices which are to be found in the more successful schools' (Ministry of Education 1959: 10 cited in Cunningham, 1988: 15). The handbook reflected a child-centred approach, uniformity of curricular provision, teacher-centred development and teacher autonomy. Cunningham (1988), however, has retrospectively questioned all of this since the content of the handbook dealt mostly with the curriculum rather than child development and, indeed, educational research conducted in the 1970s found little curricular uniformity between schools. Cunningham (1988) suggests that other unofficial texts published in the 1940s to 1960s were more influential. He assesses the merits of some of these texts noting how they helped to communicate progressive ideas and principles and thus shape primary teachers' training and practice.

In the 1960s the Labour government moved 'tentatively towards comprehensive education and curriculum reform' (Tomlinson, 2005: 21). The primary sector had remained neglected until this time when the move to comprehensive education liberated primary schools from the shackles of the 11 plus examination. For the first time in its brief history primary education was seen in its own right as a major stage of educational importance. Simon (1991) illustrates how a small minority of schools had deliberately moved away from streaming pupils and towards a new pedagogic approach in primary, with 'informal classrooms' and teachers as facilitators of learning. New ideas in primary teaching to make learning more attractive were experimented (Spear, 1999). However, a major report celebrated and endorsed the emerging progressive curriculum and methods and helped to transform primary education and pedagogy. The report *Children and Their Primary Schools*, commonly known as the Plowden Report (CACE, 1967), was published following a three-year government-appointed enquiry.

This particular shift in the curriculum is located in particular changing societal and economic circumstances of its time. From 1944 onwards changes are evident in lifestyles and living standards, the status of children and the family, popular culture and cultural trends, advances in technology and communications and the role of the mass media. The progressive approach of Plowden, so named after Lady Bridget Plowden the Central Advisory Council for Education's chairwomen, placed the individual child at the centre and promoted self-expression, discovery learning with an emphasis on process rather than its products, individual autonomy and choice, personal growth and first-hand experience. This approach inspired many teachers, though not others (Richards, 1999). The enquiry ensured that resources were shifted to the primary sector budget. What followed were extensive building projects, the expansion of teacher training and nursery education (see Chapter 5). The report advocated greater parental involvement and targeted extra allowances and resources for deprived areas recognized as Educational Priority Areas (David, 1980). Compensatory education and positive discrimination were thus deployed by the Labour government to combat educational disadvantage (Tomlinson, 2005). The recommendations of Plowden (CACE, 1967) were incorporated into a White Paper (see Chapter 1) (DES, 1972) and a more child-centred approach was adopted in primary education, though many of its intentions were never fully realized because of the changing economic circumstances of the 1970s (Wilkinson, 1999). The dominant discourse on primary education as iterated in Plowden (and mooted in the 1931 Hadow Report) was the belief that primary children required an education that was specifically adapted to the stage of their intellectual and physical development. This discourse prevailed until the 1970s.

From 1944 to the mid-1970s teachers enjoyed much freedom over what to teach and a relatively high degree of what Grace (1987: 208) terms 'legitimated professionalism' whereby they established autonomous and effective control of the curriculum. Teachers were seen as having professional knowledge, integrity, expertise and autonomy in the classroom, which Grace (1987: 218) describes as 'the heartland of teacher professionalism'. Other than RE, the 1944 Act had not specified any curricula requirements; teachers thus had control over curricula content and pedagogic methods (Lawton, 1980). They drew on public and political support, expanded their control over curriculum and pedagogy (while working within the frameworks of public examinations and, while it operated, preparing children for the 11-plus) and were responsible for assessment up to the age of fifteen. Primary teachers were regarded as generalist teachers whose professional expertise was in assisting children's learning. The Schools Council for the Curriculum and Examinations was set up in 1964, an advisory body represented mainly by teachers, whose very being crystallized a degree of professional autonomy for teachers (Simon, 1991). The relationship between teachers, LEAs and the Ministry of Education (later DES) at this time was one of 'partnership' (Coulby, 1989a). In a discussion of education in the 1960s Simon (1991: 311) observes:

> The curriculum (or what went on in schools) was the specific responsibility of the teachers – not of the local authorities (though their role here was unclear) and certainly not of the state – or the central government. That was an essential factor underlying the functioning of the 'partnership'.

Topic work, which was essentially thematic, cross-curricula and had its roots in progressive education, came to epitomize primary education.

The late 1960s saw changing economic conditions fuelled by declining world economies, which impacted funding for education. Despite the massive investment in the post-war years, education was considered expensive while standards remained poor and by 1970s the social-democratic ideology of 'equality of opportunity' was deteriorating. Lowe (1993), however, documents a positive improvement on pre-war educational standards at each level after 1944. Reading standards improved considerably and more children were gaining academic qualifications. Nevertheless there was mounting public concern over education and educational standards. It has been argued that the spectre of falling standards in education 'was being addressed by rhetoric rather than evidence' (Bennett, 1992: 65). However, as Pring (1992) observes, regardless of the 'truth' of these assertions what was more important was the effect of such allegations upon public perceptions of the educational service. The economic crises of the 1970s, rising unemployment and increased international competitiveness fuelled discontent, and in terms of 'value for money' (Lawton, 1980: 11) education was not delivering its promises. The period 1974–1980 was characterized by calls for educational reform, greater accountability of the education service and teachers and there was public concern over standards. Attempts were also made to provide empirical numerical and descriptive data of levels of attainment *actually* reached by pupils and schools (Richards, 1999).

By the mid-1970s equality meant 'equality of outcome' rather than 'equality of opportunity' (Lowe, 1993). In 1974, largely due to concerns about the education of socially disadvantaged and ethnic groups, the Assessment of Performance Unit (APU) was established within the DES with the following brief:

1. To identify and appraise existing instruments and methods of assessment which may be relevant for these purposes
2. To sponsor the creation of new instruments and techniques for assessment, having due regard to statistical and sampling methods
3. To promote the conduct of assessments in co-operation with local education authorities and teachers
4. To identify significant differences related to the circumstances in which children learn, including the incidence of under-achievement, and to make the findings available to all those concerned with resource allocation within the Department, local authorities and schools. (Chitty, 1989: 79–80)

The establishment of the APU is significant as it marks the first attempt to monitor national standards. However, as David (1980) observes, the unit exceeded its terms of reference and attempted to devise tests of attainment to evaluate the standards of all pupils at different stages of their education. At the same time, a number of LEAs were testing pupils to evaluate school performance in terms of measurable outcomes and others were evaluating teachers' professional performance by gathering descriptive data through more inspections (Richards, 1999). All these developments were partly in response to public and political concern over educational 'standards', originally enunciated by a series of *Black Papers*[4] (Cox and Dyson, 1969a,b, 1970; Cox and Boyson, 1975, 1977), published by right-wing academics and policy groups. Denouncing politicians, journalists and employers furthered the general disillusionment, with education criticizing child-centred, progressive education and advocating a return to traditional teaching methods and disciplines. Linked to the perceived 'crisis' in education was that of the William Tyndale Junior School, Islington, whereby radical progressive methods were utilized by teachers against the wishes of parents (Simon, 1991). This particular 'affair' was captured in sensationalized headlines and marks the beginning of the scrutinizing media coverage of education we are familiar with today (Jones, 2003). Another significant report of this period was the Bullock Report, *Language for Life*, published in 1975, and it investigated the teaching of English and the acquisition and use of the entire range of language skills. It surveyed 2,000 primary schools and made a series of detailed recommendations including, significantly, a system of monitoring. All these various strands outlined above served to fuel general dissatisfaction with education and primary teachers. The standards or levels of competence which should be reached by pupils and schools were debated from this period onwards (Richards, 1999).

Jones (2003) purports that by the mid-1970s schooling in England was simultaneously 'radical and conservative'. Schooling was

> home to curriculum experiment, yet in primary schools, ten years after Plowden, it was still dominated by a traditional pedagogy and a narrow, highly traditional focus on reading and writing... It was based on a commitment to equal opportunity yet continued to produce large numbers of unqualified school leavers. (2003: 94)

Primary education post-Plowden is often perceived somewhat idealistically and romantically as a 'Golden Age' of teaching and learning, where progressivism was commonplace. Campbell (1993: 216), however, explodes the myth contending:

> The curriculum was narrow, emphasising literacy and numeracy through repetitive exercises; despite encouragement, work in science was patchy and haphazard; standards in the social subjects were lower than might be expected; pedagogy was often characterised by an undifferentiated focus in the middle levels of attainment... Plowdenesque progressivism flowered largely in rhetoric.

Indeed, educational research (e.g. Alexander, 1984; Galton et al., 1980) and major HMI surveys (DES, 1978a, 1981) later revealed a narrow concentration on basic skills and showed the idyllic image of primary schools in the late 1960s and 1970s to be somewhat mythical, identifying serious inconsistencies across schools in curriculum breadth, balance, quality and management. As such, an unprecedented speech by Prime Minister James Callaghan at Ruskin College in 1976 sparked what has come to be termed the 'Great Debate' about education (DES, 1977), bringing education into the full arena of public debate and where it has since remained. The 'Ruskin speech' focused on public concerns about falling standards, pupil dissatisfaction, the economic relevance of education and social failure. Jones (1992: 98) identifies the main issues highlighted in the speech:

> First there was concern over 'methods and aims of informal instruction ...' Secondly, there was a 'strong case for the so-called core curriculum of basic knowledge'. Thirdly, there was the question of 'monitoring the use of resources in order to maintain a proper national standard of performance'. Fourthly, linked with standards, there was 'the role of the Inspectorate in relation to national standards and their maintenance'. Fifthly, there was 'the need to improve relations between industry and education'. Finally there was the problem of the examination system.

Standards in education became a major issue of government concern (Chitty, 1989) and the Ruskin speech set the agenda for education policy that would ensue in the following years (Williams et al., 1992). Educational and industrial organizations were consulted, as were parents (DES, 1977). Teachers' professional expertise was questioned; they were openly criticized and this reflected a trend towards limiting the boundaries of their autonomy and increasing government intervention in education. The influence of the child-centred approach, though only fully adopted in a minority of primary schools (Simon, 1991), was prevalent and it was argued that progressive teaching failed where inexperienced and less able teachers adopted these informal methods. Whitty (1990: 23) suggests 'trendy teachers' were perceived as 'subverting traditional moral values and selling the nation short'. Secondary schools were criticized because pupils' skills were failing to meet the needs of employers and the requirements of new workplace technologies. A more disciplined structure of learning at all stages in the system was called for along with a 'core curriculum' of basic knowledge and more vocational training (Lowe, 1993). Critics were concerned about the 'secret garden of the curriculum' (Simon, 1991: 448), a term coined by the Conservative Minister of Education Sir David Eccles. There were calls for the DES to have greater involvement over the shaping of the curriculum and more control over LEAs and teachers, and, more generally, there was growing pressure for accountability. Silver (1990: 2–3) sums up the approach to education from 1960s onwards:

> New emphasis on approaches to the 'world of work' began to influence school curricula and confuse decade-old distinctions between education and training ... Priorities moved from 'access' to 'excellence' or 'standards', from 'liberal' to more 'vocational' messages.

Indeed, it was becoming apparent that the role of schools was to prepare pupils for the workplace and, due to the unpredictability of society, their learning for life. There are other significant markers that need to be highlighted as these furthered political pressures in the drive for greater consistency and progression in the primary curriculum. First, a study by Bennett (1976) sparked concern and controversy about teaching styles and pupil progress. Second, the ORACLE project (Galton et al., 1980), which investigated primary practice, drew attention to considerable problems in the curriculum. It also highlighted the lack of whole class interaction, which was connected to the higher cognitive performance by pupils. Third, the HMI survey *Primary Education in England* (DES, 1978a), which focused on the junior phase (7–11 years), provided evidence of low expectations of pupil performance by teachers (especially in inner cities), lack of curricula progression, a narrow focus on the basics of English and maths and inadequate and inconsistent provision of other subjects (Campbell, 2001).

Finally there were a number of notable documents (DES, 1981, 1985a,b) which essentially proposed broad frameworks with the *Third Report of the Education Select Committee* (House of Commons, 1986), making the case that children should be entitled to common curriculum. This was to be broad, balanced, modern and under the charge of the secretary of state. The proportion of time then spent per week on English and mathematics equated to approximately 40 per cent, which was far greater than other subjects (approximately 10 per cent each for Physical Education (PE), art, history/geography; approximately 25 per cent for science, technology, music, RE and other teaching) and signified an unbalanced curriculum heavily weighted towards the basics (DES, 1987a). Campbell (2001: 33) describes how 'gentle persuasion delivered a professional consensus about the broad objectives for the primary curriculum' and pupil entitlement. 'Gentle persuasion' for change, however eventually gave way to political pressures for reform.

Conservative policies (1979–1997): Centralization and control

The 1988 ERA is another landmark piece of legislation which signalled substantive change (Flude and Hammer, 1990). Between the Ruskin speech and the ERA, there were growing concerns about the primary curriculum and pedagogy; change was therefore almost inevitable, but the extent of reform was unprecedented. Among its many far-reaching reforms the ERA empowered the secretary of state for education to prescribe a 'balanced and broadly based curriculum' for maintained schools. Campbell (2001: 31) conceptualizes this move by the government as the 'colonisation of the primary curriculum', whereby from 1976 onwards the balance of power shifted away from LEAs, schools and teachers towards central government. Three new bodies were established: the NCC, Curriculum Council for Wales and the SEAC (appointed by the secretary of state) to advise the secretary of state who made ultimate curricula decisions (Coulby, 1989b). The ERA created greater central control over educational content, changing quite dramatically teachers' ways of working and their professional discretion; however, primary teacher resistance to the National Curriculum was momentary.

The National Curriculum was introduced for all maintained schools in England and Wales. It incorporated core subjects (English, maths and science) and foundation subjects (art, geography, history, music, PE and technology; plus a modern foreign language for children over the age of eleven). Each subject (core and foundation) was to be allocated 'reasonable' time. Curricula commonality and progressive stages, it was proclaimed, would also ensure continuity when children moved schools, rather than having gaps or repetition in their education. While curricula content was specified, its organization, textbooks/materials to be used and particular teaching approaches, however, were left to teachers' professional discretion although Coulby (1989b: 69) maintains, 'the National Curriculum itself represents a severe restriction on what can be taught in schools'. The highly detailed National Curriculum was phased into primary schools; in 1989 three subjects were introduced into Year 1 and by 1993 all nine subjects were in Years 1 and 4 though the number of subjects varied in the other year groups (2, 3, 5 and 6). Ring-binders for each subject were distributed to schools; these contained Statutory Orders giving teachers information about programmes of study, attainment targets, the 10 (later 9) successive levels of achievement with level descriptions relating to student progress. Topic work which had characterized primary education was thus potentially threatened. This move towards subject organization in the primary curriculum can be traced back to the HMI primary survey (DES, 1978a) where concerns had been raised (Dadds, 1993). Webb (1993: 249) found that teachers in her 1992 study were gradually and regretfully moving away from 'broad-based topics to subject-focused topics' in order to 'achieve National Curriculum coverage and facilitate the assessment and recording of attainment'. To reflect this initial teacher training changed to focus on the production of subject specialists (instead of the generalist primary teacher), with the emphasis on teaching rather than pupil learning.

The ERA established a mandatory national system of pupil assessment, in the form of SATs. In primary schools children aged seven-years-old (Key Stage One, Year 2) and eleven-years-old (Key Stages Two, Year 6) were examined in the core subjects. Children were assessed against the expected 'standard' for their age. As such, the majority of children would be expected to achieve between Levels 1 and 3 at the end of Key Stage One and between Levels 2 and 5 at the end of Key Stage Two. As Brown and Lauder (1992: 23) suggest, 'The notion of standards has come to be defined in terms of standardisation: the selection and packaging of knowledge into discreet subject areas, the labelling of students with and IQ score, and badges of ability gained by amassing qualifications.' While purported to provide merely 'objective' indicators of quality, in practice SATs have provided crude and often misleading data with no attempt to allow for different levels of funding or the social composition of pupils (Gillborn and Youdell, 2000). League tables encourage school competition through exposure to market forces and performance indicators of this kind have become central to evaluating performance. These assessment procedures ensured that educational outcomes or 'standards' of different age groups could be measured across schools providing comparative information and ensuring schools' accountability (Butterfield, 1995). Adaptations to the curriculum and testing in the late 1980s and early 1990s led to 'deluge of directives' from government (Webb and Vulliamy, 1996) to clarify and extend the ERA, with 'non-statutory' advice from the NCC and SEAC to accompany the ring-binders. Whereas up to the ERA there had been some reluctance by policy-makers to determine methods or the 'how' of teaching in schools, increasingly however, the then Secretary of State for Education Kenneth Clarke intervened both in the content and pedagogy of the primary curriculum attacking child-centred education as thwarting effective delivery. As such, a review was commissioned which resulted in the publication of a document *Curriculum Organisation and Classroom Practice in Primary Schools* (Alexander et al., 1992). This document, alternatively known as the Three Wise Men Report, focused on the nature and quality of primary pedagogy, reviewing evidence and making recommendations. The Dearing Review (Dearing, 1993), also commissioned by the secretary of state, was designed to slim down the curriculum as it was known to be too unwieldy. It proposed, for example, 'discretionary time', the rhetoric of which freed schools from the shackles of prescription for the equivalent of a day a week, although in reality this was not possible (Campbell, 2001). The revised National Curriculum, introduced in 1995, had less prescribed content, with some changes made to testing arrangements. In 1999 a further major review to scale down the National Curriculum was undertaken by the Qualifications and Curriculum Authority (QCA), which also more clearly specified its aims and purposes.

New forms of school inspection emerged in 1992 through the establishment of Ofsted, which replaced HMI. Ofsted monitors activities in schools and ensures the proper delivery of the curriculum. Arguably, this new form of external surveillance and control was to ensure that schools were complying with the government's agenda. Ofsted initially published inspection reports on every school every four years, which has led to public 'naming and shaming' of schools. 'Failing schools', those failing to meet required standards and sitting towards the bottom of league tables, are thus more easily identified.

Leading up to the change of government in 1997, there are a number of significant developments that can be determined from the post-1979 period of Conservative governments. Any curricula experimentation by teachers was not allowed after 1989; the ERA coupled with the 'imposition' of a National Curriculum effectively terminated the relative freedom enjoyed by teachers in the post-war era. The notion of teachers as independent, autonomous professionals, which had been established in the preceding decades when they had expanded the curriculum, demanded greater resources, and monopolized provision (Ozga, 1995) was completely eroded. As had begun in the mid-1970s, 'ineffective teachers' were blamed throughout the 1980s for the decline in British industry and commerce and the high numbers of young unemployed who lacked sufficient skills and knowledge (Coulby, 1989a). This populist position fed parental and public concern and was perpetuated by a concerted press campaign. Central control of education under the Conservatives was tightened, although the actual impact of the National Curriculum in primary schools at this time remains unclear. Some studies reported change along the lines of government policies (e.g. the Bristol 'PACE' project, Pollard et al., 1994); others, however, indicate continuity with previous practice (Campbell and Neill, 1994). What is certain is that on the eve of the 1997 general election, there was renewed impetus for change; the anticipation and expectation was that a Labour government would be different.

Over to you ...

Locate and read the chapter by Jim Campbell
See: Campbell, J. (2001), 'The colonisation of the primary curriculum' in R. Phillips and J. Furlong (eds) *Education Reform and the State. Twenty-five Years of Politics, Policy and Practice*, London: RoutledgeFalmer.
Campbell discusses what he terms the 'colonisation of the primary curriculum'.

1 What do you think he means by this?
2 In your opinion, is his view justified?
3 How applicable is the term 'colonisation of the primary curriculum' for understanding the present situation in schools?

New Labour policies (1997–2010): Tighter governmental control

In the closing decades of the twentieth century, the restructuring of world economies and the introduction of new technologies simultaneously created greater political uncertainties and demanded highly skilled, flexible and differentiated labour forces to secure future economic success. Governments in countries around the globe were aligning the aims of their respective education systems with the perceived needs of their country's industry and economy. As such, education policy was given a very high profile in the UK under the New Labour government of 1997. The expectation of many was that far-reaching changes would be made in the education sector by the incoming government. New Labour's early educational reforms, however, largely consolidated those of the previous Conservative administration. Policy reversals were notably the abolition of the nursery voucher (see Chapter 5) and Grant-Maintained Schools and phasing out the Assisted Places Scheme. Otherwise, almost all the other reforms and measures introduced by the Conservatives continued in place. Perhaps the most notable difference was the reluctance by New Labour to rely merely on market forces to raise standards in schools, and to intervene more directly in education. While there was greater delegation of powers to schools, there was simultaneously increased centralization and accountability through the meeting of nationally set targets. The publicly stated objective of the Conservative's ERA had been to 'raise standards', but in schools such expectations appeared to have fallen somewhat short. When international comparisons were made with other industrialized countries (particularly those in Southeast Asia), standards in schools in England (and Wales) were not rising fast enough (DfEE, 1997a: 78–84) and the achievement of pupils in terms of human capital formation was presented as 'just not good enough' (DfEE, 1997a: 10, para. 9). Further government intervention, it was purported, was thus warranted in the processes of schooling and the control of teachers' work to ensure that the government's ultimate aspirations of 'raising standards' in schools were to be met and what New Labour described as a 'world-class education service' was achieved. Education was given more prominence for economical purposes, but those charged with the responsibilities of producing the workforce, namely teachers, were publicly criticized with scathing attacks on the profession from policy-makers (Rafferty and Barnard, 1998; Webster and O'Leary, 1999).

During its first term in office (1997–2001) primary schools were targeted by New Labour as a site for modernization (DfEE, 1998a). 'New' extra funding came into the education service and the neglect by policy-makers that the primary phase had endured over the previous twenty-five years or so ended. 'Modernization' of the primary curriculum entailed greater flexibility for teachers, but a more prescriptive primary pedagogy with the introduction of the centrally determined strategies. The work of the Literacy Task Force, set up initially by the Labour Party in 1996, came to fruition in the National Literacy Strategy. The National Numeracy Task Force was established in 1998 by Secretary of State David Blunkett. In the pursuit of raising standards in primary schools, the government intervened directly with the introduction of the Literacy Strategy (DfEE, 1998b) and Numeracy Strategy (DfEE, 1998c), which detailed content and methods for the daily teaching of literacy and numeracy. This level of intervention and prescription was, arguably, far from modernizing and harked back to the nineteenth-century system of the Elementary Code. Teaching materials and training were developed for teachers, while the revised programme for trainee teachers focused on the standards and strategies. Teachers' work intensified (Forrester, 2000), which resulted for some as stress and burnout because of the pressure to maximize pupil outcomes (Galton and MacBeath, 2008). The message from New Labour was evident, however; teachers could not be trusted in realizing the world-class education system the government envisaged or implement the top-down, standards agenda; intervention and prescription were therefore deemed necessary and were enforced by Ofsted. Furthermore, the chief inspector of schools at that time, Chris Woodhead, was a known traditionalist with an aversion to progressive education (see Woodhead, 2002). Without a doubt, New Labour's ideological approach shifted the primary curriculum further away from child-centredness. The focus on literacy and numeracy was to be at the expense of subjects such as music, art and PE, which were squeezed and hence distorted the 'balanced' curriculum. Primary teaching became more 'test orientated' as league table performance reflected Key Stage Two test scores. Teachers' pay became linked to their performance in 2000 (Forrester, 2005), and many felt compelled to teach more to test requirements in order to meet the required standards. Again, there is some resonance here with the nineteenth-century system, payment by results.

Government targets for Key Stage Two required that 80 per cent of pupils reached the expected standard for their age (Level 4) in literacy by 2002 (attainment was 63 per cent in 1997) and 75 per cent reached the expected standard for their age (Level 4) in numeracy (attainment was 62 per cent in 1997) (Docking, 2000). Blunkett's promise in May 1997 to resign from his post as secretary of state for education and employment if these targets were not met in 2002 caused problems for the then Secretary of State, Estelle Morris, when the results fell short. It was apparent to policy-makers by 2000 that improvements in SATs had probably reached a plateau and continual improvement was impossible due to the constraints of social structures beyond the school gates (i.e. communities with high deprivation, low aspirations). In 2002 attainment in literacy was 75 per cent and 73 per cent for numeracy (Smithers, 2002). While politically the numeracy and literacy targets may be important indicators for policy-makers, in the short term they represent a somewhat narrow definition of primary education. The strategies were subsequently brought together under the umbrella of the Primary National Strategy (DfES, 2003a). An evaluation of the strategies by Ofsted (2005) found that improvements in literacy and numeracy teaching were substantial though identified weaknesses associated with poor management of the strategies in schools. A significant review (Earl et al., 2003) found that while there was more whole-class teaching (i.e. teacher-centred pedagogy), the effect of the strategies on pupil learning was less clear. The realization that target setting was failing in the standards agenda was coupled with pressure from elsewhere; the think-tank Demos, for example, expressed concerns about the mismatch between the curriculum and the needs of a global economy and post-industrialism where innovation and creativity are vital for business success. Also, other high performing Asian economies such as Singapore were giving greater prominence to creativity, problem-solving and project work in the school curriculum (Tan and Gopinathan, 2000). Creativity, greater autonomy for teachers, less prescription and fewer targets were advocated in *Excellence and Enjoyment* (DfES, 2003a), the introductory document of the National Primary Strategy, as was an individualized form of learning conceptualized as 'personalised learning' deemed vital for the 'knowledge economy' (Hartley, 2003). The emphasis on creativity and personalized learning is, however, at variance with the narrow standards agenda. It is interesting to note, however, that while New Labour's view of personalized learning was presented as 'not a return to child-centred theories' (Miliband, 2006: 24), the five components of personalized learning identified, such as, 'accommodating different paces and styles of learning' (2006: 24) and 'every student enjoying curriculum choice, a breadth of study and personal relevance' (2006: 25), do correspond very closely to the tenets of progressive, child-centredness. Thus, this once again this provides evidence of the inherent tensions that operate within the curriculum. In 2007 further guidance was provided in terms of what to teach and how to teach it due to New Labour's continued 'drive to raise standards and personalise learning' (DfES, 2007b).

The shortcomings of the Literacy strategy led to a government-commissioned review into the teaching of early reading. The Final Report (Rose, 2006) recommended synthetic phonics as the preferred way of teaching reading and this was to be adopted by all schools in England. Wyse and Goswami (2008), however, question the research base for this intervention and demonstrate it is not supported by empirical research evidence. The role of phonics in the teaching of reading has remained controversial. Teachers have been impelled to adopt the teaching methods for reading promoted by successive governments, but this restricts how they teach and indicates a lack of trust in teachers' professional judgement.

The most extensive, comprehensive enquiry of primary education since Plowden, the Cambridge Primary Review (CPR), was undertaken between 2006 and 2009 by a team of academics and professionals led by Professor Robin Alexander. This was a major independent review, funded by the charity Esmée Fairbairn Foundation, and enquired into the 'condition and future of primary education'. The CPR generated a phenomenal mix of evidence from thousands of written submissions, surveys of existing research and soundings held in different locations. It produced thirty-one interim reports and forty briefing papers; there were numerous regional dissemination conferences between 2009 and 2010, many media articles and a substantial final report (Alexander, 2009) comprising twenty-four chapters, seventy-eight formal conclusions and seventy-five recommendations for policy and practice. The reviewers condemned what they regarded as a 'state theory of learning'. While the CPR generated extensive media coverage, some of the findings were hijacked along the way and presented, by the tabloid press especially, in a sensationalist and scaremongering manner. Such reporting inevitably impacted negatively upon the already uneasy relationship between the CPR team and government, as ministers were obliged to respond to the media hype that hurled criticism at 'failed' government initiatives (Alexander, 2010). Given the extent and breadth of the CPR, it is very difficult to summarize its research, analysis, conclusions and recommendations in this space. Notably, however, and in relation to some of the issues raised in this chapter, the Final Report concludes that the emphasis on tests, targets and prescriptive methods has probably contributed to depressed standards overall by constricting teachers, thwarting their creativity and diminishing their ability to teach. The report purports, 'Children will not learn to think for themselves if their teachers are expected merely to do as they are told' (Alexander, 2009: 496).

The CPR had a broad remit of ten educational themes. The Interim Report by Wyse and colleagues (2008), which reviewed published research for the third theme, illuminates some of the complexities surrounding the primary curriculum and assessment. Solutions to the identified 'problems' in primary schools included extending the Foundation Stage to age six, developing a curriculum which comprised eight domains of knowledge and targeting pupils from deprived backgrounds. Both New Labour and Coalition governments were hesitant to take on board the CPR's findings and recommendations, nonetheless the review opened up the debate about primary education and brought it visibly into the public gaze. In September 2013 the Cambridge Primary Review Trust[5] (CPRT), a not-for-profit company sponsored by the education company Pearson, was launched and succeeds the CPR. The CPRT's mission, as successor, is to build upon the CPR's work in pursuing high-quality primary education for all children and the development of professional support services and materials.

The CPR also challenged the review conducted by Sir Jim Rose, which was New Labour's own 'independent' review of the primary curriculum in England commissioned in 2008. The Final Report of the Rose Review (DCSF, 2009) proposed six areas of learning that combined the traditional subjects: understanding English, communication and languages; mathematical understanding; scientific and technological understanding; historical, geographical and social understanding; understanding physical development, health and well-being; and understanding the arts. The new curriculum was due to be implemented in September 2011, but subsequently shelved by the incoming Conservative-Liberal Democrat Coalition government in May 2010. There was thus a great deal of uncertainty about the future of the primary curriculum at this time.

Coalition policies (2010–2015): More change, or more of the same?

The Document *The Coalition: Our Programme for Government* (Cabinet Office, 2010) was published almost immediately after the general election in May 2010. It was 'inspired by the values of freedom, fairness and responsibility' (2010: 8) and set out the Coalition government's priorities. The section on 'Schools' which comprised seventeen bullet points gave the first indication of the new government's educational agenda. Two of these have particular relevance to this chapter relating to the curriculum and assessment:

> We will promote the reform of schools in order to ensure that new providers can enter the state school system in response to parental demand; that all schools have greater freedom over the curriculum; and that all schools are held properly to account. (2010: 28)
> We will keep external assessment, but will review how Key Stage Two tests operate in future. (2010: 29)

In its 2010 pre-election manifesto, the Conservative Party had outlined its intentions to reform the National Curriculum and organize the primary curriculum around traditional 'subjects like Maths, Science and History' (Conservative Party, 2010: 52).

Michael Gove was appointed as the secretary of state for education, and he embarked upon a crusade of ambitious curricula reform, which was also driven by his own educational experiences and strong personal opinions of what constitutes a 'good' education: traditional, rigorous and academic. The Coalition's intentions were presented in *The Importance of Teaching, The Schools White Paper* (DfE, 2010a), which proposed the new 'rigorous and stretching curriculum' (2010a: 8). This is a momentous and wide-ranging document for education. It signalled the course of action to be taken and its authoritative tone pronounced:

> a tighter, more rigorous, model of the knowledge which every child should expect to master in core subjects at every key stage … the National Curriculum will increasingly become a rigorous benchmark, against which schools can be judged rather than a prescriptive straitjacket into which all learning must be squeezed. (2010a: 10)

The schools' White Paper contained proposals to reduce prescription and review and reform the whole National Curriculum for five to sixteen-year-olds in England. It later became more apparent that reducing the curriculum involved a 'strong focus' on 'core knowledge' and 'a concomitant downgrading of the development of skills' (Brundrett, 2015: 51). A discourse of 'freedom', imbuing liberation and empowerment for schools and teachers over how they organize and teach the curriculum can be discerned; this discourse was also espoused by Gove in numerous subsequent policy speeches and statements. It should be noted, however, the aspiration for 'freedom' is not new in education policy documentation, but featured significantly, for example, in New Labour's *Excellence and Enjoyment* (DfES, 2003a). Content analysis of the schools' White Paper undertaken by Lumby and Muijs (2014) reveals forty-one references to 'freedom'; the word 'free' is mentioned twenty-four times and 'Free Schools' (see Chapter 9), that is, new schools offering greater autonomy, are formally introduced. While the idea of freedom is proposed, and freedom-associated words are peppered throughout the document, freedom itself appears to subsist within the constraints of structure and is inextricably tethered to accountability. The schools' White Paper also contains inconsistent logic such as the advocacy of the National Curriculum review to reduce 'prescription and allowing schools to decide how to teach' (2014: 10) yet is contradicted elsewhere by the stipulation of certain teaching methods such as 'systematic synthetic phonics as the proven best way to teach early reading' (2014: 22–23).

A comprehensive review of the whole National Curriculum was announced in January 2011 (DfE, 2011b). Professor Tim Oates of the University of Cambridge was asked to chair the panel of experts overseeing the review. He was known by Gove for a publication regarding the shortcomings of the National Curriculum and his work on international comparative education (see Oates, 2011). The expert panel of four members, all eminent professors of education, was to be supported by an advisory committee comprising 'teachers, academics and business representatives' (Brundrett, 2015: 51). Their remit included drawing on ideas from other 'jurisdictions' (i.e. international high-preforming education systems) and worldwide best practice in order to provide evidence to support the development of the new curriculum. In an interim report to ministers, the expert panel provided advice on the framework for the National Curriculum and outlined its overarching principles, aims, structure and key issues such as pupil progression. During the summer of 2011, however, the DfE was already developing draft programmes of study for the new curriculum on what children should know (James, 2012). It later transpired that two members of the expert panel were concerned that the panel's views were not advancing the development of the programmes of study in accordance with the principles agreed in the interim report. They contended the curriculum lacked breadth and there was too much prescription such as the year-by-year structure. They were concerned about transitions from the early years into Key Stage One and also the pace of the review when time was needed for proper deliberation of the evidence and the legitimacy of the reforms (James, 2012). Such was their concern: they tendered their resignation in October 2011, although Gove persuaded them to complete their work and their resignations were withdrawn. This somewhat desolate situation is summed up by Brundrett (2015: 53) who asserts:

> When two of the most distinguished academics in the field, who are world-renowned scholars employed at prestigious institutions, resign from the committee set up to advise on the development of the new curriculum, it is not only an embarrassment, it also raises questions about what has emerged and the process by which decisions were reached.

The panel's final report (DfE, 2011c) was published in December 2011 and Gove formally responded to the report in June 2012. At the same time, the DfE released draft programmes of study for primary mathematics, English and science. These were met with some resistance from the main teaching unions and professional associations (Stewart and Ward, 2012). During 2012 and 2013 there were further rounds of consultation, redrafting and circulation of the proposed curriculum and programmes of study. While the proposals received some support, they continued to be criticized by teachers' organizations, subject specialists and many academics (Bassey et al., 2013) for ignoring expert advice. Brundrett (2015: 53) condemns Gove's 'combative style' and the propensity to bypass the expert panel whose 'views were first sought, then dismissed and finally derided'. This reveals how the curriculum remains a site of conflict over what constitutes knowledge and, thus, can never be politically neutral.

The renewed emphasis on the 'basics' is evident in the final version of the new National Curriculum (DfE, 2013a) with two statutory appendices on spelling and on vocabulary, grammar and punctuation attached to the Key Stages One and Two framework document. The new curriculum came into effect in maintained primary schools in England from September 2014 and, for the core subjects of English, maths and science, in September 2015, by which time there was a Conservative government in office.

Pause and ponder

1 What do you consider makes an effective primary curriculum for the twenty-first century?
2 Who do you consider is best placed to construct the curriculum in primary schools?
3 How much freedom do you consider should be afforded to individual teachers in determining approaches to teaching and learning in their classroom?

Shackled to curriculum reforms is the matter of assessment which has remained controversial in primary education and also had an increasingly deleterious effect since the introduction of SATs (Bangs et al., 2010). The pressures of preparing pupils for national tests are, arguably, contrary to a broad and balanced education and also lead to erroneous league table rankings. Such was the consternation about SATs; they were boycotted in May 2010 by the National Union of Teachers (NUT) and the National Association of Head Teachers (NAHT). In a subsequent press release the government reported more than 4,000 primary schools had taken industrial action; 26 per cent of the maintained sector.

As pronounced in the schools' White Paper Lord Paul Bew, a cross-bench peer and Professor at Queen's University, was asked to chair a review of the effectiveness of the existing Key Stage Two tests. The government acknowledged they caused 'excessive rehearsal and repeated practice of tests, eating into valuable teaching time and creating a very narrow curriculum for some children in year six' (DfE, 2010a: 16). The review team's recommendations (Bew, 2011) were accepted by the government. Statutory assessment was endorsed as necessary for external school-level accountability and to support a culture of high expectations for all pupils. It was advised, however, that attention be given to progress made as well as attainment in order to provide a representative picture of a school's performance. Other changes included teacher assessment of writing composition to replace the existing writing test, and a new test to assess skills in spelling, grammar, punctuation and vocabulary. The impact of these changes in primary schools will remain to be seen.

2015 onwards: Conservative policies – Centralization and fragmentation

The new primary curriculum incorporated two major changes in its structure: languages became part of Key Stage Two and computing replaced information and communication technology. The levels which have been used since the ERA to report the results of National Curriculum tests are not aligned to the new curriculum and are now obsolete; schools are free to design their own system for assessing progress. However, it is unclear how benchmarking between schools will ensue and it will be interesting to see how the profession initiates alternative arrangements. The new curriculum is criticized on a number of grounds not least because of its remote relevance to the needs of the twenty-first century but because 'they are about unpicking comprehensive and progressive education and reinstalling the virtues of a post-1944 system' (Ball, 2013: 14–15). There are concerns about the curriculum's emphasis on subjects which reflect a neo-conservative position, its lack of clear aims and values and question the appropriateness of its knowledge-intensive nature (Brundrett, 2015). The extent to which the curriculum has actually been influenced by international best practice, as claimed (Ball, 2013), is also questionable. Both Gove and Morgan have been quite vociferous about school autonomy being accompanied by robust accountability. Ball (2013: 106) surmises 'the dualities of freedom and control … run through the methods of reform, both a "giving away" and "taking away" of professional judgement and teacher autonomy'. Despite the rhetoric advocating more freedom for teachers, the reality is that prescription restricts the decisions teachers can make about their lessons and how to best assess what pupils have learned. All of this de-professionalizes teachers and yet what is perhaps most poignant is teachers' acquiesce to the revised curriculum which, as Brundrett (2015: 56) observes, 'has been implemented by teachers in schools with surprisingly little protest, an ataraxy quite possibly born out of exhaustion from multiple and overlapping processes of innovation and change'.

The primary curriculum is different from the elementary education offered in the late nineteenth and early twentieth centuries. However, it is possible to discern elements which reverberate with the different priorities accorded to the primary curriculum over time and which have been reviewed in this chapter. Teachers' professionalism and professional autonomy have undoubtedly been challenged by policy reforms prescribing a more government-directed approach to curriculum and assessment, the emphasis on basic literacy and numeracy and on a strong subject-based curriculum, all of which resonate with earlier government priorities. Greater exertion of power, centralization and control over schools and teachers, arguably, demonstrate further 'colonisation' of the curriculum (see Campbell, 2001). Yet this is a very important juncture in the evolution of the primary curriculum and it will be interesting to see what transpires in the future. The primary phase is positioned between the Early Years Foundation Stage (EYFS) and secondary education, and thus should there be any fundamental adaptations to their curricula, then the primary curriculum may have to be refashioned in order to provide continuity and coherence to children's learning. However, while maintained schools are required to follow the new curriculum and the changes are intended to raise standards, the educational landscape is inconstant. Academies and Free Schools, along with independent schools, can choose not to follow the National Curriculum. They must provide a broad and balanced curriculum nonetheless and teach English, maths, science and RE. The expectation for schools not following the National Curriculum is that the performance of students will be improved through curricula innovation. This state of affairs suggests waning importance of curricula commonality, as postulated through the ERA, and a diminishing 'national' curriculum, given the expectation that primary schools will, or will be required to, convert to academy status (see Chapter 9). What seems to be transpiring is a more fragmented system of education provision, not all too dissimilar to what existed before the Elementary Act of 1870.

Pause and ponder

The first aim of the National Curriculum in England:

3.1. The national curriculum provides pupils with an introduction to the essential knowledge that they need to be educated citizens. It introduces pupils to the best that has been thought and said; and helps engender an appreciation of human creativity and achievement. (DfE, 2013a: 6 [3.1])

1 The new curriculum has a greater emphasis on 'essential knowledge', what counts as essential knowledge, in your opinion? What should children learn?
2 Do you see any problems with the claim 'the best that has been thought and said'?

The structure of the National Curriculum in England:

3.4. The Secretary of State for Education is required to publish programmes of study for each national curriculum subject, setting out the 'matters, skills and processes' to be taught at each key stage. Schools are free to choose how they organise their school day, as long as the content of the national curriculum programmes of study is taught to all pupils.

1 Do you see any contradictions between the secretary of state for education 'setting out the "matters, skills and processes"' and 'schools are free to choose'?
2 How does this structure resonate with the 'autonomy' and 'freedom' for teachers, which is espoused in the schools' White Paper?

Notes

1   The statutory curriculum is outlined in the Education Act 2002.
2   The Code of Regulations or Elementary Code contained the aims of the elementary school, comprised the curriculum and prescribed nationally what teachers taught in their schools.
3   *Suggestions for the Consideration of Teachers and Others Concerned in the Work of Elementary Schools* written primarily by HM inspectors was first published by the Board of Education in 1905 following the Code of 1904. It showed 'effective' teaching although shaped opinion and policy rather than practice. A subsequent edition (1937) and reprint (1942) changed little.
4   The term 'Black Paper' intentionally signalling contrast with Government White Papers.
5   See http://cprtrust.org.uk/

Further reading

Alexander, R. J. ed. (2009) *Children, their World, their Education: Final Report and Recommendations of the Cambridge Primary Review*, Abingdon: Routledge.

Apple, M. W (2004) *Ideology and Curriculum*, 3rd edn, London: RoutledgeFalmer.

Cunningham, P. (2012) *Politics and the Primary Teacher*, London: Routledge.

5

Developments in Early Childhood Education and Care

Chapter Outline

Introduction

Developments in early years – early childhood education and care – are complex, and it must be acknowledged from the outset of this chapter that changes over time are not the product of government policies alone. Crucially, the work, actions, writings, theories, beliefs and values of key early years pioneers and protagonists, and the lesser-known personalities, have been extremely influential. Space limitations, however, preclude their discussion and analysis here. The chapter's intention is to comprehend the evolution and development of policies for early years in the English system. Similar reforms have been introduced in Wales, Scotland

and Northern Ireland albeit with subtle differences (see Boyd and Hirst, 2015)[1] including the legislative framework. The forms of early years provision for children below the compulsory school age are diverse and can be broadly categorized in three sectors: public (i.e. maintained services, funded by local authorities or central government), private (fee-paying) and voluntary (such as playgroups). Publically funded services can be further characterized as social services or education services. Within education services three types of provision can be discerned. There are local authority maintained nursery schools, nursery classes linked to a primary school and reception classes of primary schools. The private sector comprises childminders (who look after children in their own homes), private nurseries and nursery classes within an independent school. Voluntary provision is most commonly in the form of playgroups or community nurseries. Provider diversity could be explained by the relatively low levels of public funding and thus the growth over time of the private and voluntary sectors in response to demand. Provision encapsulates some tensions within policy: first, the extent to which early education matters and whether this responsibility lies with parents or the state. Successive governments during the twentieth century often supported the principle of nursery education, but the funding required to put ideas into practice has not followed. Second, whether an early years' policy should focus on preparing children for school or should concern the issue of providing day care for working parents is a moot point. Finally, there are structural tensions as historically there has been a system split in England between early education and childcare places.

Under-fives and education: Changing attitudes

The notion of 'childhood' is a socially constructed concept, a discrete stage in the life cycle (Boronski and Hassan, 2015). Children were once regarded as 'little adults' or 'incomplete adults' who were the possessions of their parents and thus could be exploited by them for financial gain. During early industrialization and increasing urbanization in the UK, many working-class parents depended on their children's employment for survival. Child labour was prevalent, for example, in agriculture, mining, factories and mills. It was only gradually that children became an issue of public interest. Such acknowledgement by the state evolved due to changes in employment patterns and availability of work, evolving ideas of the family (and parental duties and responsibilities) and shifting attitudes towards child-rearing and motherhood. It is in the early part of the twentieth century that there was a perception that the well-being, raising and education of young children are also seen as the responsibility of the state (David, 1980). As such, increasingly governments have intervened, regulating and legislating on matters traditionally regarded as private (individual or family) concerns and which were previously not considered politically or economically relevant. Over time, the concept of childhood has developed alongside assumptions that children need to be cared for, require protection and should receive formal education.

The legacy of pre-school provision and nursery education for young children in England is important for the understanding of the present situation and comprehending the development, organization and availability of early childhood services and early education. At the beginning of the twentieth century, a system of state education was established in England and Wales following the Elementary Education Act (1870) (see Chapter 4) and similar legislation passed in 1872 for Scotland. Elementary schools were of low status and sometimes referred to as 'all-age' schools, since what was offered was considered a basic, sufficient education for working-class children. The 1870 Act set the obligatory age of school attendance at five years, the assumption being that the sooner working-class children completed their elementary education, the sooner they would be ready for employment (Baldock, 2011). Most working-class children would be in paid employment after thirteen and providing income for their family. A later Code[2] of 1872 set the age of three as the minimum age for a grant to be paid to the school for children attending. The ages of three and five, from this point onwards, became of substantial importance; first, in terms of grouping children and, second, for system organization purposes. Children between the ages of three and five could be admitted to elementary schools. Many children of this age attended elementary school if their parents were working and who might otherwise keep their older children (usually daughters) away from school to mind their younger siblings. Some parents supported the idea of beginning formal education early or because schools were cleaner environments for children than their own homes (Baldock, 2011).

Moss and Penn (1996) maintain that some two-year-olds and 50 per cent of three- and four-year-olds were attending infant classes in elementary schools by 1900. This situation caused pressure on the system, as classrooms were often overcrowded. In addition, teachers did not generally know how to manage younger children, believing they should be able to cope with normal lessons and school instruction (Baldock, 2011). This crisis led to the Board of Education (the government office) requesting information from its women inspectors of HMI regarding the education of young children. The corresponding report *Children under Five in Public Elementary Schools* (Board of Education, 1905) pronounced the instruction in elementary schools as unsuitable. It was in the late nineteenth and early twentieth centuries that the terms 'nursery school' and 'nursery education' were starting to be utilized (Baldock, 2011). The HMI inspectors advocated separate nursery schools, which were in the same building or near to elementary schools. They believed separate provision, a different style of teaching, and their own facilities could better meet the needs of young children (Moss and Penn, 1996). The prevailing belief was, nonetheless, that in homes where parents looked after their children properly that was the best place for them. Where care was perceived as lacking or for poorer children, the dominant view was that they were better placed with teachers, particularly in terms of their health care (David, 1980). Through the procedures of another Elementary Code (1905), LEAs could now refuse to admit to infant classes children who were under-five. At the same time, however, LEAs were not given any additional funding from central government for nursery provision.

The government-appointed Consultative Committee to the Board of Education produced a substantial report entitled *Upon the School Attendance of Children below the Age of Five* (Board of Education, 1908). As such, the committee took evidence from a range of different witnesses including medical officers, LEA representatives, inspectors and teachers. By the early twentieth century much more was understood by doctors and educationalists about the necessary environmental surroundings for the proper physical and mental development of young children. Doctors thought attendance at school below the age of five detrimental to children's health as they were deprived of sufficient fresh air and exercise. Educationists expressed concerns about the unsuitability of elementary schools, whose training and instruction caused very young children unnecessary mental pressure and undue physical discipline, such as having to sit still at a desk. The document captures, on moral, physical and mental grounds, the committee's concerns about children under-five attending elementary school. Some public provision for younger infants was advocated where the home environment was deemed 'imperfect' (1908: 16). While it was recognized that some mothers would work in paid employment and thus be away from the home, it was deemed 'unsatisfactory' that children might be left 'unattended' inside or outside the home. Some children were looked after by neighbours or a professional minder although the report cautions these were often 'ignorant women' (1908: 18). As such, the report deliberates the premises, curriculum, apparatus and staff of the 'ideal institution' for younger infants (1908: 20–23). Data are provided and comparisons made with Germany, Switzerland, the United States of America, Scotland and Ireland, where children start formal schooling much later than in England (and Wales).

Over to you ...

The ages shown in the table below indicate when children must start compulsory education.

In most of these countries children start school before it is compulsory. For some countries pre-primary education is compulsory.

Age	Country
Four	Northern Ireland
Five	Cyprus, England, Malta, Scotland, Wales
Six	Austria, Belgium, Croatia, Czech Republic, Denmark, France, Germany, Greece, Hungary, Iceland, Republic of Ireland, Italy, Liechtenstein, Luxembourg, Netherlands, Norway, Portugal, Romania, Slovakia, Slovenia, Spain, Switzerland, Turkey
Seven	Bulgaria, Estonia, Finland, Latvia, Lithuania, Poland, Serbia, Sweden

Source: Eurydice, Compulsory Education in Europe 2014/15

Locate the Eurydice website, which can be found at http://eacea.ec.europa.eu

Use the appropriate tabs to search by 'country' or 'topic'. Follow your own interests and find out more about early childhood education and care in different countries across Europe.

The impact of two world wars on day care and nursery education provision

As will be seen, the advent of the two world wars inadvertently impacted quite significantly upon the expansion of day care and nursery education provision. As men were conscripted for military service in the First World War (1914–1918), their departure from the labour force created employment opportunities for women. Many mothers found paid work, such as in armaments' factories, and this change in women's circumstances created an urgent need for childcare provision. As a consequence, the Board of Education funded day nurseries; by 1919 there were 174 (Randall, 2000). Women taking men's jobs was regarded officially as a temporary measure only while men were away at war. Women were expected to leave their employment immediately when the men returned, the prevailing ideology being a woman's (mother's) rightful place was in the home. Post-war, the demand for childcare provision was reduced as a consequence, although nursery education advanced albeit somewhat haphazardly through policies of expansion and contraction. The case for nursery education was stated in the Education Act (1918) and the Hadow Report (Board of Education, 1931), *The Primary School*. The expansion which occurred during the war years was curtailed by economic cuts in public expenditure (known as the Geddes Axe of 1922). There was then a favourable period of growth under the Labour government in 1924, but further curtailment in the early 1930s due to the recession as economic problems impacted educational expenditure.

The Hadow Report (Board of Education, 1933),[3] *Infant and Nursery Schools,* reveals perceptions relating to the importance of children's health. Randall (2000) observes how education policy-making at this time remained influenced by the medical profession who endorsed, for health and welfare purposes, the benefits of nursery education for children from disadvantaged homes. Although universal provision is resisted, the report nevertheless promoted nursery education. The report states, 'it seems highly desirable that it [nursery education] should be developed separately, and be left free to perfect its methods, and to fulfil its special purpose' (Board of Education, 1933: 188). Randall (2000: 33) observes nursery expansion was 'cautiously encouraged' after 1936 and by 1938 there were 118 nursery schools with almost 170,000 under-fives in a pre-school class of some description.

The evacuation of children from cities to rural areas during the Second World War (1939–1945) led to the setting up of 450 day nurseries, which provided 14,000 places for children under-five. Also, 230 residential nurseries and 430 residential nursery schools accommodated 60,000 children (David, 1980). David (1980) explains how the evacuation scheme transformed the relationship between the state and the family whereby the state intervened and took full responsibility for the welfare of many pre-school children. She also notes the government was primarily concerned with care and health measures, rather than the education of young children. Nevertheless, nursery provision expanded, albeit hastily and lacking proper planning (Moss and Penn, 1996) and was influenced by women's participation in a range of non-traditional work settings which was both necessary and encouraged by government. As with the First World War, there was again reliance on women's labour. Their (re)entering of the workforce in large numbers influenced the growth of nurseries and the provision by government of nursery schools, meals and health care. Moss and Penn (1996) explain how while there were official recommendations to open more nursery schools, there was disarray among the various government departments for education, health and employment as to who bore the responsibility and funded this provision. Moss and Penn (1996) also allude to young mothers who preferred not to leave their children for long hours in war nurseries, which could be quite dismal places. These mothers were not unduly disappointed when many nurseries closed down after the war.

Responsibility for the provision of nursery classes and schools was left to the discretion of LEAs through the terms of the 1944 Education Act. In the years following the Second World War, attempts were made to keep women in the home and reinforce women's dependent status through welfare policies (Arnot et al., 1999) although many having experienced paid work loathed a return to 'a life of closed domesticity' (Maguire, 1996: 26). There was an expectation in the post-war era that mothers would commit themselves to their children's education at home and at school (Arnot et al., 1999). However, women's economic activity rates subsequently increased due, in part, to changing attitudes regarding women's paid work and a changing occupational structure. The increase of services through the development of the welfare state and labour shortages in developing manufacturing industries generated work opportunities deemed 'appropriate' for women (Arnot et al., 1999). Women were increasingly recruited for a variety of jobs, although these were often low-paid and low-status jobs. Demographic changes, the subsequent post-war 'baby boom', saw rapid increases with 'almost one million extra children' in 1954 than in 1945 (Lowe, 1993: 208). Randall (2000: 88) observes how governments have repeatedly 'been most concerned to provide childcare when real or anticipated labour shortages have put a premium on ensuring mothers' availability for paid employment'.

After 1944: Slow and fitful developments in policy and provision

In the thirty years following the Second World War, there was political consensus in the UK and policies were guided by the principles of freedom and 'equality of opportunity'. Alongside a democratic state, education was seen as a vehicle by which societal inequalities could be offset. It is in this period that the Plowden Report (CACE, 1967) (see Chapter 4), a three-year government-appointed enquiry about primary schools, was published. The Plowden Report postulated positive intervention and additional resources, including the building of new nursery schools, for socially disadvantaged localities (identified as Educational Priority Areas). Primary schooling was perceived in Plowden as continuing on from nursery education; this is a different view from most European countries where nursery was mostly separate from primary and also full-time (Moss and Penn, 1996). Plowden recommended the expansion of part-time, rather than full-time, nursery education for three- and four-year-olds. This stance exemplifies the principle of minimum separation of mothers from their children, a view which echoed the proceeding Hadow Report (Board of Education, 1933):

> It is harmful to remove a child too suddenly or for too long from his [sic] mother, part-time attendance should be the normal pattern of nursery education. (CACE, 1967: 123)
> The place for the young child is with his [sic] mother in the home. (CACE, 1967: 120)

The recommendations indicated a role for early childhood education and care in policy and these were included in a subsequent White Paper (DES, 1972) and Circular (DES, 1973). Margaret Thatcher, the then Secretary of State for Education and science, outlined the ten-year educational plan and substantial increased expenditure in five areas of education, including nursery education. The plans included free places for all three- and four-year-olds where parents wanted it and a building programme, although the preference for nursery classes within primary schools to avoid a change of school was expressed, rather than separate nurseries. All LEAs were required to take a more comprehensive approach to expansion and include more fully in their plans the voluntary sector (notably playgroups) and private nurseries. The emphasis in policy at this time was helping families in deprived areas, diversity of provision, efficiency and improved standards in the education and care of children. Thatcher's free entitlement and expansion objectives were never fully achieved, however, because of the economic circumstances of the 1970s which brought economic curtailment and contraction. Nevertheless, Baldock (2011) contends the foundations were put in place for a new approach to provision during the 1970s.

Demographically, there was also a decline in birth rates in 1970s and 1980s, and primary schools began taking many four-years-olds out of pre-school and into reception classes to compensate numbers. McGillivray (2007) draws attention to the lack of debate by policy-makers at the time regarding the relevance and suitability of education for four-year-olds in reception classes in schools. This situation might be regarded by some as a shortcoming in policy and hence neglect. Conversely, however, it could be argued that early education was left alone, as it had been through the twentieth century, allowing practitioners to continue to use their own professional discretion to develop educational practices using child-centred methods.

The Conservative government, led by Prime Ministers Margaret Thatcher and later John Major, set in motion some key reforms for early education and childhood services, many of which were picked up and expanded upon later by the New Labour government. Good-quality pre-school education and care was coming to be seen as pivotal to providing a better start in life for deprived children. The 1989 Children Act covered a wide range of practical measures concerning care and protection, including parental responsibilities and the regulation and inspection of childminding and day care by local authorities. Greater cooperation between authorities and providers was advocated and there was the first attempt to define goals for early learning (Baldock, 2011). The quality and attributes of educational experiences offered to three- and four-year-olds in the late 1980s were ascertained and presented in the Rumbold Report (DES, 1990). This inquiry considered in particular 'content, continuity and progression in learning, having regard to the requirements of the National Curriculum' (DES, 1990: 1) and, as Baldock (2011: 70) states, was 'a crucial victory in setting off the idea of introducing the new National Curriculum in nursery classes and schools'.

Free nursery places were provided by the maintained sector and via funding from LEAs; these were more prevalent in disadvantaged urban areas. They were staffed by qualified teachers (graduates, usually with B.Ed.) and supported by qualified nursery nurses (with NNEB or BTEC qualifications). Premises were maintained by the LEA, often purpose-built or adapted for their purpose and properly resourced. Alternative provision was offered by the private sector and voluntary organizations. In these settings, staff, usually women, were not necessarily trained or well qualified but were generally low paid. Playgroups, though normally run by a playgroup leader, often relied on the goodwill of parents (usually mothers) for staffing and other volunteers (usually local women). A review by Sylva (1994) of various studies conducted in Britain in the 1970s, 1980s and 1990s illustrates how pre-school education, particularly that of high quality, is beneficial in terms of educational, cognitive and social development and, regarding investment costs, produces later economic savings to society. Research findings show a positive link between pre-school education and educational outcomes and the impact of early education is strongest in children from disadvantaged backgrounds. Sylva (1994) notes that a study in 1988 found the playgroup movement was the largest provider of early learning places in the UK.

Policy interest was somewhat galvanized in the latter years of the Conservative government. In 1994 the introduction of Childcare Disregard (£40 of childcare costs) for families claiming family credit and housing benefit was introduced to enable low-income parents to work and thus to lessen the reliance on state benefits (Hansard, 1993). Thatcher and Major pursued the ideology of free market enterprise (see Chapters 1 and 3); the expansion of nursery education was expected to be achieved through competition between the maintained, private and voluntary sectors. As such, private nursery provision grew rapidly, quadrupling the number of places between 1989 and 1997 (Moss, 2014). There was a greater number of working mothers and so demand for nursery places grew. However, the system remained fragmented with low levels of public funding and significant shortcomings in the provision of childcare services and early education.

The (much-criticized) nursery voucher scheme experiment

The Nursery Education and Grant-Maintained Schools Act in 1996 signified the policy priority of nursery education. The Act entitled all four-year-olds in England to early education and included the nursery voucher scheme. The scheme was devised to facilitate choice, encourage provider diversity and enable parents to gain access to part-time nursery education for their children in non-maintained nursery provision, such as playgroups and private nursery schools. Parents received a voucher worth £1,100 towards the cost of nursery education which could be 'spent' at a registered institution according to their personal preferences. The nursery voucher scheme is a good illustration of Conservative ideology; neo-liberal market policies were used to encourage choice and competition (see Chapters 1 and 3). It was assumed that parents would act as responsible consumers and use their voucher to choose a suitable provider from the range of pre-school settings. Quality in the pre-school education sector would be improved, it was presumed, as providers competed for parents' custom. Quality was to be assured through external accountability; Ofsted was given the statutory duty of inspecting and reporting on funded nursery education. Thus, national inspection was extended into the private and voluntary sectors. Quality provision is henceforth advocated as advantageous to child development. Campbell-Barr and Nygård (2014: 353) suggest this kind of policy rhetoric is a 'persuasive mechanism' to assure parents, but is couched within a model that reflects parents as 'workers' first and foremost.

The voucher entitled parents to free part-time nursery provision for the three terms following their child's fourth birthday. The providers would then claim back the voucher 'money' from government. However, the vouchers had an inadvertent effect on LEAs' and parents' actions as their value of £1,100 was insufficient (by £500) to cover the actual cost, at the time, of educating a child in a maintained nursery class (Chitty, 2009). Anxious to safeguard their funding, LEAs encouraged parents to send their children early to reception classes as primary schools moved to a single intake. Chitty (2009: 158) explains how the scheme resulted in 'the unofficial lowering of the school starting age to 4' and parents 'felt under pressure to secure a place at the school of their choice a year later'. Many four-year-olds were already being admitted to primary school reception classes in England and Wales even before the voucher scheme was piloted (Moss and Penn, 1996). According to Staggs (2012) schools often did not change their practices to cater for the younger four-year-olds in reception.

The nursery voucher scheme lasted less than a year; it was piloted in four English local authorities managed by Capita, a private services company, but never rolled out nationally (Ball, 2013). Randall (2000) doubts the merits of the experiment on a number of counts including its inadequate design, its resourcing, its incapacity to affect real choice for parents where there was no provision (such as in rural areas), the difficulties for private nurseries to expand with the uncertainty surrounding regular future income, the shortage of trained nursery teachers and the arrangements to assure quality. Parents with four-year-old children had received their vouchers in the spring of 1997 prior to the General Election in May, and this caused inevitable confusion among parents when the scheme was abolished by the incoming New Labour government, which proposed and subsequently implemented its own reform of early years provision.

Towards predetermined learning outcomes and a curriculum

In tandem with the 1996 nursery voucher scheme, the School Curriculum and Assessment Authority (SCAA), now known as the QCA, prepared a document for the pre-school sector in England called *Desirable Outcomes for Children's Learning on*

Entering Compulsory Education (SCAA, 1996)[4] (The Desirable Learning Outcomes were later to become the Early Learning Goals of the Foundation Stage Curriculum.) This document encapsulates, for the first time, government-specified parameters for nursery education and stated the learning goals to be achieved by children in England by the time they started school in the term after their fifth birthday. The curriculum framework (SCAA, 1996) comprised six areas of learning, namely: personal and social development, language and literacy, mathematics, knowledge and understanding of the world, physical development and creative development. This would have to be delivered by providers receiving vouchers and it was thus becoming evident to providers that greater accountability would be expected as a consequence of the increased focus and funding for the early years (Staggs, 2012). A discord between the six areas of learning and Key Stage One (ages 5–7) of the National Curriculum, which is subject-based, was apparent, however. In an attempt to reduce this tension, the QCA (1999b) subsequently revised the early years' curriculum framework.

Separate documents were prepared for Wales, Scotland and for Northern Ireland. While there is not the space here to compare the documents, or even consider the possibilities of what might constitute desirable outcomes, it is worth noting the observations of David (1998), who stresses the different values in the English and Welsh documents. She discerns the 'joyless, "input-output" model of the current approach for English provision' (David, 1998: 62) and contrasts the emphasis given to the importance of play for children in Wales compared to the English guidelines where the word 'play' is hardly mentioned. David's supposition is 'being under five in England is to be less joyful, less celebrated, less imaginative, less romantic, more pressurised, more rigid, more directed – especially towards literacy and numeracy – than early childhood in Wales' (1998: 61). The introduction of the centrally determined National Strategies for literacy and numeracy (see Chapter 4) impacted greatly upon early years. Staggs (2012) expounds the tensions and challenges faced in the morphing of the play-based and exploratory learning principles of the early years into a curriculum framework and assessment strategy. Then, having to marry this with government policy which was driven by developing measurable outcomes, preparing young children for primary school (i.e. 'school readiness') and raising standards in literacy and numeracy.

Investment, intervention and initiatives

The shape of services in the early education and childcare sector inherited by the incoming New Labour government in May 1997 was inadequate, disjointed and often arguably ad hoc. As has been emphasized already, historically there was split departmental responsibility (Moss, 2014). The Department for Education and

Employment (DfEE) was responsible for early education, which was administered and organized at a local level by LEAs. The Department of Health was responsible for day care, predominantly targeting support for disadvantaged children. Attempts were made by New Labour to unify children's services through the reorganization of government departments over a decade. All 'childcare' services were transferred in 2001 from Health to the newly created DfES. In 2003 the first Minister for Children, Margaret Hodge, was appointed, and the DfES took control of other services, including child protection along with those relating to ECM (see below). In 2007 the DCSF was created and assumed responsibility for almost all non-health services for children and young people.

As we have seen so far in this chapter, early education and care had been long neglected despite there being many preceding commissioned inquiries, public consultations and published reports, all of which had alluded to shortcomings in provision. Moss (2014) asserts the situation in 1997 had little changed since 1979, and arguably not since 1945. All political parties had postulated the importance and provision of good-quality pre-school education during the run-up to the 1997 General Election. Indeed, the UK political parties were not alone in recognizing its growing importance. Other countries such as Australia, New Zealand and many European countries were regulating the early years' sector, albeit with different frameworks and levels of intervention (Kingdon and Gourd, 2013).

Three weeks after the 1997 General Election David Blunkett, the then Secretary of State for Education and Employment, outlined the new early years' policy, signalling its priority for government and sparking an intense period of policy development and new initiatives over the next few years. Substantial investment for early education and childcare services was pledged as was a childcare tax credit. In England, LEAs and other early years' services came together through Early Years Development and Childcare Partnerships (EYDCP) to discuss and prepare local development plans for early years and childcare services and subsequently implement the National Childcare Strategy. The idea of partnerships and cooperation are recognizable tenets of New Labour policy-making.

The New Labour administration brought in a raft of education policies in its first term of government (1997–2001) which were specifically targeted at the early years and primary phases. The White Paper *Excellence in Schools* (DfEE, 1997a) was published almost immediately. In its second chapter the document outlines the government's proposals for early years and its targets to be met by 2002, namely:

- high quality education for all 4 year-olds whose parents want it;
- an early years forum in every area, planning childcare and education to meet local needs;
- a network of early excellence centres to spread good practice;
- effective assessment of all children starting primary schools. (1997a: 22)

With the discontinuation of the nursery voucher scheme, the increased number of nursery places were funded from 1998 through the Nursery Education Grants and paid to LEAs, who were responsible for managing nursery places and working with providers to assure quality. In 1998 free early education (in England) was offered to four-year-olds albeit on a part-time basis, comprising 12.5 hours for thirty-three weeks. From 2006, this was offered to all three-year-olds as well. From 2006, this increased to fifteen hours per week over thirty-eight weeks for all three- and four-year-olds. In 2009 New Labour announced its intention to extend this entitlement to two-year-olds living in disadvantaged areas, but while this was piloted it was not implemented until the Coalition was in government.

The Green Paper *Meeting the Childcare Challenge* (DfEE, 1998d; Scottish Office, 1998) announced the introduction of the National Childcare Strategy, which carried extra funding and which was increased in the 2002 and 2004 Treasury Spending Reviews. Ball and Vincent (2005) perceive the issue of childcare received unparalleled interest from policy-makers under New Labour. They also discern early education and childcare addressed a number of agendas central to the New Labour project, notably eradicating child poverty and combating exclusion, raising standards of educational achievement and stimulating the labour market. This interest and significant investment in early education and childcare can be found in many policy statements and documents, for example:

> The Government's vision for childcare is for every parent to have access to affordable, flexible, good quality childcare. Childcare and early education produce a variety of short-term and long-term benefits for the child, the parent and the wider community. Childcare can enable parents to work or seek employment, with consequent reductions in unemployment and child poverty. (HM Treasury, 2004: 60)

Good-quality childcare, deemed as particularly beneficial for disadvantaged young children, and early education were thus regarded as having individual, family and societal benefits. Notably childcare, which was affordable and accessible, was the means by which parents, especially women, could participate in, and return to, the workforce. New Labour increased access to childcare, but was less reliant on market forces than the previous Conservative government and more disposed to intervention to stimulate the growth of private provision, such as via the Neighbourhood Nurseries Initiative and Early Excellence Centres. Early Excellence Centres (of which there were eventually 107) were formed from existing nurseries identified as being of particularly high quality. They were intended to develop models of good practice and were thus regarded as catalytic for raising quality in early education and childcare through training and outreach to local practitioners. Significantly, Ofsted was given responsibility for inspecting and regulating all early years' services, including childminders, via the Care Standards Act (2000). A Ten Year Childcare Strategy was announced in 2004 and taken forward in the Childcare Act (2006). This is the first Act concerned solely with childcare and early years.

New Labour made headway in professionalizing the early years' workforce. Research evidence from the Effective Provision of Pre-School Education (EPPE) project (e.g. Sylva et al., 2004) suggested a relationship between the qualifications of early years' staff and the quality of provision as well as highlighting differences between the maintained sector and the private and voluntary sectors. In 2005 the Children's Workforce Development Council was established to deliver the Children's Workforce Strategy; this focused on recruitment and retention, staff development, strengthening inter-agency working and developing leadership and management within the early years setting (Palaiologou, 2010). Millions of pounds were provided to develop and retain a graduate-led workforce in the private and voluntary sectors to assure high-quality provision. In 2006, £250 million was made available for local authorities, and between 2008 and 2011 £305 million funded the Graduate Leader Fund. Graduate and Early Years Professionals[5] were employed to lead practice across the Early Years Foundation Stage (EYFS) (see below) by supporting, mentoring and modelling good practice to others.

Every child matters and sure start children's centres

By 2003 New Labour's early years' polices were well underway as were those designed to better integrate and coordinate service delivery from the existing array of services, create partnerships between providers and also include the new Children's Centres and Extended Schools. A development of considerable importance which provided impetus and urgency for childcare policies was the Laming Report (DH/HO, 2003). This inquiry investigated the circumstances surrounding the death of an eight-year-old girl, Victoria Climbié, who had suffered extensive physical abuse and neglect from her guardians. This particular case drew attention to the failure of the different services to communicate information effectively, to intervene to prevent the tragedy and properly safeguard and protect children and young people. The Laming Inquiry culminated in the ECM agenda, which was revealed through a Green Paper (HM Treasury, 2003: 14) and incorporated a common set of desirable outcomes for pre-school and school-age children, specifically:

1. Being healthy: being healthy: enjoying good physical and mental health and living a healthy lifestyle
2. Staying safe: being protected from harm and neglect and growing up able to look after themselves.

3. Enjoying and achieving: getting the most out of life and developing broad skills for adulthood.
4. Making a positive contribution: to the community and to society and not engaging in anti-social or offending behaviour.
5. Economic well-being – overcoming socio-economic disadvantages to achieve their full potential in life.

Some radical reforms were proposed to foster accountability and integration at the local, regional and national level for both education and children's social services. These included a director of Children's Services and a lead local council member in each local authority (LA), a children's commissioner and a minister for children and young people and families. ECM was subsequently legislated via the Children Act (2004) and *Every Child Matters: Change for Children* (DfES, 2004a) provided the national framework for local reform. Restructuring was required to create 'a joined-up set of services' (2004a: 93) which were more accessible, flexible and proactive to local needs (see Chapter 3). The 2004 Spending Review (HM Treasury, 2004) delineated the extra resources to support the reform of children's services. Roche and Tucker (2007: 222) analyse ECM in relation to multidisciplinary approaches to work, workforce reform and 'extended schools' and argue New Labour's agenda was an example of 'radical reform, rather than an exercise in tinkering'.

Sure Start Children's Centres were first created in 2004. They were multi-agency, bringing together many different services (such as play workers, health visitors, mid-wives), to be accessible in one place to families with children under four in areas with high levels of poverty. They succeeded other early years' initiatives: Early Excellence Centres (see above); the Neighbourhood Nurseries Initiative (launched in 2001 and provided convenient and affordable childcare for working parents on lower incomes); and Sure Start Local Programmes (SSLP). The Sure Start initiative was a linchpin in New Labour's quest to preclude social exclusion by early intervention policies. The SSLP, first piloted in 1999, targeted families in the most deprived areas and provided a whole raft of services to support children and their parents with a policy goal to tackle social exclusion and counteract the damage caused by poverty in the early years. By 2003 there were 500 SSLPs in operation.

New Labour's policies on early education and childcare were based, to some extent, on research. The EPPE project (Sylva et al., 2004) is a good example of research influencing policy and practice. This was a longitudinal study funded by the DfES which investigated the academic and social development of more than 3,000 children aged three to seven in England. The EPPE project made important contributions to the subsequent development of Sure Start as its findings suggested integrated children's centres were advantageous to children's development. Initial findings from the National Evaluation of Sure Start suggested SSLPs were not impacting as intended. An interdepartmental review in 2002 prompted the change to Children's Centres. Lewis's (2011) examination of Sure Start shows how policy shifted from

2004 despite claims of continuity by policy-makers. The key focus remained, but Children's Centres were now under the control of LAs, not central government as were SSLPs. Services were universal, for all young children and their families in all communities, with 'emphasis on children's cognitive development on the one hand, and parents' employment on the other' (Lewis, 2011: 82).

A designated key stage for early years

The Foundation Stage was introduced by New Labour in September 2000 and established in the Education Act (2002). The *Early Learning Goals* (QCA, 1999c) had set out the expectations which most children should achieve by the end of their Reception year in primary school. More detailed guidance (QCA, 2000) was provided to practitioners as to what might reasonably be expected of children aged three- to five-year-olds at the different stages in the Foundation Stage. Further supplementary and practical advice soon followed (QCA, 2001). This tranche of documents was obligatory for all providers in receipt of the Nursery Education Grant and, according to Moss (2014), signalled the move towards a pre-school national curriculum. A flood of government directives, guidance and mandated change followed through the next decade. The *Foundation Stage Profile Assessment Arrangements* (DfES, 2003b) were installed via the Education Act (2002), which also extended the National Curriculum to include the Foundation Stage; the six Early Learning Goals and the curriculum guidance thus becoming statutory.

In 2008 the EYFS superseded the Foundation Stage and other documents namely *Birth to Three Matters* (DfES, 2002) and the national standards for *Full Day Care* (DfES, 2003c). The EYFS sets the standards for all early years' providers, and there was some optimism across the sector, as Roberts-Holmes (2012) affirms. The EYFS had created a distinct phase of education, which was developmentally appropriate with a play-based, child-centred approach. Nonetheless, Roberts-Holmes (2012: 39) discerns the 'pedagogic tension' in reception classes between the child-led, play-based EYFS approach with its six areas of learning and the ten subjects–based National Curriculum.

Palaiologou (2010) applauds ongoing assessment of children as integral to the learning and development process. However, she expresses pessimism regarding changes to practice by incessant monitoring and tick-boxing by teachers' observational assessments of children's progress in the six areas of learning. These were subdivided into thirteen separate sections and each one assessed on a 9-point scale (QCA, 2008) and thus created the Foundation Stage Profile of 117 statements against which children were judged on entry to school. It replaced local systems of informal 'baseline' testing in England and was extremely bureaucratic (Bradbury, 2014). The EYFS has sparked much criticism from practitioners, academics and organizations such as the Open EYE campaign and the Alliance for Childhood (and, more recently, Early Childhood Action) who regard the curriculum and its targets as too demanding for young children. However, some practitioners welcome the higher status afforded by designating the early years as a key stage in its own right and administering statutory testing (Bradbury, 2014), this responsibility and trust, arguably, enhancing their notions of professionalism. However, simultaneously, the process de-professionalizes early years' practitioners since LAs can override their judgements. Campbell-Barr and Nygård (2014) argue that the EYFS reflects a human capital agenda (see Chapter 7) and is a foundation for skills acquisition for later life in order to increase national productivity and economic competitiveness.

Over to you ...

Now read the article by Jo Basford and Caroline Bath:

Basford, J. and C. Bath (2014), 'Playing the Assessment Game: An English Early Childhood Education Perspective', *Early Years*, 34 (2): 119–132.

> Basford and Bath discuss the issue of assessment and the documentation of learning in early childhood education which they maintain is 'a way for governments to exercise direct control over the practitioners working with young children' (2014: 119). They provide an argument for the 'assessment game' and maintain that 'if practitioners are sufficiently knowledgeable, they will potentially have greater power and confidence in playing the assessment game: a game that allows them to perform the technical duties to satisfy the gatekeepers of regulation whilst also satisfying their own moral and ethical duties to encourage children and their families to participate in learning which is representative of their social, cultural and historical heritage'. (2014: 128–129)

1 What do you see as the advantages and disadvantages of assessment in early education?
2 What do you think are the implications for those who work with young children not being 'sufficiently knowledgeable' – and what does this suggest about the prerequisite education and credentials of the early years' workforce?
3 What do you consider are the main challenges currently facing early years' practitioners?

A period of 'austerity': 2010–2015

Under the Coalition, early years did not seem to be an immediate priority of policy development. It was some fourteen months after being in government before the publication of the first early years policy statement *Families in the Foundation Years* (DfE/DH, 2011a) along with the document *Supporting Families in the Foundation Years* (DfE/DH, 2011b) which was aimed at professionals in the sector. These initial early years' policies were 'co-produced' by senior civil servants working in collaboration with key individuals within the early childhood sector (Lloyd, 2015) and headed by Sarah Teather, Minister of State for Children and Families (Liberal-Democrat MP) and Under-secretary of State for Health, Anne Milton (Conservative MP). The 'vision for the system' (Teather, 2011) indicates the Coalition's propensity, at that time at least, towards social mobility as a 'rationale for its investment in early education' (Lloyd, 2015: 148).

The preceding New Labour administration had enjoyed a period of steady growth in the economy, until 2007–2008 at least, enabling it to develop an array of initiatives. While the Coalition government did continue to invest in, expand and emphasize the importance of early years, the economy was weaker and a period of 'austerity' ensued. The 2010 Spending Review outlined substantial government cuts in services such as to Sure Start Children's Centres; there were fears many would close as local councils were left to decide how to utilize their reduced funding (Richardson, 2011). The National Evaluation of Sure Start had demonstrated, over time, some significant effects and it is claimed 'the results are modest but suggest that the value of Sure Start programmes is improving' (Melhuish et al., 2010: 160). The ring-fencing of funding for Sure Start was removed; in the tougher financial climate, the Coalition refocused Sure Start with a 'new core purpose' (Teather, 2011) to target the neediest children and families. The DCSF was renamed the DfE, although its remit remains largely the same.

The EYFS was reviewed in 2010, at the request of Teather, with the intention of reducing the amount of bureaucracy and better supporting children's learning and development. As such, the Tickell Review (2011) examined the original framework for the EYFS and the revised EYFS came into effect in September 2012, and was further updated for September 2014 (DfE, 2014a). There are now seven areas of development (prime and specific) which contain seventeen aspects (sub areas). The statutory document professes the EYFS 'promotes teaching and learning to ensure children's "school readiness" and gives children the broad range of knowledge and skills that provide the right foundation for good future progress through school and life' (2014a: 5). The assessment procedures were simplified and the Early Learning Goals reduced to seventeen. While purportedly slimmed down, there is much greater attention given to children's readiness for school and the revised Profile reflects a more acute focus on literacy and maths. Ofsted was given more powers to promote best practice in childcare setting and assess provider quality – roles previously undertaken by local authorities and signifying their further decline.

The Coalition's reforms controversially dismantled many of the initiatives established under New Labour. For example, ECM, a flagship New Labour policy, was ignored in terms of its 'brand' although its tenets can still be ascertained in Coalition policy (e.g. see DfE, 2010a: 28). Despite being positively evaluated, the Graduate Leader Fund was halted (Mathers et al., 2011) as was a requirement for Children's Centres to employ a graduate. Regarding the credentials and training needs of the early years' workforce, Teather (2011) had commissioned Professor Cathy Nutbrown to lead an independent review of early education and childcare and to advise on how these, and career pathways, could be strengthened. The government subsequently rejected most of Nutbrown's (2012) recommendations, which included replacing Early Years Professional Status with Qualified Teacher Status (QTS), arguably an important means of improving service quality. Early Years Professional Status was superseded by Early Years Teacher, but did not carry QTS or the requirement of a Post-Graduate Certificate of Education (PGCE). Nutbrown was so dismayed by the government's response to the report that she published her own (Nutbrown, 2013). However, by the time of the report (Nutbrown, 2012), and following a government reshuffle in September 2012, Teather was replaced by Elizabeth Truss (Conservative MP) who, as Under-Secretary of State for Education and Childcare, held the provision of childcare as her priority for DfE early years' policy (Lloyd, 2015). Lloyd (2015) suggests there is sufficient evidence to indicate a 'policy turn' by government at this juncture. Lloyd (2015: 149) contends the Coalition's focus swung from early education towards childcare and 'shifted substantially in favour of the economic well-being rationale as the main driver for early years policy development'. Regarding the publication of *More Great Childcare* (DfE, 2013b) and *More Affordable Childcare* (HM Government, 2013), Lloyd (2015: 149) notes that significantly policy-making 'lacked input from the Department of Health or indeed participants in the co-production process. Centralized early years policymaking dominated'.

Expanding early eduction and childcare

The annual State Opening of Parliament on 27 May 2015 took place twenty days after the Conservative Party won the general election in the UK and formed a majority government. The Queen's Speech, customarily written for her by the government, announces the government's proposed policy for the next session of Parliament and signals impending legislation (see Chapter 1). Among the twenty

Bills outlined in the 2015 Queen's Speech (Prime Minister's Office, 2015) was the Childcare Bill. This Bill required local authorities to publish information about the provision of childcare and other services in their area. A key element is to provide in England an increased entitlement of thirty hours of 'free childcare' a week (for thirty-eight weeks, equivalent to the academic year) to eligible working parents of three- and four-year-olds, which had been pledged in the Conservative Party's manifesto (Conservative Party, 2015). Under the Coalition government all three- and four-year-olds in England were entitled to fifteen hours 'early education' each week (570 hours over thirty-eight weeks). This increase was met with both enthusiasm by some and concerns about funding by others (Coates, 2015). The 2015 Childcare Bill (and the subsequent 2016 Childcare Act) denotes an important area of policy. However, there remains reliance by government 'in facilitating, enforcing, and sustaining markets' (West, 2015: 31) with responsibility lying with parents to make informed and assiduous choices for their children. This assumes choice exists of course; in reality there may not always be suitable services available.

In August 2015 Nicky Morgan, the Secretary of State for Education, announced proposals to introduce from September 2016 (a year early than originally planned) thirty hours per week of free childcare (over thirty-eight weeks) for 'hardworking' parents with three- and four-year-olds.[6] The offer is worth approximately £5,000 per child, per year (DfE, 2015) and purported to ensure 'hardworking' families benefit from childcare support as soon as possible. Other policies include fifteen hours of free childcare per week to the 40 per cent of two-year-olds in areas with high levels of poverty, worth £2,500 per child, per year. Low-income working parents are further supported through tax credits and with plans in 2017 for tax-free childcare. Changes in policy have made employment more flexible. The right to request flexible working was extended to all employees with at least twenty-six weeks continuous service through the Children and Families Act (2014). This right was first instigated by New Labour through the Employment Act (2002) for parents with disabled children under eighteen and those with children under six (which over time was extended to all children under seventeen) (Pyper, 2015). The right to request is not a right to work flexibly, but nevertheless having this flexibility does not inhibit parents, particularly mothers, from working. The Shared Parental Leave and Pay initiative also provides greater flexibility for working parents if they wish. These employment-related policies contrast starkly with earlier times when the prevailing ideology saw men as the breadwinners earning a family wage and women's place as in the home. They also evidence the Conservative Party's policy rationale for 'encouraging work as a route to family economic well-being [as] a primary objective for investing in early years provision' (Lloyd, 2015: 151).

As has been illustrated in this chapter, policy-making is complicated and complex. After years of neglect, early education and childcare policy-making has intensified of late with demands for greater quality, more accountability and better outcomes. Baseline assessment, whereby children are assessed on entry to school, is encouraged for all children at the start of Reception. This is not a mandatory requirement, but is the DfE's response to the consultation on assessment in primary schools (DfE, 2014b) (see Chapter 4). Only DfE-approved baseline assessment schemes can be used from 2016[7] and, for accountability purposes, the assessment is important in terms of being able to measure pupil progress at the end of Key Stage Two. Roberts-Holmes (2015) condemns what he identifies as the 'datafication' of early years' pedagogy: the pressures to produce appropriate (good) data. He proposes the early years is now in danger of becoming the first stage in a 'delivery chain' whereby data are passed upwards and right through the entire school system (Roberts-Holmes, 2015: 313). Basford and Bath (2014) consider how early years' practitioners are now caught up in 'playing the assessment game' whereby they have to embrace the conceivably incompatible 'dissonant demands' of assessment practices, and which they have to reconcile with 'their own professional values and beliefs regarding curriculum and policy' (2014: 122). Roberts-Holmes (2015) denounces the detrimental impact of recent policy on early years by the pressures to teach systematic synthetic phonics, the emphasis on literacy and numeracy and the intensification of 'school readiness' pressures upon the earliest stage of education. While early years is regarded as a child-centred and play-based educational stage in its own right, nevertheless the 'schoolification'[8] of the early years arguably makes it subservient to the needs of the primary National Curriculum. Despite many and major policy developments in the early childhood education and care services in England, these are arguably 'missed opportunities' for 'transformative change' which have failed to integrate its separate strands into an 'integrated and coherent' whole (Moss, 2014: 357). While it may be too soon to judge the effects of current policies for early education and childcare services, it is not yet too soon to raise some critical concerns, questions and thoughtful provocations.

Notes

1   The complexity of analysing 'national' education policy is reflected in the context of devolution in the UK, whereby from the late 1990s a range of powers were transferred to the Scottish Parliament, the National Assembly for Northern Ireland and the National Assembly Wales; England remains with the UK Parliament.

2   The Elementary Code contained the aims of the elementary school, comprised the curriculum and prescribed nationally what (elementary) teachers taught in their schools.

3   The Consultative Committee conducted several different inquiries during its existence. The 1933 Hadow Report (of which there were six reports between 1923 and 1933 and named after the chairman of the committee) is of relevance here.

4   Separate documents were prepared for Wales (Curriculum and Assessment Authority for Wales, 1996), Scotland (Scottish Office, 1997) and for Northern Ireland (DENI, 1997).

5   Early Years Professional Status was a specialized graduate route for early education.

6   Full implementation of the new entitlement was planned for September 2017. Early implementation in a small number of areas was planned for September 2016. The government ran an open consultation between 3 April and 6 June 2016 to seek views on the delivery model of the 30-hour free childcare entitlement.

7   In April 2016 the baseline tests were dropped by the DfE as a study it had commissioned concluded the three different testing systems available to schools were not sufficiently comparable (see Coughlan, 2016).

8   See OECD (2006), *Starting Strong II. Early Childhood Education and Care*, France: OECD Publications.

Further reading

Boyd, D. and N. Hirst, eds (2015) *Understanding Early Years Education across the UK: Comparing Practice in England, Northern Ireland, Scotland and Wales*, London: Routledge.

Clark, M. and T. Waller, eds (2007) *Early Childhood Education and Care: Policy and Practice*, London: Sage.

6

Post-Compulsory Education

Introduction

The relationship between education and the economy has a long and chequered history dating back to the late nineteenth century. Yet such well-known links have been described at best 'tenuous' (Young, 1993) or worse, 'mythical' (Wolf, 2002). It would thus be remiss *not* to point out that the politics of education policy is influenced by a broad range of social, cultural and historical factors, as well as important economic ones, as we have sought to demonstrate throughout this book. Here, we suggest the apparent link between education and training, and the modern economy is apt to reflect the nuances of particular social, cultural and political milieu: the enduring histories and traditions of industrial economies and their respective nation states (Green, 1990). In this chapter we focus on the influence of the late-capitalist economy on the landscape of post-compulsory education and training in England, and consider why even today this mysterious relationship continues to dominate the hearts and minds of politicians, policy advisors, educationalists and critical commentators alike. More especially and fundamentally, we suggest there remains a pathological belief in the ability of education to provide a panacea for the perceived ills of the economy and contemporary society. As Prime Minister David Cameron proclaimed when he led the Coalition government:

> For youth unemployment, which has actually been going up for years in our country, the real change we need is actually in our education system to make sure we are producing young people at the age of 18 with a *real qualification* that people need in the modern workplace. (Cameron quoted in *The Telegraph*, 2011: emphasis added)

Here the term 'real qualification' is revealing, but perhaps more for what it does *not* say than what it appears to assert. The ambition to produce young people with 'real qualifications' posits an 'authentic ideal' in the future against the perceived 'inauthentic' system of the present, where an argument for 'real change' is made. Further, by implying that contemporary education is in some way 'lacking', its maligned status is affirmed, and, with this, the notion of the 'inauthentic' to produce inferior qualifications is effectively reinforced, where credentials (including degrees) are not 'worth the paper they're printed on' (Walker E., 2008). This argument forms a recurring theme throughout the chapter, as the notion of what counts as relevant and real in educational terms has tended to become conflated with the changing preferences of modern politicians, while evolving alongside more radical, structural change in the political economy – change that continues, to this day, to be influenced by the hegemony of neo-liberal ideology (see Chapter 1). For now, though, it is perhaps worth contemplating how such an idea was initially conceived, and to consider why the apparent link between post-compulsory education and the economy is perceived so remarkably precious to the future prosperity of our society?

The birth of instrumentalism: The academic and vocational divide

In the aftermath of the Industrial Revolution, modern industrial economies increasingly relied upon a separation of 'mental' and 'manual' labour as a means to justify a similar partition of academic and vocational education and training (Young, 1993). Underlying such historical divisions in the provision of formal education was a popular belief in the ability of school-based education or work-based training to provide the engine for economic growth (Wolf, 2002). This became increasingly apparent as the nature and role of the economy changed over time and with this, too, its relationship with post-compulsory education. During the last decades of the nineteenth century and throughout the early mid-twentieth century, mass production paved the way for increasing levels of specialization at work, levels which relied, in turn, on a more clearly defined and extensive division of labour – between the creative conception of tasks and their simple execution and production (Piore and Sabel, 1984). Such divisive specialization, upon which the political economy of mass production depended, made it necessary that waged labour possess no more than the most rudimentary education and work-related skills, just sufficient, in fact, to enable the routine and timely production of goods and services. In this crucial respect, it was the inertia of the capitalist economy that produced severe constraints upon the growth of formal (academic) education, where a separation of 'minds' was created (and acknowledged much later in the Crowther Report [MoE, 1959]), producing an instrumental rationale for the development of selective education: an early selection, low participation system (Finegold et al., 1990: 14).

Over to you ...

Trawl the national newspapers and find as many articles as possible featuring the virtues of academic education, and then do the same for vocational education. Using the cuttings as evidence, develop an argument both for and against the promotion of a divided system of education: academic and vocational.

Changing times, changing conditions

During the mid-late twentieth century, a radical transformation and restructuring of the nature and state of the political economy began to emerge. As patterns of trade changed, through increasing globalization (see Chapter 9), there was a marked 'shift away from the closed or walled economies of the post-war period towards an open or global economy', where 'national "champions" such as Ford, IBM, ICI and Mercedes Benz ... tried to break free of their national roots, creating a *global auction* for investment, technology and jobs' (Brown and Lauder, 1996: 2: original emphasis). This produced a significant departure from the earlier reliance on mass production (or *Fordism*, so named after Henry Ford, who created a low-cost and standardized process of manufacture) and divisive specialization, as capital became more mobile, enabling the process and techniques of mass production to be relocated in countries and regions offering 'low wage costs, light labour market legislation, weak trade unions ... and cheap rent' (1996: 2). Fundamental change in the international economy coupled with increasing competition from external foreign markets meant that many traditional heavy industries fell into permanent inexorable decline. The post-war boom had ended and mass production was proving so uncompetitive as to be gradually replaced by a burgeoning service and technology-inspired sector, demanding new 'human-capital', knowledge, skills and 'entrepreneurial acumen in an unfettered global marketplace' (1996: 3).

Thus, whereas previously the internal resistance of a more domestically contained political economy had helped determine the purpose and selective function of education, the new global order was beginning to privilege the concept of flexible specialization, especially at the turn of the twenty-first century. More than ever, this meant there was now a requirement for workers to become more adaptable and responsive to change in the so-called 'global auction' (Brown and Lauder, 1996). A continuous demand for new knowledge and skills was created along with the possibility of several changes in employment over the course of a lifetime (of which, more later). As Young (1993: 208: original emphasis) suggests, such a conception of political economy 'depends on prior education and political changes ... [in] an era of education (or more broadly human resource-led) economic growth', and where '*national systems of education and training*, rather than *national economies* ... will determine the fate of nations'. This suggests that while the union between education and the modern economy became more strongly wedded, the quality of this marriage changed substantially over time. Both formal schooling and contemporary post-compulsory education became a prior condition in the move to serve the needs of the economy and new global order.

Economic and political context

The 1970s marked a watershed in the rise of the political New Right (see Chapter 1) and its revolutionary impact on education and the economy. At the end of the 1960s, the post-war, welfare-capitalist consensus which had held sway since the end of the Second World War finally began to recoil. The oil crisis of the early 1970s represented the start of a steep decline throughout the decade matched with unprecedented social, political and economic transformation and restructuring (Brown and Lauder, 1996; Jones, 2003), signalling the end of the so-called 'golden age'. 'Mounting inflation, swelling balance of payments deficits, unprecedented currency depreciation, rising unemployment [especially youth unemployment (Finegold et al., 1990), and] bitter industrial conflicts' (Marquand, 1988: 3, cited in Chitty, 2009: 32) all served to reinforce the feeling that Keynesian social democracy had failed and had its day, and that radical economic and political change was now urgently needed (see also Chapter 6).

Emerging in tandem with the economic crisis of the period was the widely perceived calamity of state education. As noted in Chapters 1 and 5, the *Black Papers*, written by right-wing dissenting educationalists and politicians, were influential in portraying the idea that state education had descended into chaos, and that such profound destabilization was especially worrying in the context of unprecedented global economic decline. Such events proved significant as a catalyst in synthesizing several strands of thought, and in further establishing a platform for the launch of James Callaghan's (then Labour Prime Minister) Ruskin College Speech, at Oxford in 1976 (Phillips and Furlong, 2001). The speech, and well-publicized call for a 'Great Debate' on education that followed, centred on two major areas of concern: 'standards and behaviour in schools, and the supply of skilled manpower, especially scientists, engineers and technologists' (Moore, 1984: 72). As Callaghan (1976) argued at the time:

> I have been very impressed in the schools I have visited … But I am concerned on my journeys to find complaints from industry that new recruits from the schools sometimes do not have the basic tools to do the job that is required … There seems to be a need for more technological bias in science teaching that will lead towards practical applications in industry rather than towards academic studies … To what extent are these deficiencies the result of insufficient co-operation between schools and industry? … There is the need to improve relations between industry and education.

The impact of Callaghan's prime ministerial intervention reverberated throughout the education world and gave political sanction to the so-called '"discourse of derision" mounted by the *Black Papers*', as well as further impetus to an 'increasingly well-organised and articulate New Right' (Ball, 1990: 31–32). As Tomlinson (2005: 25) explains, 'Wide publicity was given to employers and business people who argued that comprehensive schools did not serve the needs of British industry, and from this time educational practices were to become more closely linked to industrial regeneration.' More than ever before, the nature and purpose of education came to be seen as a central plank of political thinking, and thus crucially implicated in the construction of other social and economic realities, in particular the view that education and training post-16 was 'failing to meet the needs of an advanced industrial economy' (Finegold, 1993: 42). In effect, Callaghan's speech served to galvanize the link between education and the economy, and further provided the logic of justification for a more directive approach to post-compulsory education and training in the context of a radically changing economy.

The New Right: Market reforms and post-compulsory education

The impact of the Ruskin speech, mobilizing a series of debates and government-inspired policy texts (e.g. DES, 1977; DE/DES, 1986), gave credence to a 'new vocationalism' at the beginning of the 1980s, forging strong links between education and industry. For the New Right, a key point of departure involved challenging the long-stranding, anti-industrial culture in Britain, by attempting to instil the 'right' sort of attitudes in young people towards business, industry and the workplace. This entailed challenging the perceived neglect of basic (work-related) skills in education (see, for example, *A Basis for Choice* [FEU, 1979]), as well as encouraging an understanding in young people about the world of work and industry, and its important role in wealth creation for the benefit of society and the economy. Refocusing teachers' and schools' attention on the value of the 'practical and vocational' alongside the 'academic' signalled the beginning of a broad shift, for the right-wing Conservative government (1979–1997) was intent on fostering a spirit of enterprise and entrepreneurship through all sectors of education (Ball, 1990). Some of these concerns were addressed through innovation and change in educational provision, for example, through the introduction of the Technical and Vocational Education Initiative (TVEI) (intended to relate education to the world of work for fourteen to eighteen-year-olds). However, TVEI did not reform the certification system, nor did it 'address broader issues arising either from the division between academic and vocational studies or from the institutional break at 16' (Finegold et al. 1990: 12). Indeed, at the time TVEI was introduced (along with a raft of other vocational programmes intended to make education more relevant to the economy), the late Sir Keith Joseph, Secretary of State for Education (1981–1986), declared that such pathways were only properly intended for the 'bottom 40 per cent' of achievers (Rowan, 1997).

A key feature of the political New Right was its fundamental faith in the 'market analogue' (Finegold, 1993) – a system sensitive to considerations of efficiency, cost-effectiveness and notions of individual learner flexibility. For perhaps the first time during the 1980s, the discipline of the market, a corrective to excessive interference of public agencies in the economy, entered the process of education and training, creating a paradigm shift (Hodkinson and Sparkes, 1995). This meant that rather than state bureaucracies taking decisions on important matters of contemporary education and training, individual market freedom would prevail, with 'choice' being given over to students rebranded as 'consumers' of education. However, the emphasis on the individual was double-edged, invoking elements of freedom *and* coercion. For example, in a government White Paper (see Chapter 1) *Working Together – Education and Training* (DE/DES, 1986: 1.4), this tension emerged through the role of the individual reconceived as autonomous learner, where in the process of learning, 'motivation is all important so that attitudes change and people acquire the desire to learn, the habit of learning, and the skills learning brings'. This perspective is especially significant for it implies that at the root of the economic problem lies something of a benign pathology: the attitudes, skills and abilities of the *individual*, whereas Stronach (1988: 60) suggests that 'the personalising of economic competitiveness (be motivated, get skilled) offers both an economics of recovery and a metonymics of blame (if *you* were trained and motivated *we* wouldn't be where we are today)' (cited in Ball, 1990: 74).

In 1988 a different White Paper, *Training for Employment*, pointed to 'the changing circumstances of the youth labour market' (DE, 1988: 6.12), from which the then Training Agency announced the introduction of the government's new Youth Training Scheme. In this, the government phased out 'paying an allowance for trainees under the rationale that in increasingly tight labour markets employers would be competing to take on young people' (Finegold, 1993: 46). To this end, in 1990 an 'individual training credit' or voucher programme was piloted, in which *individuals* would become, once again, 'more demanding consumers of training while encouraging competition among the providers by giving sixteen-year-olds a credit to cover the costs of training up to at least NVQ level II' (1993: 46). This move was perfectly aligned with the new culture of market reforms based on the binary of choice and blame, noted above. After all, with a scheme of individual credits, young people 'have consciously to choose *not* to enhance their skills' (1993: emphasis added) – that is consciously opt out of learning. Underpinning this was the Confederation of British Industry's (CBI) notion of careership in which 'pride of place' was given 'to the individual and his or her responsibility for self-development in a market environment' (CBI, 1993: 13). Accordingly, any absence of interest and motivation on the part of the learner could be attributed directly to a personal deficit. As the CBI noted, 'relevant qualifications and transferable core skills [are] needed by employers and employees alike' (1993), where the role of the individual in managing his or her own learning can be regarded as an important 'process skill' (CBI, 1989, 1993) (of which, more later).

A third White Paper, *Education and Training for the 21st Century* (DfE/ED/WO, 1991), brought yet further significant change to the landscape of post-compulsory education, at a time of wider societal and economic instability at the start of the 1990s (Hodgson and Spours, 1997). A steady rise in full-time participation post-16 in the late 1980s and into the following decade shifted the balancing point from a traditional equilibrium of 'low participation' to one of 'medium participation' (Spours, 1995). Meanwhile, the government persisted with characteristic zeal in its ideological mission to improve 'supply-side' conditions, enabling the market to function more flexibly and efficiently and emphasizing 'the power and autonomy of individual students and individual institutions' (Hodgson and Spours, 1997: 9). This was achieved through the introduction of the 1992 Further and Higher Education Act, which secured a 'quasi-market' (Levacic, 1995) in post-compulsory education. The strategic removal of sixth-form, tertiary and further education colleges from LEA control was initiated in a bid to increase efficiency and drive up quality (Hodgson and Spours, 2006). At the same time, control of the state's finances for training was strategically transferred 'to a group of new, local employer-led Training and Enterprise Councils (TECs) ... to mobilise local employers to play a greater role' (Finegold, 1993: 47). Unfortunately, the latter coincided with a weakening of the youth labour market exacerbated by the onset of economic recession in the early 1990s. This led ironically to a situation in which employers 'hunkered' down, and so the tradition of cutting training during times of financial stringency continued, for fear of a situation in which expensively trained workers might 'be poached' (Hodkinson and Sparkes, 1995: 190).

In this changing environment, the White Paper of 1991 sought to provide a more centralized approach to qualifications reform, principally through the formalization of a triple-track: academic (A-levels), vocational (GNVQs) and occupationally specific (NVQs) (Hodgson and Spours, 1997). This came against a backdrop of discussion to develop a unified system of qualifications, comprising both general (academic) and vocational education culminating in a *British Baccalaureate* (Finegold et al., 1990). The economic rationale was in tune with the feeling that alone A-levels were unable to provide 'particular capacities' and 'skills' for the workplace (this had long been the CBI's argument) (Young, 1997). In recognition of this fact, just three years earlier, the Higginson Report (DES, 1988) had advised on the reform of A-levels, suggesting that they needed to be leaner, broader and less specialized to meet the twin demands of rising participation and flexible specialization, an important prerequisite of future economic success. Despite this fact, the 1991 White Paper served to retrench them, by restricting access and participation through modified assessment (making them 'tougher') and developing a clear vocational alternative through the introduction of GNVQs (Hodgson and Spours, 1997). Moreover, as participation rates grew from 50 per cent to about 70 per cent between 1987 and 1994, the government further exercised its neo-conservative arm of 'social authoritarianism' (Johnson and Steinberg, 2004). The introduction of more structure and centralization through National Training Targets for Education and Training (originating from the CBI) and a new National Vocational Qualifications framework served to enhance the 'market analogue' as a basis to drive up standards. Thus, much like the National Curriculum had usefully created a centralized system of standardization (of curricula and assessment), to facilitate comparison between schools in a competitive market environment, so competence-related NVQs would serve a similar purpose and allow the state to play 'a less interventionist role' (Finegold, 1993: 48) in the market, while simultaneously catering to the 'job-related training needs' (Spours, 1997: 57) and demands of employers. Throughout, the focus on the responsibility of the individual would be paramount, as a 1994 White Paper, *Competitiveness: Helping Business Win*, indicated: 'a fulfilled workforce meeting *individual targets*, driven by the will to perform to their *individual best*, will be a world class workforce' (HM Government, 1994: 30).

At the end of the Conservative government's (1979–1997) political reign came the publication of the Dearing Report on 16–19 qualifications (Dearing, 1996a). Like many policy texts, both before and since, this report conveyed an ambiguous message to the debate on post-16 reform, and perhaps deliberately so in order to satisfy a broad range of 'educational and political constituencies' (Young, 1997: 25). Essentially, the report pointed towards the development of a more unified system of qualifications and their consolidation, more emphasis on 'core skills' (albeit only for those involved with GNVQs) and the need to achieve greater parity of esteem between academic and vocational pathways. This coincided with growing recognition of increasing levels of participation, along with a desire to minimize the wastage of talent (as A-levels were reaching only one in three people [Young and Leney, 1997]) and further enhance competitiveness through improved qualifications for the whole population (DTI, 1995). However, despite the call to an overarching framework for an Advanced Diploma, bringing different qualifications together (including A-levels), the reality was that many right-wing politicians remained suspicious of change, especially when such radical reform posed a threat to the selective function of A-levels, and, with this, the view that only a 'very small number of students could possibly do well at [them]' (Young and Leney, 1997: 48). As such, notions of breadth and flexibility, articulated as part of the modernizing agenda (a rhetoric to develop a high-participation, high-skill and high-wage economy), appear at odds with the divisive function of A-levels, and, correspondingly, the enduring elitist belief that enhanced participation must equate with a decline in academic standards. Indeed, the Advanced Diploma was not so much posed as a replacement for A-levels, in the way the *Baccalaureate* had been (Finegold et al., 1990), but rather as a 'weak-framework' designed to capture existing qualifications, while at the same time preserving different forms of assessment (as opposed to unitizing them) and reinforcing the value of 'core-skills' (later proposed as a qualification in 'key-skills' to link the different qualification tracks [Dearing cited in DfEE, 1997c]). In retrospect the Dearing Report (1996a) can be viewed as a reincarnation of the 1991 White Paper, which dates back to the spirit of Crowther (MoE, 1959), and before that the long history of academic/vocational divisions noted at the beginning of the chapter. This may be what David Cameron meant by 'real qualifications' and a changed education system: a return in the future to good old-fashioned elitism?

New Labour: But more of the same?

The radical reconfiguration of post-compulsory education and training along economic lines during the 1980s and 1990s created a competitive, marketized system in which educational services were rebranded as 'commodities' and sold to student-consumers in the marketplace. This transformation heralded the beginning of a new mixed economy of private and public sector institutions competing for education business in an environment in which notions of educational welfare were effectively displaced by a new *modus operandi* in which only the fittest survived (see Chapter 7). Yet while the market economy promised much in the way of addressing the inflexibilities associated with the abovementioned Fordist model of divisive specialization in a low-skill economy (by increasing participation and driving up standards), paradoxically the New Right's market reforms served only to colonize academic education and thus

> school the majority of children for a neo-Fordist economy which requires a low level of talent and skill … in the context of the global auction, the market reforms are likely to leave a large majority of the future working population without the human resources to flourish in the global economy. (Brown and Lauder, 1996: 7–8)

It is against this backdrop that New Labour's approach (1997–2010) to post-compulsory education and training, across three terms of office, signalled both points of continuity and change in relation to previous Conservative education policy. Much like their predecessors, New Labour was similarly committed to achieving higher standards in education and thus establishing 'greater relevance to economic performance' (Pring, 2005: 72). However, a distinction was in deciding how best to reconcile notions of 'competition' with the ameliorative function of education, to level the playing field in the interest of social justice (Callinicos, 2010). In essence, the commitment to a marketized system matched with a pledge to improve educational opportunities represented a 'Third Way', the birth of a new 'market socialism' (Giddens, 1998) or 'more progressive settlement within a neo-liberal era' (Hodgson and Spours, 2006: 685). In this respect, New Labour's approach to post-compulsory education (now broadened to policy for 14–19 provision) stood for more than a simple 'rhetorical repackaging' of Conservative neo-liberalism. It represented the emergence of a new statist/managerialism under Prime Minister Tony Blair, yet one with a similar political and ideological persuasion in which policy-making occurred within a single political era stretching from the mid-1980s to the present (2006).

Such political continuities met with radical economic change throughout the 1990s and into the new millennium. As noted earlier, the new global order made particular demands on the economy and worker in ways that served to transform both (Robertson, 2005), not least in terms of the belief that a 'nation's competitiveness in global markets ultimately depends on the skills of all its people' (Coffield, 1999: 480). This gave rise to a new type of 'producer capitalism', in which economic competitiveness could no longer be achieved on price alone, but rather required an improvement in the quality of goods and services, and with this an investment in 'physical and human capital … [where] the development of a highly educated workforce is seen as a priority' (Brown and Lauder, 1996: 10). In this new political economy, Toffler (1990: 18) suggests that

> knowledge itself … turns out to be not only the source of the highest-quality power, but also the most important ingredient of force and wealth … this is the key to the power shift that lies ahead, and it explains why the battle for control of knowledge and the means of communication is heating up all over the world.

The shift in the balance of power away from physical capital towards knowledge (Robertson, 2005) reflects a key point of departure in which human capital is regarded as the new 'raw materials' of late-capitalist production (see also Chapter 7). This view was articulated at the beginning of New Labour's first term through the discourse of the White Paper *Excellence in Schools* (DfEE, 1997a: 15):

> Investment in learning in the 21st Century is the equivalent of investment in the machinery and technical innovation that was essential to the first great industrial revolution. Then it was physical capital; now it is human capital.

A year later in a Green Paper (see Chapter 1), *The Learning Age: A Renaissance for a New Britain* (DfEE, 1998e), Blair proclaimed that 'education is the best economic policy we have', thus endorsing the view that education is a 'mere instrument of the economy' (Coffield, 1999: 480). As the paper (DfEE, 1998e: 1.1) suggests:

> We are in a new age – the age of information and global competition. Familiar certainties and old ways of doing things are disappearing … We have no choice but to prepare for this new age in which the key to success will be the continuous education and development of the human mind and imagination.

The strategy deployed to address such change was both complex and multifaceted – the politics of which extends well beyond the scope of this chapter. However, for post-compulsory education and training, there have been a number of key structural changes that have set a context for addressing the requirements of the 'knowledge-economy', and with this its role in providing 'continuous education' in an 'information society' and age of 'global competition' (Lauder et al., 2006). Under New Labour, post-compulsory education was characterized by an even greater degree of state 'interference', managerialism and accountability (Ball, 2007), in which the growth of powerful unelected quangos (quasi-autonomous non-governmental organizations) – so-called 'arms-length' agencies – began to multiply. Agencies such as the Learning and Skills Council (LSC), Adult Learning Inspectorate (ALI), QCA and the Teaching and Learning Standards Unit within the DfES produced increasing numbers of policy advisors, mediating between elected government ministers and education providers (Hodgson and Spours, 2006). Such complexity in the policy-making process was further compounded by the increased autonomy of individual education and training providers and, in some cases, new private ones. In the new mixed economy of public and private sector institutions, behaviour was strongly influenced by a number of 'powerful steering mechanisms (e.g. funding, targets and inspection)' (2006: 682), regulated and delivered by quangos through 'top-down' performance management (Ball, 2013).

The convergence of 'management, the market and performativity' (2013: 60) under New Labour served to increase the level of political centralization and further exacerbate the 'politicization of the policy process' (Hodgson and Spours, 2006: 682). As Blair put it in the White Paper *Our Competitive Future* (DTI, 1998: 5), 'old fashioned state intervention did not and cannot work', rather new governance, managerialism and accountability should be allowed to prevail (Ball, 2007). Thus, in a similar vein to that which had dominated the Conservative's tenure in government, significant tensions in post-16 policy continued to persist under New Labour. This was especially the case in terms of making good on the ambition to sustain competition, on the one hand, while seeking to enhance collaboration (between education and training providers), on the other – as a means to provide different local opportunities and progression routes for learners. Moreover, the promise to improve economic performance was almost constantly at odds with the aim to achieve social justice. In fact, far from addressing important structural inequalities in post-compulsory provision (Tomlinson, 2005; Ball, 2013) – as New Labour had set out to do through documents such as *Learning to Succeed: A New Framework for Post-16 Learning* (DfEE, 1999a), which had attempted to focus on 'those in greatest need', or indeed, provide assistance through the introduction of the Educational Maintenance Grants for 16–18 year olds from 2004 onwards (Pring, 2005: 72) – a culture of heightened accountability and managerialist policies consistently undermined considerations of justice. The imposition of targets, scrutiny and surveillance upon *individuals* made them responsible for *their* own learning, and for the continuous improvement of skills to ensure *their* employability in the 'knowledge economy'. In this respect, New Right policy on individualism became much deeper-rooted under New Labour, in which it became 'not the symbol of our unfinished development, but a guarantee of our permanent inadequacy' (Illich and Verne, 1976: 13), with yet greater emphasis on individuals, their skills and the value of human capital theory.

The next part of this chapter focuses on perhaps the two most enduring and often contentious strands of the post-compulsory education debate: the 'skills revolution' and reform of A-levels, both of which relate to the historical thread of this chapter. The skills revolution can be traced to the abovementioned Further Education Unit's (FEU) *Basis for Skills* (FEU, 1979), and then followed in subsequent debates throughout the 1980s and 1990s in CBI literature (CBI, 1989, 1993). In both cases, the underlying argument for the introduction of a 'skills revolution' was based on a series of international studies that show UK economy as falling behind its European competitors in Organisation for Economic Cooperation and Development (OECD) comparisons (Green, 1997).

Furthermore, there was a lingering view that a narrow and overly academic 16–19 curriculum served to compound poor workforce skills (Johnson, 2004), and thus failed adequately to prepare young people for the modern workplace, still less during times of economic recession or in the midst of rising youth unemployment. At the same time, an erstwhile but tenuous view prevailed that such skills might actually link the different qualifications tracks (DfEE, 1997c; Raffe et al., 1998); however, fundamentally, 'there was a commonly held assumption, supported by human capital theory, that raising the level of skills and qualifications within the population would contribute directly to increased productivity and economic competitiveness' (Hodgson and Spours, 2002: 31) – though, of course, some like Wolf (2002, 2004, 2007, 2015) continue to challenge this view.

Nevertheless, various reports throughout the 1980s and 1990s published by HMI, SEAC, National Council for Vocational Qualifications (NCVQ), NCC, FEU and the TA recommended that core or key skills (the semantics of which spawned yet another debate) be integrated into vocational *and* academic qualifications (i.e. A-levels), for the sake of the nation's future economic success (Hodgson and Spours, 2002). Moreover, under New Labour, twenty-five Sector-Skills Councils were set up to replace the old National Training Organisations, in which they became the 'lynchpins of a centrally planned, supply-driven training system' (Wolf, 2007: 113), demonstrating the specific skills required by employers and the sector as a whole of the education process. However, due to the practical difficulties associated with the implementation of skills in all qualifications post-16, and a feeling that A-levels might effectively dilute standards, such key/core skills were quickly exiled to the realm of vocational education, notably GNVQs. The outcome of *Curriculum 2000* served only to confirm the ambiguity around New Labour's appeal to 'key skills for all', and thereby exacerbate the long history of academic/vocational divisions in the English system.

Despite this fact, the contradictory and cyclical nature of education policy meant that it was not long before a similar crisis in skills emerged once again (Johnson, 2004). In 2003, the White Paper *21st Century Skills Realising Our Potential: Individuals, Employers, Nation* was published jointly by the DfES, Department of Trade and Industry and Department for Work and Pensions (DfES/DTI/DWP, 2003). Much like the earlier CBI versions that had sought to 'revolutionize' skills, the White Paper made yet another appeal for a 'skills revolution', focusing upon *individuals'* needs, with the aim to provide a broader framework of relevant skills matched to employers' needs (Pring, 2005). Like its predecessors, this document attempted to reinforce the value of functional numeracy and literacy (identified in the Moser Report, 1999 and later conceived as 'communication'), and ICT as core skills, along with a range of wider process-related, though often marginal, social and interpersonal skills, including 'working with others', 'learning and performance' and 'problem solving'. Critically, however, whereas previously education policy to enhance such skills was presented as a matter of generating favourable 'supply-side' conditions, orchestrated by the various quangos of central government, the Leitch (2006) review was unequivocal in stressing the importance of a demand-led system inspired by employers (Wolf, 2007). Yet, in practice this amounted to little more than 'a whole network of additional quangos' (2007: 116).

Pause and ponder

The importance of skills and the rhetoric of upskilling in a knowledge economy has featured prominently in polices of all recent governments, as illustrated in this chapter. The question of what 'skills' can be counted as 'economically valuable' remains contested in the context of post-compulsory education and training in an evolving global economy. With this in mind, reflect on the following questions:

1 Does the ambition to develop core 'skills' promote a view of 'recognition' or 'deficit-reduction' in relation to the learner?
2 How does the emphasis on 'economically valuable skills' enhance or impair critical thinking about the broader aims and purposes of education?

Tomlinson Report

Coinciding with the publication of the 2003 White Paper, *21st Century Skills Realising Our Potential*, the government commissioned a Working Group to review 14–19 qualifications, chaired by Mike Tomlinson (Working Group, 2004). The Working Group emerged following the so-called A-level crisis in 2002, in which there had been accusations of unethical practice and grade-fixing (especially in the determination of coursework grades). The Working Group consulted with thousands of young people, educationalists, policy-makers and professionals to develop proposals for a unified and multilevelled diploma system, replacing A-levels and creating a fusion between academic and vocational forms of study. The new framework would serve to encourage greater participation and retention, along with enhanced choice and flexibility, through more inclusive and progressive curricula (Pring, 2005). If followed, the ideas of Tomlinson would build upon the historical debate which had taken place since the late 1980s, culminating in the publication of the *British Baccalaureate*, noted earlier (Finegold et al., 1990).

However, in 2005 the New Labour government published a White Paper, *14–19 Education and Skills* (DfES, 2005), which rather than following the proposals of the Working Group as first anticipated, instead entirely disregarded the proposition of an overarching diploma. Here responsibility for the proposed vocational route diploma was given over 'to employers via the Sector Skills Councils' (Keep, 2005: 538). The idea of abandoning A-levels once and for all as a means to create a more flexible, inclusive and equitable system of post-compulsory education and training had, in the end, failed miserably. Just like all previous attempts at reform, it had fallen at the last hurdle; in this case, the New Labour government concerned with political popularity during the pre-election period became nervous at the prospect of ditching the A-level 'gold-standard'. As Hodgson and Spours (2006: 685) note, 'the post-Tomlinson 14–19 ... settlement of 2005–2006 can be seen to represent a clearer line of continuity with the previous administration than may be evident in other policy fields'. To this extent, 14–19 policy under New Labour was virtually indistinguishable from the neo-conservative arm of the political New Right. Thus, one wonders why the initial ideological commitment to social inclusion was eventually displaced by the inertia of neo-liberal reform.

From the Coalition to the present ... and so the cycle continues?

The reforms of Further Education (FE) exemplify some of the key features of Coalition policy notably austerity, freedom and privatization (see Chapter 1) and to which we now briefly consider in turn. First, FE endured budgetary cuts of £1.1 billion (25 per cent) in 2010, followed in the proceeding years by other major reductions in the funding of initiatives that the former New Labour government had initiated. The FE sector is commonly labelled the 'Cinderella sector' of the English education system and, accordingly, Allen (2015: R41) observes there was 'predictably little publicity or public disapproval' of the 'deep cuts' suffered in FE. There were cuts to careers advice/guidance for young people and to community learning. Adult learning grants were replaced by Advanced Learning Loans, and New Labour's flagship £1 billion 'Train to Gain' scheme was scrapped (this had provided free or partly funded training provision in the workplace), as was the Young Apprenticeship programme for fourteen to sixteen-year-olds (Lupton et al., 2015). The Coalition abolished in England the £560 million Education Maintenance Allowance (EMA) for sixteen- to eighteen-year-olds, set up under New Labour. It was replaced by a £180 million Bursary Fund in 2012, which, as Lupton and others (2015) observe, was considerably lower than EMA and received by fewer students (around 40 per cent). Second, greater freedom from direct state control is evidenced through the Coalition's termination of quangos and by the reduced function of the regulatory and developmental organizations responsible for FE. Finally, to facilitate notions of freedom, primacy was given to market competition and consumer choice to deliver socially beneficial outcomes; there was active promotion of privatization. Simmons (2013: 93) contends, however, 'The current jungle of organisations delivering education and training is both socially divisive and incredibly difficult for ordinary people, to understand ... Institutional competition and consumer choice benefit those most able to manipulate market forces.' Thus, those in possession of appropriate economic, social and cultural capital (see Chapter 3) are best placed to comprehend and exploit the different forms of education available.

After the 2010 general election, Michael Gove commissioned a review of vocational education and remarks in the foreword of the consequent Wolf Report:

> Since Prince Albert established the Royal Commission in 1851 policy-makers have struggled with our failure to provide young people with a *proper technical and practical education* of a kind that other nations can boast. 160 years later the same problems remain. Our international competitors boast more robust manufacturing industries. Our *technical education* remains weaker than most other developed nations. And, in simple terms, our capacity to generate growth by making things remains weaker. (Gove, 2011: emphasis added, cited in Wolf, 2011: 4)

Paradoxically, it is interesting to note that while the virtues of high-quality vocational education are fully endorsed throughout the report, and further positively touted as a means of entering 'secure employment or higher-level education and training', still the report recommends that all young people be required to study a core of academic subjects until they are sixteen (Wolf, 2011: 8). Indeed, we are told that

> good levels of English and Mathematics continue to be the most generally useful and valuable vocational skills on offer. They are a necessary precondition for access to selective, demanding and desirable courses, whether these are 'vocational' or 'academic'; and they are rewarded directly by the labour market throughout people's careers. (2011: 10)

The disclosure of an openly 'selective' system of post-compulsory education is in one sense admirable, but in fact no more than what most people have recognized for a very long time. The Coalition accepted in full the report's twenty-seven recommendations for changes to curricula, organization and funding. Curricula reforms to enhance the rigour of vocational qualifications subsequently reinforced requirements for English, mathematics and 'A' levels (Lupton et al., 2015). The critique of existing low-level vocational qualifications by Wolf (2011), which are said to have little to no market labour value, is underscored with the claim that 'in recent years, both academic and vocational education in England have been bedevilled by well-meaning attempts to pretend that everything is worth the same as everything else. Students and families all know this is nonsense' (2011: 9). Wolf (2011: 30) stated it was 'morally wrong' that so many courses for fourteen to sixteen-year-olds did not provide a suitable foundation for young people to progress to further study or training or to advance in the labour market. She also criticized the weightings given to non-GCSE equivalent in the performance tables and the practice of schools embracing such courses to improve their league table position. Her recommendation that vocational qualifications be removed from performative league tables is yet a further step away from neo-liberalism, but one which nevertheless fell short of Finegold and colleagues' (1990) proposals and, indeed, those of Tomlinson (Working Group, 2004), for whom change represented the entire system of post-compulsory education, vocational and academic. Funding was subsequently withdrawn from 7,000 qualifications 'deemed irrelevant or insufficiently rigorous' (Lupton et al., 2015: 45). Coalition policy endorsed the report's rigid separation of academic study and vocational training. Policy-making also rendered permissible the sifting out of school pupils identified as 'less academic' and transferring them to FE colleges 'at an early stage', thus buttressing a perception that vocational qualifications are inferior and a 'second class option in comparison to academic education' (Simmons, 2013: 92).

The Coalition's aim of enhancing the value of vocational qualifications is reflected in the creation of UTCs, which are new technical Academies catering for fourteen to nineteen-year-olds. They are each run by a trust and sponsored by universities and employers. Their curriculum comprises technical and scientific subjects that offer both a practical and academic education; the expectation is students will progress to HE or take up apprenticeships in their chosen specialist field. As with other Academies, UTCs do not have to follow the National Curriculum, adhere to LA standard hours or term dates or employ teachers with QTS (see Chapter 9). At the time of writing, there are thirty-nine UTCs in England with a further fifty-five proposed by 2017. However, as Avis (2014: 242) contends:

> the aim is to enhance the standing of the vocational against the academic rather than a serious engagement with the 16–19 curriculum and its fundamental reform. ... This absence feeds into a failure to engage with the way in which the academic/vocational divide articulates with the class structure and plays an important role in the reproduction of inequality.

Over to you ...

Locate the University Technical Colleges® website – http://www.utcolleges.org. Take a look at some of the different UTCs and note the partners involved.

1 In your opinion, what are the benefits and pitfalls of large companies being involved in the running of UTCs?
2 What would you say are the benefits and pitfalls of sponsorship on students, institutions and the post-compulsory education sector more generally?

In the scramble to address the collapse of the youth labour market and involve business and industry more fully (by altering funding systems and offering subsidies to employers who provide higher-quality apprenticeships with an element of general education), the Wolf (2011) review moved well beyond the piecemeal, 'supply-side' solutions which have dominated the sector for the last thirty years. Subsequent reforms prompted a shift of funding from workplace learning to traineeships for sixteen to twenty-three-year-olds and adult apprenticeships. Apprenticeships are currently 'policy favourite' (Wolf, 2015: 20), perceived as the key to address youth unemployment and the skills gaps. Cameron (2013) went so far as to claim 'apprenticeships are at the heart of our mission to rebuild the economy'. Simmons (2013: 91: emphasis added), however, argues:

> apprenticeships and similar forms of vocational training have been *shamelessly oversold* by the Coalition as the solution to a range of problems…the enduring problem of youth unemployment…is rooted at least as much in a chronic lack of demand for young people's labour as in any deficits in their skills, abilities, attitudes and dispositions.

Traditional models of apprenticeships were for young school-leavers as new employees, 'confined to jobs where there was a substantial corpus of vocational skills' (Wolf, 2015: 30) and where there would be a job at the end. While apprenticeships may be helpful in advancing young people into employment, Wolf (2015: 32) argues these are presently likely to be in low-cost areas, leading to low-level qualifications (typically level 2) and 'driven by funding and targets and not labour market needs'. In some cases, existing jobs may have been rebadged as apprenticeships by employers keen to acquire state funding; there is simply a 'change of formal status for employed, mature workers' (2015). This probably accounts, therefore, for the greatest increase in apprenticeships among the over twenty-fives under the Coalition government (Lupton et al., 2015). A recent review by Ofsted, which examined the quality of apprenticeships, was highly critical of 'low-level, low-quality programmes' (Ofsted, 2015: 4). The report announced, 'Inspectors identified common features in weak apprenticeship provision that failed to provide apprentices with sufficient training and devalued the apprenticeship brand' (2015: 14).

In 2015 the compulsory participation age in education was raised to eighteen – a policy initiated by New Labour. Beyond eighteen, 'the new norm for young people [is] to either go to university or into an apprenticeship' (Cameron, 2013), a view shared by all the main political parties. Given the configuration of current post-compulsory education policies, it is perhaps already clear that the tradition of inequality, which has persisted in English education for more than a century, is likely to continue for the foreseeable future. Allen (2015: R42), analysing the impact of the Coalition's education policy, concludes somewhat pessimistically that 'future governments are unlikely to reverse most reforms'. If such a situation is left unchallenged, then will it emerge that education has failed in at least two distinct senses, both as a means to address the economic imperative and as a panacea to virtuous social policy? Only time will tell.

Further reading

Acquah, D. K. and P. Huddleston (2014) 'Challenges and Opportunities for Vocational Education and Training in the Light of Raising the Participation Age', *Research in Post-Compulsory Education*, 19(1): 1–17.

Hillier, Y. (2015) 'England: Further and Adult Education', in C. Brock (ed.), *Education in the United Kingdom*, 107–130, London: Bloomsbury Publishing Plc.

Wolf, A. (2015) *Heading for the Precipice: Can Further and Higher Education Funding Policies Be Sustained?* London: The Policy Institute at King's.

Economics of Education

Introduction

Over the course of the last forty years, the relationship between education and the economy has become inseparably interwoven. Education is no longer regarded a public service or 'free good', as originally conceived in the radical reforms of the post-war settlement. It is now seen as 'big-business' (Pring, 2004), and one that continues to develop rapidly under the influence of neo-liberal politics and the evolving structural relationship between the economy and the state. In this chapter, we examine the political formation of education policy of successive modern governments and explore the increasing role of market solutions in public policy, in particular the intrusion of economics in state education. We consider how the apparent conversion in capitals from Keynesianism to neo-liberalism under the strong influence of globalization throughout the 1970s and 1980s served not only as a catalyst for economic change but also the radical reconfiguration of education policy, including its recent alignment with human capital theory. Following a more general contextualization of educational reform, we present a set of genealogies of policy discourse in HE, tracing the various moves, continuities and changes in policy-making where, over the last fifteen years, widespread systemic and institutional change has taken place (Ertl and Wright, 2008). We analyse how neo-liberal policy imperatives in HE (Deem, 2004) have led to a radical marketization of the sector, and, with this, an equally radical emphasis on commercial activity, the commodification of knowledge and creation of so-called university 'products' (Garratt and Hammersley-Fletcher, 2009). In particular, we consider how the rapid and unprecedented expansion of HE in England (David, 2010), reflected in the policy drive to ensure that 40 per cent of the workforce will acquire level four qualifications by 2020 (Fuller and Heath, 2010), has produced marked divisions between the more and less well-off, and created an inequitable system in which the virtue of welfare-capitalism has been seriously compromised.

Towards the 'Competition State': The demise of the Keynesian National Welfare State

As noted elsewhere in Chapters 1 and 6, there has been a seismic shift in the landscape of the political economy in England since the early 1970s where a conjunction of crises – financial, economic, social and political – has conspired to render the Keynesian National Welfare State (KNWS) virtually redundant. The global oil shock of the early 1970s, coupled with chronic patterns of economic and financial instability and periods of deep recession, served to exacerbate a wide range of social, political and economic tensions across the system. During the late 1960s and 1970s, accelerating inflation *and* mass unemployment (Callinicos, 2010) confounded Keynesian economists, where alongside rising taxation costs, a condition of 'stagflation' was produced, leading to a devaluation of the economy and subsequent deep recession. Notions of ungovernability (including state/union conflict), 'demographic change, inequality, rigidity, changing national identities, family instability, movements of capital, ecological problems etc' (Ball, 2007: 4), provided further tangible evidence that Keynesianism had failed and become a 'hindrance to international competitiveness' (2007: 5), where it was now widely regarded as economically and politically untenable.

The ineffectiveness of the KNWS to regulate the economic system was based upon its well-documented failure to deal with recurring patterns of crisis in the capitalist business cycle. Yet, as Gamble (2009) explains, 'there have always been debates…about whether the fundamental cause of capitalist crisis was overproduction or underconsumption. Was the problem that profits were too low to continue expanding production, or was it that there was insufficient demand to buy the products?' (2009: 47). The Keynesian solution to the 'restless dynamism' (2009) of capitalism, and its characteristic peaks and troughs, is a project of state intervention – a series of economic policies intended to suppress such booms and slumps through a range of fiscal measures (i.e. macro-economic policy in the form of government spending and/or taxation), as well as regulatory interventions to address potentially harmful fluctuations in the over-accumulation of capital. Yet, as Callinicos (2010: 37) reminds us, for Keynes, capital accumulation (the investment of capital in labour, machinery, technology and money dealing, as a means to produce 'surplus-value', i.e. profitability) is 'one of the defining features of a modern capitalist economy…it amounts to taking a bet on the future, a bet whose chances of success cannot be calculated'. This would suggest that instability and uncertainty are inherent features of capitalism, and so inevitably incapable of being managed in any complete sense (the financial crisis of 2007–2008 is a case in point). The combined effect of the inflationary expansions and employment-creating contractions that were characteristic of the mid- to late 1970s paved the way for a liberal renaissance: the rise of neo-liberal capitalism.

The ideological work of the New Right, which presents a radical coalition of neo-liberal free-market thinking and individual liberty coupled with traditional shades of neo-conservatism, has been dealt with elsewhere in this book (see, for example, Chapters 1, 5 and 6). Throughout the late 1970s and 1980s, neo-liberalism drew upon a number of influential thinkers, including Frederick von Hayek, Milton Friedman and Robert Nozick (1974). For current purposes, however, it is Hayek's work, resting on 'a critique of socialism, statism and Keynesianism' (Ball, 1990: 35), that is perhaps most relevant to the analysis of the impact of economic change on the nature and purpose of education policy.

Hayek's work was fundamentally wedded to the economic principle of free-market, *laissez-faire* capitalism. This meant that, unlike Keynes, Hayek believed that during periods of economic and financial crisis 'the state should do nothing to prevent the bust, apart from moderating the expansion of credit' (Callincos, 2010: 44), through the prudent application of monetary (rather than fiscal) policy and judicious control of interest rates (e.g. higher interest rates would increase the cost of borrowing, making it less attractive and so reduce the circulation of money in the economy). The spirit of minimal state intervention and displacement of central planning was enthusiastically adopted by the Conservative Party's opposition in the mid-1970s, under the leadership of Margaret Thatcher. When the Tories finally came to power in 1979, the full weight of Hayek's neo-liberal political and ideological framework was applied to the domestic economy. This led to the privatization of nationalized industries, support for the unfettered freedom of the individual as an economically rational and autonomous agent – for example, through the move to install 'inviolable private property rights at the heart of the social order' (Harvey, 2010: 233), via the sale of corporation housing – and explicit reinforcement of the sovereignty of free-market enterprise and competition, propagated across all sectors of society. Choice became a celebrated concept in a system in which the allocation of goods and services was determined by a quasi-market, partially free from state interference.

Pause and ponder

A society pursuing market policies sustained by competition and 'choice' is one that is arguably reserved for privileged choosers (Thrupp and Tomlinson, 2005).
Consider the above statement and answer the following questions:

1 Is the concept of 'choice' freely available to all those who want it?
2 In the statement above, what do you understand by the term 'privileged choosers'?
3 Who are the likely winners and losers in a marketized education system?

Neo-liberal economic policy and state education

A further rolling-back of the state emerged throughout the 1980s, when the Conservative government introduced free-market principles to the apparatus of state education. This was manifested in the question of how, and on what basis, should education attend to the needs of the political economy? The response relied predictably on the virtue of neo-liberalism and, with this, new autonomous individuals: the consumer and the parent. In general terms, the beginning of this trend can be traced to the 1980 Education Act, in which, perhaps for the first time, improved parental choice was actively promoted. However, this reflected only one aspect of a much broader political agenda of choice, where a whole series of charters emerged across different areas of the public sector. These included transport and patients' charters, as well as two parents' charters in 1991 and 1994, extending parental choice and rights in education. The latter came to fruition in the way parents were allowed to express preferences for schools and also set up appeals committees as a means to challenge malign or unfavourable circumstances, in which, for example, their child's entry to a (preferred) school may have been refused. This privileging of the parent as sovereign consumer was further reinforced in the middle of the decade, in which a Green Paper on *Parental Influence at School* (DES, 1984) – leading to the Education Act 1986 – sought to extend the representation of parents on school governing bodies, from two, as required by the 1980 Act, to a maximum of five elected parent governors (Tomlinson, 2005).

In political and economic terms such moves reinforced the neo-liberal pledge to roll-back the state, by blunting the power of LEAs to intervene in the running of schools, which were now becoming increasingly locally managed through the decisions of the parent/consumer. This is significant to the development of policy in HE, for it occasioned the rise of what Ball (2013: 53, original emphasis) refers to as a '*new moral environment*' and '*culture of self-interest*', in which the creation of education markets opened the door to intensive competition in the public sector, encouraging 'schools, colleges and universities to recruit students in order to maximise their "income"' and thus their internal well-being. The new ethic of '*survivalism*' (Ball 2013: 53) produced a transformation in the education system from what was originally a public service based on notions of egalitarianism and social justice to a system of values in which considerations of efficiency, marketability and open competition prevailed, with schools, colleges and universities competing aggressively for demand in local, regional and national (and sometimes even international) marketplaces. Ethically this meant that educational institutions were no longer motivated by working cooperatively, especially in the case of schools and colleges, but rather in direct competition, with teachers and lecturers doubling as business '*entrepreneurs*' (Ball 2013: 53) within their own institutions.

The introduction of the Education Reform Act in 1988 was perhaps the most profound piece of legislation and policy reform of the neo-liberal era. Not only was it symbolic of a shift further to the political right, but it signalled an even greater commodification and confusion of 'social relationships with exchange relationships' (Ball, 1990: 87) through the implementation of 'open enrolment' and LMS. In this new privatized regime, schools would be funded per capita, in terms of pupil numbers, who were now reduced to a 'form of exchange between parents and schools' (1990: 86). On this simple equation, a greater number of pupils schools were able to attract, the more money they received and vice versa, and so the power and monopoly of LEA influence on state schooling was effectively reduced, as authorities would no longer allocate pupils to schools. As Jones (2003: 107) notes:

> Conservative legislation sought to drive neo-liberal principles into the heart of public policy. An emphasis on cost reduction, privatisation and deregulation was accompanied by vigorous measures against the institutional bases of Conservatism's opponents, and the promotion of new forms of public management. The outcome of these processes was a form of governance in which market principles were advanced at the same time as central authority was strengthened.

Such direct and decisive centralization of authority is best represented through the government's move to control funding on the basis of schools becoming more effective brokers of their own competitive advantage and individual success. The introduction of examination league tables in 1992, for example, to supply market information to parents as a means to compare the performance of state schools, provided an essential basis for choice making (Ball, 2013). Schools were thus now operating not only as independent spending units with devolved budgets but paradoxically as quasi-autonomous businesses under a political regime of increasing centralization and state control. In many ways, such developments represented the beginning of what has been referred to as the 'competition state' (Jessop, 2002: 199), in which there has been a 'redrawing of the public-private divide' through the partial privatization and commodification of pupils and students reconfigured as 'products' of education. In this prevailing context, competition between institutions is regarded *de facto* as the principal means of raising standards in education, as schools, colleges and universities vie to enhance quality through results and further improve their position in the educational marketplace. In many ways, the radical transformation of state schooling represents the centrepiece of hegemonic neo-liberal reform within education, and as such is vitally important in helping us understand the environment within which change in HE has taken place. It provides not only a useful perspective on the scale of change sector-wide but an important embryonic view of what HE would later become under New Labour and, more latterly, the Coalition and Conservative governments. With these issues in mind, we turn now to analyse the beginning of the neo-liberal settlement in HE.

The development of higher education into the 1990s

A seminal 'move' in the development of HE policy emerged in 1985 with the Green Paper *The Development of Higher Education into the 1990s* (DES, 1985b), followed subsequently with the White Paper *Higher Education: Meeting the Challenge*

(DES, 1987b). The Green Paper was important for a number of related reasons, notably that it arrived in the aftermath of the Great Debate (see also Chapters 1, 5 and 6), which flagged the importance of education meeting the needs of industry and commerce and also that it emerged as part of a broader set of neo-liberal educational reforms with the aim of transforming education sector wide.

> The economic performance of the United Kingdom since 1945 has been disappointing compared to the achievements of others. The Government believes that it is vital for our higher education to contribute more effectively to the improvement of the performance of the economy … unless the country's economic performance improves, we shall be even less able than now to afford many of the things that we value most – including education. (DES, 1985b: 3)

The aim to make education more instrumentally focused was later supported in *Higher Education: Meeting the Challenge* (DES, 1987b), which overlaps with Chapter 6 on post-compulsory education and training, as well as the broader transformation of state education reported elsewhere in the book. In the first instance, this Green Paper argues that unless there is an increase in the supply of students of 'suitable quality' emerging from schools and colleges, coupled with an increase in interest from employers through the 'sponsorship of able students at universities and polytechnics', improvements are unlikely to be made in producing 'appropriately qualified manpower' (DES, 1985b: 3). In fact, the link between HE, business and industry could not be expressed more emphatically:

> Higher education establishments need to be concerned with attitudes to the world outside higher education … and to beware of 'anti-business' snobbery … the future health of higher education – and its funding from public *and private sources-depends significantly upon its own success in generating the qualified manpower the country needs … there is a growing concern that higher education does not always respond sufficiently to changing economic needs. This may be due in part to disincentives to change within higher education, including over-dependence on public funding.* (1985b: 4, 6: emphasis added)

Of particular note to the development of HE policy is the perceived importance of alternative funding mechanisms and future income streams. The turn towards a 'competition state' noted above is already implanted in the discourse (see Chapter 1) of 'changing economic needs', in which HE is identified as being slow to respond to change in the face of countervailing disincentives. Moreover, the prevailing view of an 'over-reliance on public funding' in HE marks the genesis for what is to follow later on, under New Labour and beyond in the Browne Review (of which, more later). Such strong neo-liberal sentiments, supported in the view that higher education institutions should become more entrepreneurial and fundamentally business savvy, are captured further in the perspective that 'the Government would like to see even greater vitality and flexibility' within HE. So, while universities are regarded as 'the principal guardians of pure academic excellence and the main sources of creative research', they are not seen as typical of 'the paradigm for higher education as a whole' (1985b: 5). Indeed, back in the 1980s 'polytechnics and other institutions' were believed to 'have a distinctive responsibility to prepare people for a wide range of activities, [including] provision for adult and continuing education' (1985b). This resonates strongly with the notion of a two-tier system of education not so dissimilar from that examined in Chapter 6 on post-compulsory education (and which gained some momentum under the Coalition government – of which, more later) and also signals the beginning of a journey to widen access and participation to a more vocationally relevant HE (DES, 1987b).

The twin move to strengthen education's link with the economy while also generating wider access to HE formed the conceptual basis of *Higher Education: Meeting the Challenge* (DES, 1987b). This gave political sanction to the discourse of 'flexibility', in which new vocationally oriented degrees began to emerge at the same time as academic disciplines became less dominant. In many ways, this represented the beginning of a double movement to enhance efficiency *and* quality in HE simultaneously – a policy that would later become enshrined within the Higher Education Quality Council, following the publication of the 1991 White Paper *Higher Education: A New Framework*. In the meantime, the proliferation of new degree programmes matched with increasingly flexible and imaginative modes of study could be seen to align sympathetically with the rhetoric of post-Fordism (see also Chapter 6), in which the impact of globalization coupled with increasing competition from external foreign markets served to create a new demand for 'humancapital' in the late-capitalist economy.

The concept of 'human capital' can be traced to the self-same title of Becker's seminal work (1964), in which he argued that people's knowledge and skills represent a form of capital capable of generating income just like a 'bank account, one hundred shares of IBM, [or] assembly lines' (Becker, 1993: 15, cited in Wolf, 2004: 317). Accordingly, in the neo-liberal regime, it is the added value of human beings rather than physical machinery per se that creates a competitive 'edge', and further fosters the development of new knowledge, skills and the flourishing of the entrepreneurial spirit. In turn, this generates an economy which is increasingly dependent upon knowledge – a 'knowledge economy' of scientific and technological innovation – which further aids the development of 'vitality and flexibility' in a rapidly changing global marketplace (Brown and Lauder, 1996). Correspondingly, notions of 'flexibility' are matched with the evolving vocational discourse of 'flexible specialisation', in which modern graduates are expected to be multiskilled, more responsive and adaptable (in fact, 'employable') in conditions of ongoing social and economic change.

In addition, students are expected to have greater political awareness of the impact of increasing numbers entering into HE generating a problem of escalating tuition fees. Interestingly, it was the Green Paper (DES, 1985b) which first drew our attention to the issue of 'whether arrangements less onerous to the taxpayer might be justified', suggesting that 'a greater financial engagement on the part of students would cause them to take greater care over their choice of study' (DES, 1985b: 15). This provided the genesis of a debate that is highly pertinent to contemporary HE policy and politics – that human capital of the future will need to be more responsive to changing economic circumstances and that *individuals* will take greater responsibility for decisions of personal investment, both for making rationally economic choices and in sharing the burden of cost.

Human capital formation: A theory of false assumptions?

The political discourse of education for economic growth, and its assumed dependency on the role of human capital formation, can be linked directly to the impact of global competition on the economic performance of OECD countries in the late twentieth century. According to Wolf and others (2006: 535), the notion of improved 'economic performance … has been informed by a rather simplistic version of human capital theory', in which the development of the nation's skills has come 'to be regarded as both a critical, and a sure-fire, way of improving productivity'. Thus, in a similar vein to the rhetoric of the Green Paper (DES, 1985b), various governments, dating from the early 1980s to the current moment, have actively promoted employability policies (Brown et al., 2003) on the strength of OECD comparisons and the much publicized view that human capital formation and lifelong learning are vital to sustained economic growth. More especially so in a world in which the 'increased pace of globalisation and technological change' are said to have created 'serious deficiencies in skills and competencies in the … labour force' (OECD, 2004: 2–3). The very idea that the 'welfare of individuals and … competitive advantage of nations … depend[s] on the knowledge, skills and entrepreneurial zeal of the workforce (Brown et al., 2003: 122) represents an interesting political turn, for it marks the beginning of a trend in which economic policy is strategically presented as responsible social policy. This is taken as 'good' not only for the aspirations of the *individual* and future economic prosperity of the nation but as a means to enhance public welfare and corporate social responsibility.

Ironically, however, as Wolf (2002, 2004) argues, there is scarce empirical evidence to support the view that education can improve productivity and economic performance, even though governments since the early 1980s have enthusiastically proceeded on this assumption. For example, following the Green Paper (DES, 1985b), the Conservatives released two White Papers: one announcing their plans 'to improve and develop the education and training system … [in]

response to the rising demand from employers for more and higher level skills to meet the growing challenge from overseas competitors in world markets' (DES, 1991a: 1); and a second proposing a new framework for HE (DES, 1991b). Another six years on, and Tony Blair's New Labour government announced that 'investment in learning in the twenty-first century is the equivalent of investment in the machinery and technical innovation that was essential to the first great industrial revolution. Then it was physical capital; *now it is human capital*' (DfEE, 1997c: 15: emphasis added). Elsewhere, under New Labour, we heard that 'learning is the key to prosperity. Investment in human capital will be the foundation of success in the knowledge-based economy of the twenty-first century' (DfEE, 1998e: 1). Quite apart from the idea of whether education can bring about improved economic growth, the latter contains a further questionable assumption: that formal learning, realized and measured via qualification targets, can serve as an accurate 'proxy for skills acquisition' (Wolf et al., 2006: 538). Indeed, there is little empirical evidence to support the claim that improved qualifications, creatively interpreted as improved skills, are able to contribute towards economic policy objectives (2006). In fact, where evidence does exist, it is reported to be ambiguous and contradictory (Keep and Mayhew, 2004), and so in the end while the workforce may be much better qualified, we ask whether, in fact, it is any better skilled.

Pause and ponder

Ainley (2013: 51) maintains, 'Only some of those from elite universities are likely to be guaranteed "graduate jobs". Others – possibly up to one in three graduates – are likely to be "underemployed" in jobs previously done by non-graduates, that is assuming they are able to find a job.'

1   Why is competition so fierce for graduate-level jobs?
2   Do qualifications automatically assure the reward of higher salaries for well-qualified graduates?

The National Committee of Inquiry into Higher Education – Higher education in the learning society

A year before New Labour's election victory in 1997, a series of working groups were commissioned to conduct a National Inquiry into Higher Education in the United Kingdom. The committee, chaired by Sir Ron (later Lord) Dearing, received consent from all political parties to examine, and further make recommendations on 'how the purposes, shape, structure, size and funding of HE, including support for students, should develop to meet the needs of the United Kingdom over the next 20 years' (Dearing, 1996b: 3). The extensive report, comprising some 23 chapters, 466 pages and 93 recommendations, begins by declaring that 'the purpose of education is life-enhancing: it contributes to the whole quality of life … In the next century, the economically successful nations will be those which become learning societies: where all are committed, through effective education and training, to lifelong learning' (1996b: 7). A key theme throughout is linked to the expansion of HE in which 'people in all walks of life' (1996b: 9), regardless of background, will recognize the 'need to continue in education and training throughout their working lives' (1996b). The catchphrase 'lifelong learning' is thus intended to capture and respond to 'the pace of change in the work-place', which 'will require people to re-equip themselves, as new knowledge and new skills are needed for economies to compete, survive and prosper' (1996b). That HE should respond to the needs of the economy is affirmed on the somewhat dubious view that 'experience suggests that the long-term demand from industry and commerce will be for higher levels of education and training for their present and future workforce' (1996b). As noted above, the concept of increased certification is questionable as a means to enhance productivity (Wolf, 2004), even though 'the economic imperative is … to resume growth', and the means to achieve this is by increasing levels of participation in HE to '40 per cent or beyond' (Dearing, 1996b: 9). As Wolf (2004: 330) goes on to argue, 'if chasing quantity reduces quality, societies can actually end up worse off than before in terms of the human-capital formation they seek'.

Higher education for the twenty-first century and beyond

New Labour's response to the Dearing Report (1996b) was articulated in the White Paper *Higher Education for the 21st Century* (DfEE, 1998f), which emphasized the increasing importance of higher education's role and 'contribution to the economy and its responsiveness to the needs of business' (DfEE, 1998f: 3). The principal means to achieve this – by 'increasing participation and widening access' – appears in continuation with the outgoing Conservative government's stance on HE policy (DES, 1987b). However, the emphasis on ensuring a positive entitlement for 'groups who are under-represented in HE, including people with disabilities and young people from semi-skilled or unskilled family backgrounds and from disadvantaged localities' (DfEE, 1998f: 3) provides an interesting point of departure, with a different rhetorical appeal towards inclusion, egalitarianism and the notion of social democracy. Thus, in contrast to the Conservatives, New Labour appeared committed, in their first term at least, 'to the principle that anyone who has the capability for higher education should have the opportunity to benefit from it and [we] will therefore lift the cap on student plans imposed by the last government' (1998f: 5).

Any initial move towards inclusion and social justice in HE policy-making, however, was simultaneously met with the view that such policy should also make more economic impact. Here, the apparent tensions are not so much contradictory but quite typical of New Labour thinking and the dual approach offered by 'Third Way' ideology (see Chapter 1). In this sense, the value of marketization as a model for economic success can be seen to coexist alongside enhanced state regulation. This is intended to address the corrosive effects of market forces upon the most disadvantaged groups within society. However, despite such rhetoric, we suggest the market reigns supreme. From an economic perspective, for example, the DfEE invested £3 million in the year 1998–1999 in funding the 'systematic interaction between higher education and business on skills development', and to develop regional networks to facilitate links to employability and work experience (1998f: 35). Such links to 'employability', 'human capital theory' and the 'knowledge economy', as well as the more general debate concerning the 'skills revolution', have served to transform HE in the most radical way.

Pause and ponder

The concept of 'lifelong learning' has led to the intractable view that qualification-bearing learning is a 'good thing' (Coffield, 1999).
    Think about this statement and answer the following questions:

1 What is your understanding of lifelong learning?
2 In a climate of enhanced 'choice', what are the likely consequences of choosing to opt out of lifelong learning?
3 Is it possible to favour lifelong learning while at the same time rejecting qualification-bearing learning?

Over the last twenty years, the exponential growth and the so-called massification (the move from an elite to a mass system) of higher education (Henkel, 2000; Jarvis, 2000; Morley, 2003; Barr, 2004; HEFCE, 2004) has gathered considerable momentum across the globe, literally transforming the sector, as the move to 'widen participation' continues apace. Higher education institutions 'are constantly in motion' and 'change is a permanent condition, with universities constantly responding to external and internal demands' (Delanty, 2008: 126). The resultant structural effect has produced not only greater numbers of students from a wider variety of backgrounds entering into HE but, in fact, greater political centralization as the orchestration of what counts as 'good university education' has become increasingly state managed.

In this important respect, while the sector has seen a manifold increase in the number of HE providers, and further proliferation of taught programmes with ever-more flexible forms of study, at the same time institutions have become more accountable to central government policy. This brings us to our second point: that the primacy of human capital formation has served to produce a state-informed agenda in which HE is inspired paradoxically by 'government ideas on how to promote productivity' (Wolf et al., 2006: 540). It is not, as economic sense would have it, a vision of education that is authentically 'demand-led', inspired from the bottom-up and thus shaped by the economic and business-related needs of employers. It is rather a system of governance inspired through networks in which centrally imposed policies actively structure notions of relevance and employability (Boden and Nedeva, 2010), and hence support the alignment of particular qualifications with the aim to enhance economic growth. While on first inspection the logic of this alignment may seem economically irrational, it is, in fact, perfectly consistent with the politics of neo-liberalism, in which the purpose of state-managed intervention is entirely deliberate. In essence, it helps create the supply-side conditions under which the growth of efficient economic activity is able to flourish and proceed unimpeded.

In this regard, the ideology of 'individualism', reinforced through the concept of choice and human capital formation under neo-liberal reform, reflects not only an 'economic turn' in education policy-making but a direct play towards social policy, in which individuals are forced to bear the consequences and full moral responsibility of *their* choices, especially those that reject the continuous demand for improved skills and/or 'lifelong learning'. However, it is sobering to remind ourselves that as yet there is no proven correlation between increasing numbers of graduates and improved economic success (Eggins, 2003).

A further dimension of New Labour's HE policy involved the 'commercialisation of research and knowledge' along with the launch of the 'Higher Education and Employment Development Prospectus', a venture of funded projects designed to 'make a significant contribution to promoting entrepreneurship within higher education' (DfEE, 1998f: 36). Indeed, this was a message echoed elsewhere in Tony Blair's foreword to the White Paper *Our Competitive Future – Building the Knowledge Driven Economy*:

> In Government, in business, in our universities and throughout society we must do much more to foster a new entrepreneurial spirit: equipping ourselves for the long term, prepared to seize opportunities, committed to constant innovation and enhanced performance. That is the route to commercial success and prosperity for all. We must put the future on Britain's side. (DTI, 1998: 5)

The deliberative move to combine public sector education with private sector participation became a prominent feature of the rise of the 'competition state' (Jessop, 2002) in the late 1990s and into the early twenty-first century. In economic terms it marked a significant departure in two important ways: on the one hand, a shift away from the old-fashioned model of Keynesian bureaucracy and 'big government' and, on the other, a subtle distancing from Hayekian neo-liberalism, popularized under the Conservative governments of Thatcher and Major. The 'Third Way' thus came to represent a more nuanced and sophisticated form of neo-liberal economic and social policy, a form of 'market socialism' (Giddens, 1998), or, indeed, what Jessop (2002) has referred to as the 'Schumpeterian Workfare State', based on the thinking of the Austrian–American economist and political scientist Joseph Schumpeter. Ball (2007: 5–7) takes Jessop's analysis further, arguing that the discourse of education policy under New Labour is characteristic of a number of Schumpeterian principles: namely, that the state has become a commissioner and monitor (rather than owner) of public services and broker of all social and economic innovations; that the aim of public/private partnership and, hence, shared ownership is based on innovation, competitiveness and entrepreneurship; and that the government has a role to play in investing in human resources to develop an entrepreneurial culture. Indeed, the discourse of innovation and entrepreneurship in HE has produced a condition in which 'politics and business get embedded in the "texture of texts"' (Fairclough, 2000: 158), as part of the process of thinking about, and articulating education policy. As the 2003 White Paper *The Future of Higher Education* usefully illustrates:

> Realising our vision will take time. Having presented a radical picture of a freer future, it is the duty of government to make sure that the transition is managed carefully and sensibly so that change is not destabilising. So in some areas government will want to support the way in which institutions move towards new freedoms, and develop new patterns of provision. Government also has to retain a role because it is the only body that can balance competing interests between the different stakeholders. It will also have a responsibility to intervene when universities fail to provide adequate opportunities or when access, quality or standards are at risk … We see a higher education sector which meets the needs of the economy in terms of trained people, research, and technology transfer … [and which] acknowledges and celebrates the differences between institutions as each defines and implements its own mission. (DfES, 2003d: 21–22)

Perhaps, the most radical and disruptive change in HE policy-making under New Labour came with the restructuring of funding arrangements sector-wide. Following the recommendations of the Dearing Commission (Dearing, 1996b), to move away from a block grant scheme towards a system in which funding follows the student, the New Labour government adopted a formula 'based directly on the number of students enrolled' at a particular institution (DfEE, 1998f: 53). This meant that more of the funding would now follow student demand, so that in a semi-privatized environment more popular universities would eventually become richer and more financially secure. It also suggested that HEIs were now in direct competition with one another. This meant they had to become more marketable and business-like to appeal to an expanding base of students re-clothed as 'buying consumers'. Thus, as universities became ever more concerned about their reputation and market position, branding and commercialization became increasingly prominent, with institutions repackaging themselves more distinctively as 'branded products' to be bought in the corporate marketplace.

In addition to radically revised funding arrangements, *Higher Education for the 21st Century* introduced plans to increase the cost of tuition for undergraduate students. The Dearing Commission had recommended that students pay 'around a quarter of the average cost of a course – with the other three quarters being met from public funds'. In turn, 'the Government supported this principle', stating that 'the investment of the nation must be balanced by the *commitment of the individual*' (DfEE, 1998f: 54: emphasis added). This marked the beginning of a somewhat curious but inexorable slide towards full-time undergraduate students paying more for their university education proportionately than at any point since the post-war settlement. In 2006, for example, following the 2004 Higher Education Act, a system of fees was introduced in England whereby students would now be subject to a new regime of higher variable fees. In practice, over the next few years, this meant that almost all HEIs would eventually move towards a position of charging the maximum statutory fee of £3,225 in the year 2009/2010 – the last in New Labour's term of office. More than this, however, the seismic shift in policy linked to student fees heralded a key departure from the conception of students as 'partners' in the education business to a model in which they became fully fledged 'clients'. This prompted a revision of student expectations towards 'service provision' and 'service quality', as increasing numbers of undergraduate students with more exacting standards were now able to demand better value for money and improved returns on *their* investment (Foskett et al., 2006).

The independent review of higher education funding and student finance

In 2008, the world changed in the most dramatic fashion following the collapse of the banking system, giving rise to the 'biggest global financial crash since the Great Depression of the 1930s' (Callinicos, 2010: 2). While the move towards a fully privatized system of HE was already in motion, and had been so since the radical reforms of the 1980s, the global financial crisis and subsequent economic meltdown threw the issue of HE funding into sharp relief. Indeed, it served to focus attention more acutely on the economics of HE at a time when Britain's total debt was reported to be worsening, and forecast to top £10 trillion by 2015 (Rowley, 2010). In the wake of the financial 'crash' and new era of austerity post-2008, the then New Labour government, just six months away from an historic election defeat, commissioned an independent review of higher education. Chaired by Lord Browne of Madingley, and comprising panel members from business and academe, the review made a strong case for further investment in HE, not only because it 'transforms the lives of individuals' but also because it 'drives innovation and economic transformation. Higher education helps to produce economic growth, which in turn contributes to national prosperity' (Browne, 2010: 14). While politically there is nothing new in the tenor of this economic argument, a key difference is contained in the view that *individuals* will now be responsible for such investment and that 'HEIs should persuade students that they should "pay" more in order to "get more"' (2010: 4) from their university experience. This will be done by 'ensuring that students get the benefits of more competition, by publishing an annual survey of charges, looking after the interests of students when an HEI is at risk and regulating the entry of new providers' (2010: 11). So while on the one hand HE is regarded as highly valuable, not least because it pump-primes 'future economic growth and social mobility', on the other it is seen as desirable only in so far as individuals themselves are able to pay for it, and further 'buy' into the promise of a transformed life. According to such policy, this is a life in which 'higher status jobs' and increased earnings are guaranteed to follow (2010: 14). The reality, however, was that graduate-level jobs were in astonishingly scarce supply as more graduates flooded the market. In 2011 some eighty-three graduates were reported to be chasing every job vacancy (Paton, 2011), rising in 2013 to eighty-five applicants or more for every graduate job (*Independent*, 2013). However, in 2015 the number of graduate-level openings has increased and returned to pre-recession levels: on average there are thirty-nine applications per vacancy (although this is much higher for some industries). An annual survey conducted by High Fliers Research (2015) shows graduate recruitment expanding and the number of graduate jobs available increasing. While to some extent this reflects emergence from the recent economic crisis, the point made by Ainley (2013: 47) regarding the 'often graduatised jobs in the new "knowledge economy"' cannot be disregarded. Ainley (2013: 53) maintains many graduates are in occupations for which they are overqualified and consequently, 'as graduates move into non-graduate jobs, the incomes of those with lower-level qualifications are suppressed still further as they are forced to look for lower-paid employment, whilst many young people cannot find any work'.

Returning to the Browne Report, in comparison with the policy under New Labour, the report steps further towards the political right in advocating a 'direct funding relationship between student and HEI' (Browne, 2010: 10), albeit one that is initially closely monitored:

The relationship between students and institutions will be at the heart of the system. We are reducing the reliance of the system on funding from Government and control by Government. Nevertheless there is an important role for regulation to look after students' interests and the ongoing public investment in higher education. We propose a new HE Council with five core responsibilities: investing in priority courses; setting and enforcing baseline quality levels; delivering improvements on the access and completion rates of students from disadvantaged backgrounds; ensuring that students get the benefits of more competition in the sector; and resolving disputes between students and institutions. (2010: 45)

The current system in which 'institutions are funded by the HEFCE [Higher Education Funding Council for England] on the basis of a notional annual allocation of undergraduate places' (2010: 32) will transform into one where open competition is more actively encouraged between universities, and where growth in more successful institutions is promoted rather than stifled: 'Institutions will face no restrictions from the Government on how many students they can admit. This will allow relevant institutions to grow; and others will need to raise their game to respond' (2010: 33). The move to a more overtly marketized system is thus intended to raise the barrier on student numbers entering into particular prestigious institutions, in two important ways. First, to allow all successful universities to expand and grow, much in the way that successful businesses do by selling popular products, and second, to enable students from wealthier backgrounds to obtain a university education if their families are willing to pay more for extra places – the suggestion of which stirred up a political furore, leading to a partial retraction from the Universities Minister David Willetts (Mulholland and Vasagar, 2011).

The wholesale privatization of higher education promoted in the Browne Review, and implemented by the Coalition government since October 2010, took a further curious and problematic turn. The radical overhaul of student funding arrangements resulted in universities having the freedom to charge between £6,000 and £9,000 for student (annual) tuition fees, as a means to replace lost state funding (Coughlan, 2010). Lifting the cap on undergraduate tuition fees caused problems, politically, for the Liberal Democrats whose 2010 pre-election manifesto pledged to abolish tuition fees. However, despite this awkward political setback for the Liberal-Democrats, the party was able to influence a more sympathetic repayment schedule for students and also to accentuate HE as a vehicle for social mobility.

While the Coalition government was initially clear to point out that only in exceptional circumstances would universities be allowed to charge the highest fee of £9,000, in practice the withdrawal of public funding served to reinforce the sovereignty of the market, and with this focus the gaze of university vice-chancellors on 'client perceptions' of quality. In practice, it is virtually impossible *de facto* for institutions to charge any *less* than £9,000 a year for tuition fees, without at the same time implying certain degree courses are substandard, or, indeed, of lower quality than competitors charging the maximum market rate. This produced a situation, contrary to the government's intention where universities competed on price, in which 'with more universities than expected charging the maximum £9,000 a year for tuition, universities minister David Willetts' is seeking a way to reduce the liabilities of the government-backed Student Loans Company by turning to the UK's major banks to provide loans at preferable rates' (Boffey, 2011: 6) Sir Steve Smith, the president of Universities UK and vice-chancellor of Exeter University, indicated that 'the proposal to allow banks to exploit the student market carried huge risks and could create a two-tier system', potentially allowing wealthier students to buy their way into university education (2011). This suggests that students from wealthier homes are able indirectly to gain a significant advantage in a privatized system over their less affluent peers.

Policy formation beyond the Browne Report

University enrolments have remained buoyant despite the higher tuition fees. While the number of part-time and mature undergraduates dropped by more than a third, the proportion of applicants from low-income families has increased (Lupton et al., 2015). The mission of the Office for Fair Access, the 'Access Agreement', HEI outreach work, annual bursaries and the creation of the National Scholarship Programme (NSP)[1] may have removed barriers and encouraged greater participation. The latest available data at the time of writing shows record HE entry rates (over 40 per cent) in 2015 for eighteen and nineteen-year-olds living in England, although these figures camouflage some regional variation (UCAS Analysis and Research, 2015a). A closer examination by gender, however, reveals a 3 per cent increase for men and a 6 per cent increase on 2014 entry for women, with 60,000 more women than men starting degree courses in autumn 2015 (Woolcock, 2015). In terms of access by different socio-economic groups, the latest figures available (UCAS Analysis and Research, 2015b) show a substantial increase in 2015 in the application rates across the United Kingdom of eighteen-year-olds from the most disadvantaged areas. In England,

> the application rate of 18 year olds from the most disadvantaged areas has increased from 12.2 per cent in 2006 to 21.0 per cent in 2015. This means that 18 year olds living in the most disadvantaged areas in England are 72 per cent more likely to apply to higher education in 2015 than nine years ago. (2015b: 24)

Nevertheless, those living in advantaged areas are still more prone to apply to HE. The period 2006 to 2011 saw a steady rise in applications from eighteen-year-olds in the most advantaged areas in England; there was a dip in application rates in 2012. The application rate for this group in 2015 shows a further decrease by 0.2 percentage points, which is lower than in 2010 and 2011. Yet, in 2015, those from the most advantaged areas remain 2.4 times more likely to apply to university than those from the most disadvantaged areas. However, in 2006 the likelihood was 3.8 times more, so the increase in application rates in the most disadvantaged areas has helped to reduce the difference (2015b). Yet, as Boliver (2013) contends, HE participation rates have increased substantially since the 1960s, when they were around 5 per cent. Today participation is approximately 40 per cent. Whereas traditional concerns focused on access to HE per se, Boliver (2013: 345) argues the more pertinent issue is regarding 'access to the UK's more prestigious universities'. Not only are those from lower social class backgrounds less likely to attend prestigious HEIs but 'graduates of more prestigious universities have been shown to be more likely to secure professional and managerial jobs and to earn higher salaries' (2013: 345).

This situation, of the more affluent prevailing over the less well-off, is in danger of being replicated in relation to the stakes and relative position of universities competing in the new market environment. For example, the private run-for-profit university BPP launched a bid to run ten publicly funded university institutions, where 'under the model, universities would control all academic decisions, while BPP would be responsible for managing the campus estate, IT support, the buying of goods and services and other "back office" roles. BPP would not hold equity in the universities' (Shepherd, 2011). In 2013 BPP[2] gained full university status and, with tuition fees at about £5000, BPP is substantially undercutting other universities. Creating more universities is part of a growing trend in the United Kingdom, which has been facilitated by government to encourage greater competition and diversity as well as generating more private sector involvement and investment within HE (Temple, 2014). Concerns have been expressed by the University and College Union 'that this move could open the floodgates for more for-profit companies to become universities. A quick glance across the pond warns us of the risks associated with that sort of move' (Sellgren, 2013). Citing BPP and the for-profit University of Law[3] as examples, Temple (2014: 164) cautions 'the legal and ownership positions of private universities and colleges cannot be regarded as stable when they can be bought and sold (and presumably closed if they become unprofitable) without hindrance'.

The Coalition government's White Paper *Students at the Heart of the System* (BIS, 2011) codified the preceding Browne Report, and was the eleventh new 'framework' for HE since 1963, the Robbins Report (Watson, 2014). Accordingly, the White Paper promulgates more 'alternative providers' in HE; what is actually being asserted is more private, for-profit provision. Although, as Temple (2014: 167) observes, 'the absence of a clear rationale: the precise problems the private providers are expected to help solve is never set out.' The 2011 White Paper, one of the Coalition government's early policy statements, promised a free market in HE and strengthening the priority of competition as a means to improve quality and drive up standards. However, as Scott (2011: 2) cautions, it may well deliver the very opposite, for instead of one 'simple limit' being placed on 'overall student numbers, there are three caps' – A cap for 'top' students, typically those with AAB grades at A-level, entering Russell Group universities; a cap for 'cheap' students, typically those applying to institutions that charge less than £7,000 per annum; and a third cap for the rest. As Scott (2011) elaborates:

> the white paper promises deregulation … yet it is difficult to discover any significant relaxation of bureaucratic controls … to implement the proposals the government will have to give itself (or HEFCE) new legal powers over universities … far from disappearing HEFCE is to become the lead regulator. This is nationalisation with a vengeance … the white paper promises it promotes social mobility. Again, it does the opposite … it will simply lead to a further polarisation of students with 'top' universities crowded even more with 'good' students – in other words those who by and large are socially privileged enough to have attended 'good' schools (many of them private).

Willetts (2013) forged ahead with reforms to provide alternative HE providers to 'take on' established universities and offer students 'a more genuine choice'. The proposition of a new partnership model in the context of HE raised concerns that such relations might ultimately blur accountability and hence impact negatively on educational quality.

Over to you …

The publication of an 'alternative' paper by academics – *In Defence of Public Higher Education* – challenges the market-led vision for HE and its reliance on the underpinning theory of human capital investment. Several hundred academics have signed the document. Locate the paper on the Internet by searching for its title; the paper was published in *The Guardian* on 27 September 2011. The paper is substantial, but the first pages provide a useful summary. Read the nine propositions about the value of public higher education.

1 How do these relate to your own views of the purposes of HE?
2 To what extent are ideologies reflected in these propositions?
3 If you had to create a proposition in defence of HE, what would it be?

Higher education: Where are we now?

Higher education is, arguably, experiencing a time of unprecedented change in its history. The period 2009–2011 is aptly described by Scott (2014: 52) as a 'watershed moment' as it incorporates the reform of HE and student funding, which changed the policy landscape. Scott (2014: 54) deems these reforms not as a 'revolution' in English higher education', but as the 'unintended impact' of a culmination of separate and uncoordinated policy changes over several decades by various governments. The origins of the current turbulence can be traced back to three discrete critical moments in HE history. First, the Robbins Report (CHE, 1963), which reviewed full-time HE in Britain in the early 1960s and sparked the move from an elitist to a mass system in HE. Robbins acknowledged students in HE from working-class backgrounds performed as well as their middle-class counterparts and recommended a massive expansion of HE in order to tap into the 'pool of ability' from lower socio-economic groups. The rationale for a huge increase in public expenditure to support this would 'be remunerative both in its absolute effects on the general productivity ... and in helping to maintain our competitive position in the world at large' (CHE, 1963: 273 cited in Callender, 2014: 165). Thus, the development of human capital, discussed above in this chapter, is evident in Robbins as is a social-democratic view of education whereby those who have the ability (qualifications) and desire to benefit from HE should have opportunities for access. Callender (2014) points out the emphasis of the public benefits of higher education underpinned the Robbins Report and also drove its recommendations and policies at the time. Second, significant shaping of HE policy occurred through Thatcher's Conservative policies to reduce public expenditure. Finally New Labour's 'Third Way' and its 'widening participation' agenda further moulded the sector. Scott (2014: 54) proposes that these discrete policies served to produce a 'perfect storm', now being experienced in HE in England.

The HE policy landscape continues to be fashioned by a series of particularly complex factors. First, devolution has undoubtedly increased diversification in HE policies with universities in England especially affected by the change in funding arrangements. Second, the changes made to student funding have not gone unchallenged; students (and academics) across the HE sector have continued to make their objections known about tuition fees, education cuts, privatization in universities and privatization of the student loan book (Lewis et al., 2010; Collins, 2011; BBC, 2012; Sabur, 2013; Taylor, 2014). Additionally, students' expectations of their HE experience have been augmented undoubtedly because of the anticipated debt they will incur; they thus presuppose 'value for money'. The relevance of their degree to future employment prospects is also amplified as students are 'desperate to find vocational relevance in what they are offered' (Ainley, 2013: 54). These kinds of responses are not unsurprising given the recent direction of policy which promotes a marketized system, propagates the private individual financial benefits of HE and postulates social mobility. As such, the National Student Survey (NSS),[4] which garners students' perceptions of their experiences, has come to be regarded as the measure of 'consumer' satisfaction of HE provision in the United Kingdom. While criticized for various methodological and conceptual reasons (Yorke, 2009; Cheng and Marsh, 2010), nevertheless the

NSS is an influential instrument in the HE sector. The NSS results are widely publicized, inform world league tables and are used by HEI providers as drivers for improving quality and performance. Programmes that receive relatively weak ratings by students are likely, thus, to encounter some institutional pressure. Equally, there is some consternation among lecturing staff, who feel the pressures of consumer evaluation and consumer demand through formal mechanisms such as the NSS, and have professional reservations about the developing 'narrow definition of student needs – put crudely, giving students what they say they want' (Temple, 2015: 176). Third, further marketization of the sector is being facilitated through the different levels of fees being charged, the involvement of new providers of degrees such as private colleges and expanding provision of HE in FE. At the time of writing, it is too early to determine the extent to which the reforms are successful in creating a competitive market and improving the student experience. This leads to the final factor, privatization. Potential problems associated with the accountability of private, for-profit, alternative HE providers were alluded to above in this chapter and, unfortunately, have already begun to emerge. Private institutions are not subject to monitoring by government in the same way as public universities. In 2014 it became apparent that the dropout rates for such were five times higher than public universities (over 20 per cent); some students are bring subsided by the taxpayer (i.e. they are in receipt of cheap loans and grants), but do not undertake meaningful study; and many were not registered to take recognized examinations (Malik and McGettigan, 2014). At the time of writing, the Minister of State for Universities and Science Jo Johnson is due to publish a Green Paper by the end of 2015 which is expected to include proposals that facilitate the opening up of new institutions (Coughlan, 2015).

The 2011 White Paper reforms and other subsequent policy interventions have not necessarily achieved the changes for HE envisaged by policy-makers. Callender and Scott (2014: 216–217) note 'a failure in terms of detailed policies' and remark:

> levels of overall funding are regarded as precarious and temporary … Fees are not variable in any meaningful sense. Instead institutions have 'priced' to the cap … a market has failed to develop: there is little evidence that student preferences have significantly changed … The institutional landscape has remained essentially unchanged.

Nevertheless, they argue 'the cumulative effect of these measures is likely to have an important impact on both institutional priorities and organizational cultures' (2014: 217). Yet, while universities may well become more efficient businesses in the longer term, whether in the end the market can deliver a high-quality, fair and sustainable system of higher education for everyone, regardless of social background, remains, at best, an open question.

Pause and ponder

Writing on further and higher education funding policies Wolf (2015: 76) pronounces:

> The current situation [in FE and HE] is financially unsustainable. It is deeply inegalitarian in its allocation of resources. It is also inefficient and bad for the 'human capital development', which increasingly drives and justifies education policy. In post-19 education, we are producing vanishingly small numbers of higher technician level qualifications, while massively increasing the output of generalist bachelor's degrees and low-level vocational qualifications. We are doing so because of the financial incentives and administrative structures that governments themselves have created, not because of labour market demand, and the imbalance looks set to worsen yet further. We therefore need, as a matter of urgency, to start thinking about post-19 funding and provision in a far more integrated way.

1 Do you agree/disagree with Wolf's analysis?
2 What does Wolf mean by 'bad for the "human capital development" '?
3 In your opinion, what should post-19 funding and more integrated provision look like?

Notes

1   The NSP ceased for new undergraduates in 2015–2016 following the spending review decision made in June 2013 to repurpose funds to a Postgraduate Support Scheme. Between 2012 and 2015 the government contributed £200 million to the NSP.
2   BPP University is owned and operated by BPP Holdings Ltd., which in 2009 was itself acquired by the American for-profit higher education company Apollo Global.
3   The University of Law was the first 'for-profit' university in Britain (November 2012). Originally called The College of Law, it was bought in 2009 by Montague, a private equity company who then sold it in June 2015 to Global University Systems.
4   The NSS is an annual survey operated by the market research company Ipsos MORI. It has been undertaken by most HEIs across the United Kingdom since 2005. Final year undergraduates are invited to report on their experiences of their programmes (courses).

Further reading

Ball, S. J. (2007) *Education plc – Understanding Private Sector Participation in Public Sector Education*, London: Routledge.

Callinicos, A. (2010) *Bonfire of Illusions – The Twin Crises of the Liberal World*, Cambridge: Policy Press.

Temple, P. ed. (2012) *Universities in the Knowledge Economy: Higher Education Organisation and Global Change*, London: Routledge.

Wolf, A. (2002) *Does Education Matter? Myths about Education and Economic Growth*, London: Penguin.

8

Inclusive Schools: Special Educational Needs and Disability

Introduction

Inclusion is a wholly contested concept as is the idea of inclusive schools. Nonetheless, various factors have contributed to the move towards inclusive education, and while not a linear process, this is regarded as a general trend from the later part of the twentieth century. The present circumstances in education have been shaped over time by a complex assortment of ideas, individuals, ideologies and incidents, which together have fashioned policy 'problems' and 'solutions'. As such, there was a time when the segregation of children considered 'abnormal', 'mentally defective', 'idiots', 'imbeciles' and 'feeble-minded' meant that they were excluded from education or educated separately. Today such labels are derogatory, demeaning and offensive. When investigating the development of policies around special educational needs (SEN) and inclusion, one of the more uncomfortable aspects is probably contending with the negative terminology that has been used at different times. While the morals and ethics surrounding the use of such labels could be questioned, nonetheless, it should be kept in mind they are characteristic of prevailing discriminatory attitudes of their time.

Today, it is more commonly accepted that children who have severe learning difficulties are entitled to education provision and also that many children with all kinds of special educational needs and disabilities are included in mainstream education. So how did we get to the notion of inclusive schools and special educational needs? 'Special educational needs' is a term best associated with Mary Warnock, who, in the late 1970s, recommended the 'integration' of children with SEN in mainstream schools. It was recognized at this time that some children were being marginalized within the education system or excluded from it entirely. Following on from what came to be known as the *Warnock Report* (DES, 1978b), there was less emphasis on the segregation of different groups of children and much greater emphasis on their integration in mainstream schools. This form of provision developed during the latter part of the twentieth century as did the consequent idea of inclusion, which can be understood as 'transforming mainstream in ways that will increase its capacity for responding to all learners' (Ainscow, 2016: 86). In this chapter we take a retrospective view of policy developments which have sought, at different times, to segregate and then include children with particular needs. We have selected some of the key policy moments, legislation and documents which illustrate societal and political attitudes and policy developments of their time. Along this 'historical road' (Ainscow, 2016: 86), we track developments encapsulating SEN, integration, inclusive education and the notion of educational equity.

From the management of the 'abnormal'

We begin first by examining how people regarded as being different to what society deemed as 'normal' were considered and managed. Armstrong (1998) recounts how up until the end of the eighteenth century 'insanity' and 'idiocy' were largely accepted as part of everyday life. So, those with impairments were not segregated in society, but were part of the 'marginalised labouring peasantry' who could earn a living by working or begging (Boronski and Hassan, 2015: 146). At the beginning of the nineteenth century, UK society and the nature of work were being transformed by the many changes brought about through industrialization and urbanization. It became a commonplace requirement for workers to be capable of operating machinery in factories and mills, for example. Industrial expansion and economic success also required controlled and disciplined workers who would adhere to the demands of capitalist production. Such dramatic change in society made visible those who could not conform to or were physically and/or mentally incapable of meeting these expectations. This was a stance that came to be differentiated as 'abnormal', 'mad' and 'defective'; the inflicted were subsequently 'perceived as a threat to the new social order and consequently requiting confinement and treatment' (Armstrong, 1998: 33). The management of the 'abnormal' was legislated via The Idiots Act (1886), which distinguished between 'lunatics' and 'idiots'. Idiots were placed in a registered hospital or institution, 'imbeciles' were recognized as a subgroup less defective than idiots and the 'feeble-minded' were considered both an educational and economic problem (1998). The expertise of doctors was drawn upon to classify, allocate appropriately and then institutionalize those with individual deficits. Thus, workhouses and asylums incarcerated the 'defective' and 'useless'. Those considered fit to be productive would be trained and offered work (Boronski and Hassan, 2015). Thereon, segregation on the grounds of difference was normalized in British society.

In the mid- to late nineteenth century, a compulsory system of state education for the 'masses' was in process of formation. The 1870 Elementary Education Act, which ushered in elementary education in England and Wales (see Chapter 4), recognized from the outset the unsuitability of teaching children with disabilities in large classes. The solution was a segregated form of education in special schools. At this time there was emphasis on the medical condition of a child rather than on its educational opportunities, and, as such, children were often denied access to activities in the local school. SEN developed through a 'medical' model of disability whereby the pathology was seen to reside within the person – that is, it was considered there was something wrong with the individual child. The Elementary Education (Defective and Epileptic Children) Act of 1899 introduced special schooling for the 'feeble-minded' (Armstrong, 1998). This was, in one sense, a 'humanitarian mission' (Boronski and Hassan, 2015: 146) to support those who were unfortunate to have physical and/or mental impairments. In another sense it fostered the needs of capitalism whereby children would receive a 'basic' form of education and, as workers, be able to contribute to the economy. They could thus earn their own livelihood and would be a lesser drain on society (David, 1980).

The Butler Act and the matter of 'handicaps'

The next major piece of legislation for England and Wales that is highly relevant to SEN policy developments is the 1944 Education Act (Butler Act). This established an entitlement of every child to statutory education at primary and secondary school (five to sixteen) and also gave LEAs responsibility to decide whether a child needed 'special educational treatment' (Simon, 1991: 75). Similar provision was made for children in Scotland via the 1945 Education (Scotland) Act (Hodkinson, 2015). There were contradictions already developing in special education policy before the 1944 Act (see Armstrong, 1998) and so this legislation was regarded as important in being able to ease such tensions. The Butler Act established eleven categories of 'handicap', which were set out in the *Handicapped Pupils and School Health Service Regulations* of 1945. Children were delineated as either 'blind, partially sighted, deaf, partially deaf, delicate, diabetic, educationally subnormal, epileptic, maladjusted, physically handicapped, children with speech defects' (Hodkinson, 2015: 76–77). This categorization was 'the product of different competing professional interests' (Armstrong, 1998: 39) and it also buttressed the view of the time which located 'disability of mind or body' firmly within individuals. The diagnosis of a specific handicap was to ensure relevant support could be allocated; the practice was to assign (or prioritize) one category for 'special' provision to be made. This, of course, overlooked the complex needs of some children who had one or more of the pre-designated handicap categories. The medical model also explicitly juxtaposes children who are perceived as 'normal' and those who are considered 'handicapped'.

The 1944 Education Act was at the centre of social reforms after the Second World War and, according to Armstrong (1998: 36), embodied a 'new philosophy of social inclusion'. The post-war era was one of optimism for the future and it was perceived that education could act of the vehicle to address society's inequalities and shortcomings. The consensus about the purpose of education circled the idea that every child should have equal educational opportunities. The idea of separate provision for children of different abilities, as symbolized in the tripartite system, dominated thinking at the time, however. Separate provision for children with physical difficulties; severe, moderate and mild learning difficulties; and behavioural problems were taught either in special units within mainstream schools or in special schools, all of which served to reinforce divisions. Once a child was attending a special school, the transfer to mainstream schooling was very rare and thus segregation was sustained.

Towards SEN and integration

Through the 1960s there were, gradually, changes in societal views towards disability (Boronski and Hassan, 2015). These changing attitudes are also discernible in The Plowden Report (CACE, 1967) (see Chapter 4), which rejected the idea that educational 'handicap' arises from individual deficits. Rather the report recognized 'there should be collective responsibility towards those individuals who experienced learning difficulties in their education' (Armstrong, 1998: 38). The 1970 Education

(Handicapped Children) Act transferred, from the health authorities to LEAs in England and Wales, the responsibility for the education of mentally handicapped children in all establishments, and thus signified the move-away 'treatment'. Similar legislation was passed for Scotland in 1974. At this time many children considered to be 'backward', 'subnormal', 'maladjusted' or 'remedial' were accommodated in mainstream schools, but would be withdrawn from ordinary lessons and taught separately in special classes or designated remedial units by remedial teachers who provided additional support with basic skills. There was a need to address what was being recognized as outmoded views. As such, a Committee of Inquiry into the Education of Handicapped Children and Young People was set up in 1974. This was at the request in 1973 of Margaret Thatcher, then Secretary of State for Education and Science. The committee's remit was

> To review educational provision in England, Scotland and Wales for children and young people handicapped by disabilities of body or mind, taking account of the medical aspects of their needs, together with arrangements to prepare them for entry into employment; to consider the most effective use of resources for these purposes; and to make recommendations. (DES, 1978b: 1)

The committee was chaired by Mary Warnock, then senior research fellow, St. Hugh's College, Oxford, and comprised various experts from education, medicine and psychology. Significantly, the involvement of experts from the fields of medicine and psychology reflects their dominance on issues connected to disability up unto this time (Boronski and Hassan, 2015). Four years on, the committee's report (known commonly as the Warnock Report) offered an alternative framework, which was not based on the medical model of disability, and introduced the concept of 'special educational needs'. The Warnock Report asserts 'the general aims of education are the same for all children' (DES, 1978b: 203), although it considered 'modification may be necessary' (1978b: 207). It acknowledged 'a continuum of special educational need rather than discrete categories of handicap' (DES, 1978b: 327), although it acknowledged the crudeness of a continuum 'which conceals the complexities of individual needs' (1978b: 6). Nevertheless, the report proposed abolishing the eleven handicap categories associated with the 1944 Act. Thus, there was a shift in thinking away from the idea of individual deficit and towards a generic concept emphasizing educational criteria. Hereafter, educational need was to be established in the context of the child's interaction with the school and learning environment (Wedell, 1988). Furthermore, the committee estimated up to 20 per cent of the school population experienced learning difficulties due to SEN during their school career which 'needed special attention for varying periods of time' (DES, 1978b: 40). Two per cent of these were catered for in special schools, but it was argued such schools 'would not necessarily be suitable for up to one in five children of school age, who present a very much wider range and variety of educational needs (1978b: 50). It was proposed, in chapter 3 of the Warnock Report (1978b), that children assessed as having special educational needs would be given a 'statement': this is essentially a record of a child's needs. A detailed assessment of learning needs procedure was proposed and a statement compiled if the needs could not be met within the resources of the ordinary school. There would be a multi-professional assessment and a process that included parents in the assessment and decision-making. Notably, advocating the involvement of parents in this way was a new approach which the report set in motion (Armstrong, 1998). The extension of special needs assessment procedures and provision was also to include pre-school age children and young adults in FE. The Warnock Report envisaged most children with SEN being educated alongside their peers in mainstream schools and having their needs met. As such three 'not discrete, but overlapping' forms of integration were distinguished:

> The first form of integration relates to the physical LOCATION of special educational provision. Locational integration exists where special units or classes are set up in ordinary schools. It also exists where a special school and an ordinary school share the same site ... its SOCIAL aspect, where children attending a special class or unit eat, play and consort with other children, and possibly share organised out-of-classroom activities with them. The third and fullest form of integration is FUNCTIONAL integration. This is achieved where the locational and social association of children with special needs with their fellows leads to joint participation in educational programmes. (1998: 100–101)

Despite the philosophy encapsulated in the Warnock Report, it can be criticized on a number of grounds: first, for its own use of labelling as SEN itself is seen as denoting categorization and indeed the report identifies different 'levels of ability and disability' (1998: 208) as well as various types of learning difficulties. Second, the report makes several references to the need for 'adequate resources', but otherwise the matter of financing the integration was, arguably, largely neglected:

> The provision of special facilities of a comparable standard to those in the best existing special schools will involve a very considerable amount of public expenditure and whether or not such expenditure is justifiable will be a matter of judgement by those responsible for the allocation and management of public resources. (1998: 118)

Third, the Committee could have recommended closing down all special schools, which would have achieved full inclusion and a fully comprehensive system. Moreover, the Warnock Report is significant in its implications and its subsequent influence cannot be underestimated. It shifted the ideological focus, influenced subsequent policies for SEN and disability and promoted the idea of integration. However, Simon (1991: 456) claims at the time 'nothing whatever was done, or achieved' by the Labour government's Secretary of State for Education Shirley

Williams, who instigated instead another round of consultations. It was for the next (Conservative) government to take Warnock's recommendations forward, but who acted upon 'the barest minimum of these proposals' (1991).

The 1981 Education Act incorporated Warnock's recommendations, both of which promoted the right of children with SENs to be educated in ordinary schools (Wedell, 1988) and thus both are significant in changing perceptions. Special needs were henceforth conceived as educational, not medical, criteria, and educational need was no longer tied to a handicap. This signifies the move away from the medical model embodying conditions and treatments towards a social one, whereby appropriate adjustments were made by schools to improve provision. Boronski and Hassan (2015: 146), however, maintain 'negative labels and pathological terms' continued (and still continue) to 'dominate academic and professional practice and this has a strong influence on common-sense assumptions held by policy-makers and the public'. The Act established a new framework for management of the assessment and decision-making regarding SEN (Armstrong, 1998). It set out in law the assessment procedure leading to a statement and the duty of LEAs to integrate children with SENs into mainstream education. This was based on the presupposition that children with SEN would receive appropriate provision and resources in order to be educated alongside their classroom peers. The belief being they would engage in the regular activities of the school, to the greatest extent possible, and with the proviso that the learning of others was not adversely affected. Critics argue that the usual practice by LEAs and educational psychologists in matching needs with existing provision still continued (Daniels et al., 1995). Boronski and Hassan (2015: 162), however, discern these constituting factors provided 'a get-out clause' if these requirements could not be met efficiently as LEAs were not under any legal obligation to make the necessary changes to facilitate integration, and thus was a weakness of the legislation. Research conducted at the time regarding the implementation of the legislation reveals the Act was 'largely ineffectual' in bringing about change because many cases were rejected by LEAs, parents often lacked basic information due to poor communication by LEAs and 'professional staff were able to avoid their responsibilities' (2015). Indeed the removal of the 'barriers' seemingly created by LEAs was to become, as we discuss later in this chapter, a prevailing feature of policy. Simon (1991: 487) contends the extra financial resources needed to 'shift organisational structures [and] also attitudes in a new direction, involving the humanist perspective of bringing children with special educational needs together with all others' was not forthcoming. Thus, the 1981 Education Act, arguably, suffered most from the 'financial squeeze' (Simon, 1991: 487) imposed by the new Thatcher government.

As noted already above, the idea of integration was espoused in the Warnock Report and, as a concept, is grounded in the educational and moral virtues of 'equality of access' and 'opportunity for all'. However, while integration may be considered both progressive and egalitarian, it requires proper and adequate funding in order to realize the merits of 'access' – as full participation, and 'opportunities' – as leading to more equal outcomes. One of the criticisms of the 1981 Act was that resources remained concentrated in special schools. As such, this led to LEAs and schools making idiosyncratic decisions regarding priorities in order to develop their own resources, policies, support mechanisms and practices, which were enacted 'through a complex network of school based, school attached and outreach services' (Wedell, 1988: 21). Other criticisms were that segregation and integration existed side by side in mainstream schools, and also teachers lacked insufficient training. Support teachers worked alongside ordinary classroom teachers and could be used in an advisory capacity. Nevertheless the research literature suggests many teachers felt (and still feel) ill equipped to educate these children adequately and deal with the multitude of special educational needs presented in their classrooms. Moreover, the responsibility rested with parents to fight for their child to be integrated into a mainstream school (Boronski and Hassan, 2015).

Education reforms and SEN

Immense changes in education were brought about by the Conservative government in 1988. The Education Reform Bill that led to the ERA 'had been pushed through parliament at great speed' (Simon, 1991: 549); it paved the way for the education market which was influenced by New Right ideology (see Chapter 1). This was not a market in the true sense, however, but highly structured with indicators that measured performance and, from 1992, was regulated through routine Ofsted inspections. For schools, the managed market translated into the balance of power shifting from LEAs, who had controlled much of the day-to-day running of the system, towards central government on the one hand and locally towards head teachers on the other. Decentralization, encompassing delegation and autonomy, and centralization, which strengthened political control, thus occurred simultaneously and worked together. Particularly significant was LMS, which devolved to schools from LEAs control of their budget, as well as financial accountability. What transpired in terms of resource implications for SEN was a reduction in LEA support services. In some schools, as well, funds designated for SEN were being utilized elsewhere in the school. Consumer choice was regarded as a vehicle for improving education (and the public services more generally). Pupils were evaluated through national assessment procedures and their results subsequently published in league tables in England and Wales for public scrutiny, providing consumers of education with comparative data. In the education marketplace schools competed for pupils through open enrolment, as is the neo-liberal approach. Inevitably, the emphasis on output and testing created pressures on schools to focus on their performance. This had a number of repercussions, including schools marketing themselves in order to attract parents and admit pupils whose performance is likely to reach high standards and an increase in pupil exclusions particularly those with statements. Daniels and others (1995: 208) argue the 'most powerful indicator of school effectiveness which is likely to be available ... will be the eventual pattern of aggregated subject attainment scores'. What followed was an increase in referrals by schools to obtain formal statements for some pupils so as to augment their budget as well as exempting them from annual returns so they did not depress results (1995). It is against this demand-led, customer-oriented backdrop that developments in SEN post-Warnock must be considered.

Through the ERA the Secretary of State Kenneth Baker introduced a National Curriculum which 'promotes the spiritual, moral, cultural, mental and physical development of (all) pupils at a school' (Wedell, 1988: 19). Wedell (1988) emphasizes the resistance to an amendment to the Bill which added the word 'all' to this sentence. He (1988: 19) claims the Bill appeared to have been drafted within 'a different conceptual framework' to those adopted by the 1981 Act and the Warnock Report which prefigured it. The Green Paper to the National Curriculum (DES, 1987c) only made a small mention of SEN in relation to pupils with statements. So when the Bill was first introduced to Parliament (see Chapter 1), it contained a 'sparse reference' to SEN (Wedell, 1988: 19). However following the parliamentary debate another section was included enabling schools to 'modify or "disapply" or adapt the National Curriculum in certain cases' (Letch, 2000: 108). Wedell (1988: 19) notes there was 'no explicit recognition of the continuum of SENs written into the Act, nor a commitment to the promotion of integration, either within the compulsory school age range, or in further and higher education'. Nonetheless, 'all' emphasizes a universal entitlement and the expectation that all children in maintained schools would follow the National Curriculum and partake in the associated national tests. Boronski and Hassan (2015: 166) contend 'we have an inclusive philosophy that works according to a system which measures all children against a notional norm outside of which children with SEN are more likely to fail'.

Now having unprecedented powers, the secretary of state continued unabated with the publication of a White Paper, *Choice and Diversity and New Framework for Schools* (DFE, 1992a), and a Green Paper, *Special Educational Needs: Access to the System* (DFE, 1992b). The resulting 1993 Education Act attempted to remedy some of the shortcomings of previous legislation. It introduced a new system of tribunals to hear parents' appeals and established a tighter time frame to facilitate a swifter statementing process and it was made obligatory for the secretary of state to issue a Code of Practice, which would be periodically revisited and revised. The 1994 *Code of Practice on the Identification and Assessment of Children with Special Educational Needs* (DFE, 1994) duly followed. This reiterated the Act's tenets and provided 'practical guidance to LEAs and schools on their responsibilities to children with SEN' (Letch, 2000: 109). The Code provided for schools and LEAs to make greater provision and parents to have greater involvement in decisions. It also set out more clearly the specific roles and responsibilities of schools, notably the role of the special educational needs co-ordinator (SENCO; Letch, 2000). The 1996 Education Act offered further guidance for teachers and other professionals to enable them to make accurate decisions regarding whether or not a child has a SEN (Hodkinson, 2015).

The Act also enshrined in law a clear definition of SEN (and which was later reinforced in legislation in 2001):

> A child has 'special educational needs' for the purposes of this Act if he has a learning difficulty which calls for special educational provision to be made for him [sic]. (Education Act, 1996: Section 312 (1))

The policy rhetoric suggested entitlement for all; however, the Conservative reforms of the time, especially those of the Thatcher government, arguably thwarted the development of a more equitable SEN policy.

Pause and ponder

According to Norwich (1994: 293):

> Underlying … different conceptions of differentiation are different views about 'difference' which are in tension. The can be represented as the tension between a negative view of 'difference' as indicating lower status, less value and perpetuating inequalities and unfair treatment, versus a positive view which sees 'difference' as recognising what is relevant to an individual's learning and development. The difference can be seen as posing a dilemma in education over how difference is taken into account – whether to recognise differences as relevant to individual needs by offering different provision, by that doing so could reinforce unjustified inequalities and is associated with devaluation; or, whether to offer a common and valued provision for all, but with the risk of not providing what is relevant to provisional needs.

Norwich presents a 'basic dilemma' in policy between individuality and equality.

1 In your opinion, is this a fundamental contradiction in policy?
2 Do you think treating all learners as the same and at the same time differently is compatible?
3 Can this dilemma be reconciled?

Fostering inclusion

Hodkinson (2015: 85) argues the roots of inclusion can be traced to the later 1800s as evidenced in the ambitions of those 'educational pioneers' who pushed for a non-segregated schooling system and helped to develop provision for those who were otherwise excluded from education plans. A more contemporary analysis can be charted from *The Salamanca Statement and Framework for Action* (UNESCO, 1994). This emanated from a World Conference on Special Needs Education held in Salamanca, Spain, involving ninety-two governments and twenty-five international organizations. The Statement promotes the importance of principles, policy and practice in SEN noting:

> The trend in social policy during the past two decades has been to promote integration and participation and to combat exclusion. Inclusion and participation are essential to human dignity and to the enjoyment and exercise of human rights. Within the field of education, this is reflected in the development of strategies that seek to bring about a genuine equalization of opportunity. Experience in many countries demonstrates that the integration of children and youth with special educational needs is best achieved within inclusive schools that serve all children within a community. It is within this context that those with special educational needs can achieve the fullest educational progress and social integration. (UNESCO, 1994: 11)

The Salamanca Statement, a fifty-page document, calls for united and international action to promote inclusive practices worldwide, acknowledging that the responsibility should not fall on governments alone; rather, it requires 'the co-operation of families, and the mobilization of the community and voluntary organizations as well as the support of the public-at-large' (1994: 37). We examine in the next section of this chapter the incoming New Labour government's commitment to inclusion and its support for taking forward the ideas contained within the Salamanca Statement, which postulated:

> The development of inclusive schools as the most effective means for achieving education for all must be recognized as a key government policy and accorded a privileged place on the nation's development agenda. (1994: 41)

Aside from the Salamanca Statement, this period of policy change in the 1990s can be attributed to a number of other contemporary issues and contributing factors. Boronski and Hassan (2015) discern, first, the demands for civil rights for disabled people by groups and organizations who were starting to collectively challenge prejudiced attitudes and practices. Second, changing societal attitudes were leading to the reconsideration of procedures and the effectiveness of segregation by professionals and practitioners working in the area of SEN. Third, and as already outlined above, they recognized the international impetus for change (see also

Chapter 9) which promoted the fostering of strategies by national governments to further educational rights and equality. Key to this agenda are, for example, the United Nations Convention on the Rights of the Child (UNICEF, 1989) and the Education for All initiative (World Education Forum, 2000), in which six goals were identified and pledged to be met by 2015.

Pause and ponder

The Salamanca Statement advocates the following:

Educational policies at all levels, from the national to the local, should stipulate that a child with a disability should attend the neighbourhood school, that is, the school that would be attended if the child did not have a disability. Exceptions to this rule should be considered on a case-by-case basis where only education in a special school or establishment can be shown to meet the needs of the individual child. The practice of 'mainstreaming' children with disabilities should be an integral part of national plans for achieving education for all.

In your view, do policies implemented by the UK government since the Salamanca Statement work towards this view of inclusive education?

Having been out of government for some seventeen years, the 'New' Labour Party entered office in 1997 with great ambitions for education. Ainscow and others (2011: 12) consider New Labour was 'notoriously hyperactive' over the following eleven years in government and launched numerous initiatives. The core values of New Labour politics namely – community, inclusion, fairness and social justice –underpinned its policies for education (Driver and Martell, 1998). New Labour placed educational provision within a broader social inclusion agenda which included a framework of equal rights initiatives for disabled people. More children with disabilities attended mainstream schools and so, for some children, the rhetoric of inclusion did become a reality (Tomlinson, 2005). In keeping with the main policy drive for excellence in education, the Green Paper *Excellence for All Children: Meeting Special Educational Needs* (DfEE, 1997d) was published[1] in England. This provided a clear indication of the government's 'broad commitment to equity in and through education variously badged as "inclusion" or "social inclusion"' (Ainscow, 2016: 174). The Green Paper also proposes the removal of 'barriers which get in the way of meeting the needs of all children' and the government's intention to redefine 'the role of special schools within this context' (DfEE, 1997d: 5). Thus, greater inclusion was advocated, but also the continuation of a dual system accommodating both special and mainstream schools. The consultation period was followed by yet another publication, *Meeting*

Special Educational Needs: A Programme of Action (DfEE, 1998f). This document outlined measures to be taken to implement the Green Paper's proposals. The subsequent Bill in 2000, applying only to England and Wales, led to The Special Educational Needs and Disability Act (SENDA) 2001, which promoted greater inclusion. Importantly, the Act coupled SEN and disability and made it unlawful to discriminate against any disabled student in their admissions policies and service provision. Boronski and Hassan (2015: 165) thus observe how the 'get-out clause', the 'blatant feature of the 1981 Education Act which allowed LEAs to escape their duty to integrate, was rescinded'. A revised (2001) Code of Practice on SEN was also published and provided greater practical advice and guidance for professionals working in LEAs, schools and early years' settings.

Three years on, a report by Ofsted (2004) drew attention to the disparities and confusion in the current provision. While it was found that schools considered they were inclusive, only a small number were judged to be meeting SEN well. So, to further its strategy for inclusion and provide policy clarity, the government published *Removing the Barriers to Achievement* (DfES, 2004b), which also connected up with ECM agenda (see Chapter 5). *Removing the Barriers* explained how government aimed to tackle educational disadvantage and child poverty, as well as proposed better integration of children's services, the need for early intervention polices and better teacher training which provided 'a good grounding in core skills and knowledge of SEN' (2004b: 51). The launch of a new *Inclusion Development Programme*, designed 'to help schools become more effective at responding to the needs of individual pupils', was also proposed (2004b: 31).

As we have alluded so far, numerous guidance documents and many initiatives for schools aimed to promote inclusion. It is interesting to discern, however, when examining New Labour's documents how the focus on policy steers towards meeting the individual needs of the child. There are also many references made to different medical conditions. Some examples include:

> Effective inclusion relies on more than specialist skills and resources. It requires positive attitudes towards children who have difficulties in school, a greater responsiveness to individual needs. (2004b: 26)
>
> With autistic spectrum disorder, increasing numbers of children are being identified, presenting a wide range and complexity of needs. Children with behavioural, emotional and social difficulties pose similar challenges, too often leading to exclusion from school. Overcoming speech, language and communication difficulties is crucial to enabling children to access the whole curriculum. Children with moderate learning difficulties in mainstream schools are the largest group with SEN but too often can find their needs overlooked. (2004b: 31)
>
> For parents of children with severe autism, for example, we know that joint working between the school, speech and language therapy services and short breaks providers is essential to meeting their child's needs. (DfEE, 2011d: 99)

> Early identification of learning difficulties or disabilities can be vital to a child's learning and life chances. In some areas, major breakthroughs have recently been made. In particular, the screening of newborn babies means that deafness and hearing problems can now be diagnosed months or years earlier than in the past. (HM Treasury, 2003: 27)

We will return to the idea of individual need and the matter of 'diagnosis' later in the chapter. For the moment, and in the next section, we wish to draw attention to and briefly contemplate two issues in New Labour's policy-making whose consequences endure. As such, we examine the tensions between the inclusion and standards agendas and the ineffective deployment of Teaching Assistants (TAs) who provide support for pupils with SEN; these issues reveal on the ground some of the arguably unintentional consequences of policy impacting practice.

The unintended consequences of policy?

First, New Labour's overarching aim in education was to develop a 'world-class' education system and this required raising achievement in schools. To this end the government promoted a 'standards agenda' and the policy push was target setting. Commenting on New Labour's policies for inclusion, Ainscow (2016: 169: original emphasis) states:

> The government has argued that the raising standards *is* about equity: that a powerful emphasis on raising attainment will not simply benefit children who are already performing at a high level but is of even greater benefit to previously low-attaining children.

The means of achieving equity through raising standards ran concurrently with its agenda for inclusion. This dissonance, arguably, created a policy tension between standards on the one hand and inclusion on the other. The apparent discord was exacerbated further as policies of inclusion, which promote educating children together in mainstream, coexisted alongside education policy priorities to meet the needs of the economy (see Chapter 7). Thus, human capital formation, which links directly to economic performance, underpinned New Labour's policies and successive governments' policies, but is, arguably, not fully reconcilable with an inclusive agenda. Ainscow's study (2016: 174) is one example, among many, which illustrates how the performative context in education which encapsulates test scores, exam results and inspection outcomes as the 'sole criteria for determining success … acts as a barrier to the development of more equitable education system'. Dealing with this policy contradiction could go some way to explaining the limitations of equity-oriented policies. However, Ainscow and others' (2011) research explains how contradictions in policy cause teachers and schools, who are charged with their implementation, to find their own responses; this, in turn opens up spaces to develop local responses that tackle aspects of educational inequality.

Second, we examine how New Labour restructured the teaching workforce and consider the subsequent ramifications. The re-modelling of the workforce in the early 2000s aimed to reconfigure teachers' work, enabling them to concentrate more on teaching and learning. As such, New Labour brought more TAs into schools to support and work alongside regular teachers in the classroom. Numbers were increased by New Labour during its time in government, and successive governments have also continued to follow suit. Since 2000 TA numbers have increased from 79.0 thousand full-time equivalents (FTEs) to 255.1 thousand FTEs in 2014 (DfE, 2015). Of these 166.2 thousand FTEs are in primary schools, 53.9 thousand FTEs in secondary schools and 62.4 thousand FTEs in special schools. The total number of school support staff including auxiliary staff is 232.0 thousand in 2014 (DfE, 2015). A fundamental role of TAs has emerged in relation to providing a high amount of support for pupils with SEN, with and without statements. According to Webster and Blatchford (2015), TAs 'have become an essential way in which teachers deal with problems connected to the inclusion of pupils with statements'. This 'unintentional drift [in schools] toward a model of TA deployment' (2015) separates pupils with SEN from their peers, their teachers and the curriculum. It raises questions about pupils with SEN being supported by those whose level of pedagogical knowledge and quality of training is inferior to teachers, which has further implications for teachers' professionalism. Webster and Blatchford's (2015) research, across six LAs, investigated the deployment of TAs in primary schools and the educational experiences of forty-eight Year 5 pupils (aged nine and ten-year-old) with the highest levels of SEN. Their findings show 'when compared to the experiences of pupils without SEN, pupils receiving a high amount of TA support have a different – and less effective – pedagogical diet' (2015: 337). This suggests a variance of experience of pupils with SEN compared to their peers. Further, the research serves to illuminate how TAs are being ineffectively deployed by schools to the detriment of the pupils experience, not that a 'problem' resides in TAs per se. Webster and Blatchford (2015: 340) call for schools 'to widen their models of SEN provision and reconfigure overall pedagogical supports'.

A new approach to special educational needs and disability?

The Coalition's 'ambitious vision' (DfE, 2011d: 13) for SEN was articulated in its 2011 Green Paper, *Support and Aspiration: A New Approach to Special Educational Needs and Disability*. This was in response to the notion that existing provision was based on a model introduced thirty years previously, and was 'no longer fit for purpose' (Perry, 2014, cited in Hodkinson, 2015: 124). The Green Paper shares many messages and attributes which have informed recent policy-making. For example, the Coalition's preference for the market and the primacy of diversity and choice for parents feature fairly extensively in the document:

> We will remove the bias towards inclusion and propose to strengthen parental choice by improving the range and diversity of schools from which parents can choose. (DfE, 2011d: 17)
>
> No one type of school placement (such as full inclusion in mainstream provision, special schools, or specialist units in a mainstream setting) is the most effective at meeting children's SEN. (DfE, 2011d: 20)
>
> We believe that real choice for parents requires a diverse and dynamic school system that offers a wide range of high quality provision and that has the autonomy and flexibility to respond effectively to parental choice. (DfE, 2011d: 51)
>
> We will explore ways to make it easier for special schools and special Academies to enter the market to offer alternative provision. (DfE, 2011d: 72)

The Coalition's policy priority of marketization has seen the encouragement and development of different types of schools. To this end, there has been a rapid growth in the number of Academies following the expansion of the programme through the 2010 Academies Act. This Act enabled school types previously barred, such as special schools and also pupil referral units, to seek academy status. The Act allowed for the development of more specialized Academies and introduced Free Schools, a new type of Academy (see Chapters 3 and 9). Furthermore, the legislation requires that Academies of all types adhere to SEN legislation; and thus, regarding admissions policies, they have the statutory duty to admit children with statements. Policies have worked towards creating more school diversity and parents do now have greater choice in terms of their right to express a preference for mainstream or special schools. Inclusive education is thus a greater reality now for children with SEN. However, the realization of their stated preference cannot be guaranteed, as parents may have their choice fulfilled if, exceptionally, the 'efficient education' of other children would be affected (Hodkinson, 2015: 129). Hodkinson (2015) also contends that due to 'budgetary constraints', achieving the flexibility and responsiveness needed to accommodate every child's needs with a school of their choice is still highly problematic.

The re-focus on individual need is evident and we return to our earlier point regarding references about diagnosis and disability in recent policy documents. The Green Paper (DfE, 2011d) makes reference to, for example:

> Maternity services help to prepare and support families who have a baby diagnosed with a foetal anomaly in prenatal screening, or where an impairment is diagnosed postnatally. (2011d: 30)
>
> diagnosis of autistic spectrum disorder in children and young people. (2011d: 31)

The aims which permeate the schools' White Paper (DfE, 2010a) to reduce bureaucracy, lessen government prescription and create greater freedom for schools also feature in *Support and Aspiration:*

> we propose to:... reduce bureaucratic burdens by simplifying and improving the statutory guidance for all professionals working with children and young people from birth to 25 with SEN or who are disabled so that it is clear, accessible and helpful, and withdrawing guidance that does not provide useful support to professionals. (DfE, 2011d: 93–94)
>
> Rather than directing change from Whitehall, we want to make it easier for professionals and services to work together, and we want to create the conditions that encourage innovative and collaborative ways of providing better support for children, young people and families. (2011d: 93)
>
> Head teachers have been overwhelmed with top-down initiatives rather than having the freedom to drive improvements. (2011d: 57)

The rhetoric emphasizes the need to enable schools and practitioners, rather than politicians, to do more and bring about meaningful change in their own educational contexts. It will therefore be important for schools to embrace these opportunities and create the appropriate culture and ethos for learning so that the aspirations of children and young people can be met.

The reforms to provisions for children with SEN and disabilities were legislated through the Children and Families Act (DfE, 2014c) with effect from September 2014. It replaces earlier descriptions in previous legislation (1996 and 2001) and defines SEN as follows:

> A child or young person has special educational needs if he or she has a learning difficulty or disability which calls for special educational provision to be made for him or her. (DfE, 2014c: Part 3, 20 [1])

Among the key changes in the Act are the new single assessment process and the Education, Health and Care (ECH) plan which replaces the statutory SEN assessment and statement. Moreover, there are new rights bestowed upon children and young people including beyond the age of compulsory schooling.

Over to you ...

Locate some of the key documents featured in this chapter; search by their titles as most are available online.

1 What objectives are outlined and how far have they been realized?
2 Have policies turned out differently to what was proposed or intended?
3 Consider the reasons why this may have happened.

Towards educational equity ...

This chapter has explored the policy move from the segregation of children from their peers, now regarded as a denial of human rights, and towards a model of inclusive education. However, some would argue the drive for inclusive schools has not gone far enough and does not yet match the expectations set out in the Salamanca Statement (Hodkinson, 2015). In this sense, although various factors have contributed to a move towards inclusive education, such moves have not been fully followed through and completed.

There was an interesting adjunct to the inclusion debate in 2005 when Mary Warnock, now Baroness Warnock, reflected on her original ideas and recommendations some thirty years on. As the architect of the 1978 Warnock Report, her ideas, and those of the committee she led, were enshrined in the 1981 Act. This Act represents a watershed in the education of children with disabilities, fuelling the move towards integration and later towards inclusion. Her essay/pamphlet '*Special Education Needs: A New Look*' (see Warnock, 2010) published in 2005 contains her reflections on the more contentious elements of the original report and the subsequent application of her ideas in practice. Her revised ideas caused some controversy at the time, being highly publicized as constituting a 'U-turn' (Telegraph, 2005). Indeed, Warnock recognizes the 'seeds of confusion' which, she says, were planted in 1978 and which 'still bedevils the field of special educational needs to this day' (Warnock, 2010: 18). She feared the desire to 'avoid categories of disability' (i.e. the removal of the eleven handicap categories) and their replacement with special education needs 'led to a tendency to refer to children with very different needs as if they were all the "same"'. She also considered 'the statement of special education is beset with confusion' (2010:19). Warnock, however, regards the most 'disastrous legacy of the 1978 Report [as] the concept of inclusion (formerly known as integration)', the premise of her argument being that small special schools should be 'invented' to serve a wider variety of need (2010: 44). Since this proclamation some of Warnock's concerns have been subsequently revised and legislated, though not necessarily as a direct result of her publication. In recent education policy documents, as illustrated above, the identification of different disabilities and medical conditions is much more explicit. For example, legislation has replaced statements with EHC plans, and there is encouragement of special Academies 'to offer alternative provision' (DfE, 2011d: 72). There also seems to be a return to former ideas where individual need is emphasized rather than learning environments adapting to meet the needs of children with SEN. Debates, struggles and confusion over inclusion continue to persist and will no doubt do so as policies of different kinds, ambition and intentionality serve to exacerbate or ameliorate existing problems in education. A corollary implication is that it would therefore seem likely there is still much to be done in realizing a coherent strategy forwards and, more importantly, achieving greater educational equity.

Pause and ponder

1 How have policies influenced the education of children with SEN since 1870?
2 What factors generated moves towards inclusive education?
3 Why, in your opinion, have these moves not been completed?

Note

1   In Wales, *The BEST for Special Education* was published in 1997 for consultation, followed in 1999 by *Shaping the Future for Special Education*. The subsequent Bill applied to England and Wales only.

Further reading

Ainscow, M. (2016) *Struggles for Equity in Education: The Selected Works of Mel Ainscow*, Abingdon, Oxon: Routledge.
Armstrong, A. C., D. Armstrong and I. Spandagou (2009) *Inclusive Education: International Policy & Practice*, London: Sage.
Hodkinson, A. (2015) *Key Issues in Special Educational Needs and Inclusion*, London: Sage.

Globalization and Policy-Borrowing

Introduction

This chapter begins by examining the nature and meaning of globalization: its characteristics, complexity and pervasive influence. Then an international, comparative stance is adopted to show that, in spite of the influence of globalization, significant differences remain in the construction of policy between different education systems. The chapter draws attention to a variety of nuanced perspectives to identify key differences in the overlapping discourses of globalization, policy-learning and policy-borrowing. Particular cases, which focus on the creation of different types of schools, curricula and the management of performance, are drawn upon to illuminate instances of policy convergence and divergence. The chapter highlights the tensions and points of resistance that impede the transfer of policy from one context to another. 'Policy networks' and 'policy entrepreneurs' are significant in the international flow of policy, and such roles are also given consideration. Through a variety of cases, the chapter contrasts the idea of 'imitation, emulation or copying' (Dale, 1999: 9) in policy (bilaterally from one country to another) with more implicit notions of globalized change.

Globalization: Definitions and its characteristics

Defining 'globalization' is not a straightforward endeavour, as it is a widely used term that encompasses multiple meanings and interpretations. At the outset, one might even contemplate and deliberate whether globalization actually exists – is it tangible? Globalization might constitute an ideology, a discourse, a phenomenon, a trend, a process – or perhaps something else? Nonetheless, despite these various characterizations it is pragmatic, as a starting point, to comprehend globalization as a concept which describes the way in which the world appears increasingly as a single social system. At its broadest, globalization is associated with the increasing interconnectedness and integration of contemporary world society (Held et al., 1999) and 'the intensification of consciousness of the world as a whole' (Robertson, 1992: 8). Typically the concept is used to interpret the vast economic, political and cultural changes which have been experienced globally particularly since the late 1990s onwards.

In the 1960s Marshall McLuhan coined the term 'the global village' to refer to the way in which the electronics revolution had transformed time and space. Since then, 'globalization' has been utilized to explain the interconnected nature of the world and the growing interdependence of communities and countries. Burbules and Torres (2000: 12) maintain the process of globalization is evident in 'the changes in communication technologies, migration patterns, and capital flows'. McGrew (1992: 65–66) suggests:

> Globalisation refers to the multiplicity of linkages and interconnections that transcend the nation-states (and by implication the societies) which make up the modern world. It defines a process through which events, decisions, and activities on one part of the world can come to have significant consequences for individual and communities in quite distant parts of the globe.

However, Watkins and Fowler (2003: 31) contend 'developing countries have been progressively integrated into a global economy since the discovery of the New World more than five centuries ago'. Contemporary understandings of globalization arguably stem from the early 1970s and the world oil crisis which prompted important technological and economic changes (Burbules and Torres, 2000). Also in the 1970s and 1980s there was a dramatic intensification of globalization due to shift to 'post-Fordist' methods of production (Murray, 1989) (see Chapter 6) and development of the information society, cultural globalization and post-modern culture (Harvey, 1990). Especially notable are the explosion of 'globalization theory' and a proliferation of academic literature about globalization from the 1990s onwards. A review of relevant literature uncovers varying definitions, and as these become more explanatory and encompassing, the complexity of globalization becomes more apparent. Rothenberg's (2003: 4) analysis, for instance, offers the following:

> Globalisation is the acceleration and intensification of interaction and integration among the people, companies and governments of different nations. This process has effects on human well-being (including health and personal safety), on the environment, on culture (including ideas, religion, and political systems), and on economic development and prosperity of societies across the world.

Rothenberg accentuates the dynamism of globalization by emphasizing its 'intensification and acceleration'. The speeding-up aspect of globalization has been explored at length by Harvey (1990), who attributes this type of change, referred to as 'time-space compression', to the increasingly abstract activities of the global exchange of capital. Giddens's (1990) examination of 'modernity' is similar to Harvey's in terms of the connecting up of the local and the global and the increased pace and scope of change. Giddens (1990: 14) engages with the concept of 'time-space distanciation', the process by which new technologies reorganize time and space. He argues that geographical distance has changed dramatically in the modern era. The shrinking world is due to the development of information and communication technologies whereby global communication networks, such as the Internet, provide new and ever-faster modes of connecting people and societies. According to Giddens (1990: 64), globalization 'stretches' the connections between different social contexts and regions, resulting in 'local involvements (circumstances of co-presence) and interaction across distance (the connection of presence and absence)'.

Definitions are clearly varied and address different aspects of globalization. It is the view of globalization as an economic phenomenon, however, which best exemplifies the increasing interconnectedness and independence between nation states, the transcendence of power above that of national boundaries and time–space compression. Hence, for some authors, the main driving force of the world's contemporary interconnectedness is due to the expansion of globalized chains of production and consumption fuelled by the expansion of neo-liberal economic thinking and practice. Economic definitions of globalization can thus be understood as the formation of internationally integrated economies characterized by openness to international trading and increasingly greater movement of capital and labour across national borders (Burbules and Torres, 2000). Capling and others (1998: 5) explain economic globalization as

> The emergence of a global economy which is characterised by uncontrollable market forces and new economic actors such as transnational corporations, international banks, and other financial institutions.

National governments around the world have been guided by the perceptions of a global economy and post-industrialism where knowledge, information and creativity are vital for economic success. Economic prosperity is dependent on the knowledge of workers and hence there is a critical role for education in the development of 'human capital' (Williams, 2009). What has ensued is essentially a global policy discourse encompassing highly skilled, adaptable workers functioning in a knowledge economy/learning society. Whereas many nation states (including the UK) previously based their policies on Keynesian macro-economics (see Chapter 7), state ownership and economic planning, these ideas are no longer regarded as pertinent in a world characterized by flexibility, de-regulated markets, increased insecurity and political uncertainties (Henry et al., 2008). Neo-liberalism has permeated policy-making, thus globalizing the world economy and capital mobility; the consequences are characterized by greater interdependence and instability. As such, Giddens (1994) sees the increasing role of 'action at a distance' whereby the actions that take place in one nation state can have profound consequences for another.

Trade has created links and interdependence between producers and consumers that are often geographically distant. These trade relationships can often be thought of as 'transnational' as they involve multinational and transnational corporations (e.g. BP, Toyota, Apple, Microsoft, Kraft) which can undermine or at least bypass interstate relations. Similarly, supranational agencies such as the World Bank, International Trade Organisation, International Monetary Fund, World Trade Organisation and the Organisation for Economic Cooperation and Development have arisen prominently to operate above and across national boundaries in what Rosenau (1992) refers to as 'governance without government'. Their dominance significantly weakens national power, national sovereignty and national prominence which, according to Castells (1997: 121), creates the 'powerless state'. However, while relinquishing national political power, on the one hand, the world's richest countries have arguably opted into and promoted supranational agencies as a means of preserving their own privileged positions within the world economy (Cerny, 1997). While the world's major economies may share a common ideological response to global problems, and to some extent cede authority to international organizations, it is not a case of relinquishing all political capacity. Nation states respond in different ways in that the effects of globalization are mediated through different national societal peculiarities and idiosyncratic cultures (Dale, 1999). Nation states do therefore continue to maintain their distinctiveness, although, as Ball (1999: 200) points out, it is the way in which supranational agencies 'represent the accepted, collective wisdom of "the west"' that is significant.

Beck (2000a,b, 2006) provides an alternative perspective; his analysis of globalization differs somewhat from those theorists who focus on the nation state. Beck's concerns predominantly span global insecurities and the increase in risk that extend into what he refers to as the 'second age of modernity' (Beck, 2000a).

He is primarily interested in what he sees as shared global problems: ecological and environmental problems and climate change; war, terrorism, armed conflict over resources and weapons of mass destruction; and issues connected to poverty, health and human rights. Beck appeals for a common awareness which leads on to a cosmopolitan consciousness of community. He argues that the problems are global and therefore cannot satisfactorily be addressed by individual nation states. Beck thus emphasizes the desirability of transition from national to cosmopolitan society and politics:

> The question I want to put on the agenda is: how to imagine, define and analyse post-national, transnational *and* political communities? How to build a conceptual frame of reference to analyse the coming of a cosmopolitan society (behind the facade of nation-state societies) and its enemies. (Beck, 2000a: 90)

Besides the economic and political characteristics of globalization, other authors focus on its cultural and social aspects. Rizvi (2000: 208–209) provides a flavour of the cultural dimensions in which globalization operates and permeates contemporary societies noting, 'Practices that are transcultural, emerging out of rapid flows of cultures across national boundaries, not only through global media and information technologies but also through the movement of people … for a range of purposes including migration, tourism, business and education.' Stiglitz (2002: 214) offers a positive analysis in social terms stating, 'Globalisation has brought better health, as well as an active global civil society fighting for more democracy and greater social justice.' Castells (2000: 164), however, provides an alternative perspective to Stiglitz, purporting the emergence of a 'Fourth World' which comprises, 'multiple black holes of social exclusion throughout the planet. The Fourth World comprises large areas of the globe … it is also present in literally every country, and every city, in this new geography of social exclusion'.

Pause and ponder

Spend some time thinking about the nature and meaning of globalization. In order to come to your own judgement, you might want to consider the following:

1 What are the main benefits of globalization?
2 What are the potential problems?

Globalization has enabled markets to expand so that we have a 'global economy', but globalization affects countries or people in different ways.

1 Who benefits most from globalization?
2 Who has the most to lose?

There are different theories of globalization within the literature as the excerpts above show; 'globalization' is an inexact term with multiple meanings. In terms of the drivers of globalization, the literature typically cites the influence of single causes, for example, capitalism (Wallerstein, 2011), technology (Rosenau and Singh, 2002) or political factors (Gilpin, 1987). Other authors, however, such as Giddens (1990) and Robertson (1995), suggest multiple causes to account for globalization and cite a complex set of interconnecting processes. Globalization thus remains a contested concept (Rizvi, 2004).

Homogenization and differentiation

The interconnectedness of the world via globalization simultaneously brings about homogenization (sameness) and differentiation. In terms of evidence of 'sameness', one can consider the nature of global brands, commodities and images. For example, McDonalds, Disney, Nike and Coca Cola are well-known global brands; the particular symbols associated with them are widely acknowledged and their meaning understood globally. So, for instance, the bright yellow 'M' associated with McDonalds, and which is symbolic of American culture, would be instantly recognizable worldwide to anyone already familiar with it; they would immediately know that that particular icon signifies 'fast food'. Such is the power of this phenomenon that in the 1990s Ritzer (2008: 1) coined the term 'McDonaldisation' which means 'The process by which the principles of the fast-food restaurant are coming to dominate more and more sectors of American society as well as the rest of the world.' McDonaldisation has become incorporated in the academic and public lexicon as an 'exorable process' (2008: 2) to explain the increasing homogenization and standardization across all countries where tastes and systems alike are being controlled and developed by large corporations. In a similar vein Bryman (2004) created the term 'Disneyization' of society, which is a comparable analysis of global society. There are other shared elements of life that might be considered the same worldwide too such as: city life, religion, the existence of human rights and so on. However, at the same time, there is also differentiation and the reworking of the global in relation to local circumstances, what Robertson (1995) refers to as 'glocalisation'. So, remaining with some of the examples given above, there are country-specific menus in McDonalds designed specifically to suit particular national and cultural tastes; Italian children have renamed Disney's Mickey Mouse 'Toplino'; the practice of Islam is quite different in different countries; and there are different interpretations of human rights. Robertson (1995: 30) thus cautions:

it is wrong simply to read off from the global to understand what is happening locally. And it is wrong to assume the local is detached from what is happening globally; rather what is happening needs to be increasingly understood as glocalisation involving 'the simultaneity and the interpenetration of what are conventionally called the global and the local'.

As can be seen, globalization is not a homogenous, consistent or linear process; it is multifaceted. There is little consensus with respect for definitions, characteristics, explanations and influences, and it has had, and can have, positive and/or negative effects on societies. In recent years globalization has been given considerable attention by theorists and education policy-makers alike and a rational question would be, what is the impact of globalization on education? Largely due to the inextricable links between the economy and education, the performance of education systems is regarded as a benchmark for national economic success. It is to the relationship between globalization and education that the chapter now turns.

Globalization and education

The impact of globalization is probably the most significant challenge currently facing national education systems. Certainly, in the field of comparative and international education current literature examines the global influences which challenge considerably and significantly the sovereignty and importance of the nation state in education. Increasingly, multilateral agencies such as the United Nations Educational, Scientific and Cultural Organization (UNESCO) and the OECD shape, determine and mandate global educational policy debates and agendas (Resnik, 2006). Much of UNESCO's work involves information sharing and setting standards in education as a means of creating enhanced provision of education driven by notions of equality of opportunity and as a liberal internationalist ideal (Jones, 1988). The Paris-based OECD was one of the earliest facilitators of bilateral funding for cross-national testing and comparative studies. Its Programme for International Student Assessment (PISA) surveys, undertaken every three years since 2000, measure literacy in reading, mathematics and science for fifteen-year-old students. Commission agencies produce the tests and the results provide statistical information enabling politicians and policy-makers to compare different countries' education systems and socio-economic performance. While PISA data should not be regarded as 'global league tables that praise or shame countries' (Sahlberg, 2013), the data are often used by policy-makers to justify change for national education policies or provide support for an existing policy direction (Grek, 2009). Certainly PISA results have been exploited by UK policy-makers who make selective comparisons in order to rationalize education reforms and restructuring. The PISA tests propagate the continued focus on the economic imperatives of education, economic prosperity and the need to adopt 'best practice' as promoted by the OECD. Arguably, this is driven by 'an ideology that accepts economic growth and competitiveness as the sole aims of schooling' (Wilby, 2013: n.p.).

Over to you ...

Find out more about the PISA survey by visiting the website at http://www.oecd.org/pisa/
Use the menus provided or the search function to explore:

- 'About PISA' – see 'What the assessment involves'
- PISA products – check out the 'Test questions'
- 'Key findings' – use the menu provided to look at the rankings by country/economy

The most recently published results available at the time of writing are from the fifth survey in 2012 undertaken by sixty-five countries and economies. The 2012 survey involved approximately 510,000 students aged between fifteen years and three months and sixteen years and two months. The focus of the 2012 survey was mathematics, which the OCED (2014: 6) claims is 'a strong predictor of positive outcomes for young adults, influencing their ability to participate in post-secondary education and their expected future earnings'. The 2012 results (2014) show Shanghai in China topped all three of the PISA rankings in reading, mathematics and science, with Hong Kong and Singapore ranking second and third, respectively. The East Asian countries of Japan, Taiwan and South Korea are unfailingly just beneath those at the top. In previous surveys Finnish students have consistently performed well in the PISA tests, coming out top overall and hence attracting the attention of policy-makers across the globe (Helle and Klemelä, 2010). In 2012 Finland was fifth in reading and sixth in science, but its drop from sixth place for mathematics in 2009 to twelfth in 2012 caused its national media to conclude the 'Finnish school system has collapsed' (Sahlberg, 2013). The performance of students in England, Scotland, Northern Ireland and Wales places the UK 'among the average, middle-ranking countries' (Sahlberg, 2013), although Welsh students are below the OECD average in all three subjects. Regarding the performance of students in reading, the 2012 results placed the UK at twenty-third which is a marginal improvement on its twenty-fifth place in 2009. However, the UK rankings for reading in 2006 were seventeenth and seventh in 2000. In Mathematics the UK is positioned twenty-sixth, slightly higher than the twenty-eighth place in 2009, but in 2006 it was placed twenty-fourth and eighth in 2000. In science the trend for the UK is downwards, to twenty-first place in 2012, down from sixteenth in 2009, fourteenth in 2006 and fourth in 2000.

Inevitably the results for the UK caused some wrangling among MPs of different political parties and comments from the various teaching unions as to whose education policies are to blame (Coughlan, 2013). However, the PISA rankings should be read with caution. Meyer and Benavot (2013: 9) examine the role of PISA and suggest 'PISA's dominance in the global educational discourse runs the risk of engendering an unprecedented process of worldwide educational standardization'. Yet the PISA survey and the data produced are highly esteemed internationally, and so despite the emphasis on and investment in education by current and former UK governments, this external and very public evaluation of the 'national' system(s) does not bode well for policy-makers.

Over to you ...

Locate and read the letter from academics from around the world written to Dr. Andreas Schleicher, the director of the Programme of International Student Assessment. The letter, published in *The Guardian* on 6 May 2014, expresses concern regarding 'the negative consequences of the Pisa rankings' and its 'deficits and problems'.

See http://www.theguardian.com/education/2014/may/06/oecd-pisa-tests-damaging-education-academics.

1 What arguments are put forward to support their concerns?
2 In your opinion, are these justified?
3 What do you regard as the relative strengths and limitations of evaluating education systems worldwide by assessing the knowledge and skills of fifteen-year-old students?

Locate and read the article by Sean Coughlan (2013), 'UK makes no progress in Pisa tests':
See http://www.bbc.co.uk/news/education-25187998.

1 What does the analysis suggest about (a) the UK's investment in education and (b) a policy that has unqualified teachers in the classroom?
2 Do you agree or disagree with the view 'the danger in the exaggerated importance that politicians attach to Pisa, is that implicitly they are pushing the world to a narrow and particular view of education'?

The OECD engages in educational standard setting in what is known as 'educational multilateralism' (Mundy, 1998). Standard setting in education is thus elevated beyond the nation state, and, as Resnick (2006) shows, member governments of the OECD increasingly view the relationship between education and the economy in new ways. From a neo-Marxist perspective these multilateral organizations are viewed as 'instruments of Western neoimperialism' (Mundy, 1998: 449) in the global spread of educational policies and practices. Hurst's (1981) analysis unpacks the contradictions and conflicts associated with multilateralism as understood by neo-Marxists as well as those taking a more liberal perspective. A neo-Marxist interpretation surrounds 'power, knowledge and wealth [whereby] "aid" is used by the rich to pacify or exploit the poor' (Hurst, 1981: 120). Thus, neo-Marxists would argue there is gain by some and loss by others. A liberal perspective, however, would emphasize the social welfare foundations of these international organizations, including the United Nations Children's Fund (UNICEF), so that poorer nations can become wealthier without impairing the rich. Thus, the liberal view regards aid as the vehicle by which the rich utilize their wealth and knowledge to assist the poor and ignorant.

A key issue for this chapter therefore is unravelling to what extent globalization and/or global factors affect, influence and shape national education policies and the consequences for national education systems. In order to do so, the notions of policy-borrowing and policy-learning are explored.

'Policy-borrowing' and 'policy-learning'

From the 1980s onwards greater emphasis has been given to economic competitiveness by nation states worldwide. Governments, most notably those of Westernized countries, have simultaneously prioritized national economic needs and aligned the aims of their education system with the perceived needs of their country's economy and in relation to the development of human capital (see Chapter 7). The New Public Management (Hood, 1995; Ferlie et al., 1996) emerged in the public services of the Westernized world as an organizing mechanism as governments pursued and continued to strive for enhanced efficiency, quality and performance in order to become more economically competitive in the global marketplace. 'New' managerialism emerged due to an increased concern with service quality and measurable outcomes (Pollitt, 1993; Zifcak, 1994) as did a culture of 'performativity'; these global phenomena (Yeatman, 1994) have infiltrated and saturated societies. As a direct consequence, national governments have actively restructured their education systems in the pursuit of greater efficiency and effectiveness, often identifying what they perceive to be similar weaknesses in their systems and similar sets of problems (Halpin and Troyna, 1995). As a means of improving their own provision of education, national governments may look beyond their own system and towards educational ideas and 'policy solutions' in operation elsewhere. This kind of activity has duly accelerated the trend of cross-national education policy-borrowing (Halpin and Troyna, 1995). However, policy-borrowing of this kind is not a recent phenomenon. For example, a reading of the parliamentary debates leading up to the 1870 Elementary Education Act provides evidence of UK policy-makers looking towards the education systems of Germany and the United States, for example, for policy ambitions (Hansard, 1870).

Phillips (2011) examines the nature of policy-borrowing in terms of the process of educational transfer between nations, arguing that this can take different forms and, as such, postulates a 'spectrum of educational transfer'. This is a five-point spectrum, ranging from 'Imposed', which Phillips identifies as the totalitarian or authoritarian 'post-conflict occupation of or political domination of one country by another', through to 'Introduced through Influence' – a general influence of educational ideas and methods (Phillips, 2011: 4). It is this latter element of the spectrum along with the penultimate element, 'Borrowed Purposefully', signifying the 'intentional copying of policy/practice observed elsewhere' (Phillips, 2011: 4), which is of particular relevance to this chapter. Particular 'cases' which provide different examples of purposeful borrowing will now be examined in turn.

Cases of purposeful policy-borrowing

Dale and Ozga (1993) undertook a comparative study of the impact of 1980s education reform in New Zealand and in England and Wales. They point out that New Right thinking (see Chapters 1 and 3) influenced the decision-making in policy at the time; in other words, there is some ideological similarity underpinning the policies of these nations. This can be seen, for example, in the measures taken in New Zealand and in England and Wales to devolve more power to schools (decentralization) and facilitate greater consumer choice. However, the respective policies exhibit clear differences since policies in England and Wales display a tendency towards both the neo-liberal and neo-conservative strands of New Right thinking. This is evidenced in particular policies stemming from the 1988 ERA for England and Wales such as LMS, which resonates with the neo-liberal strand, and the National Curriculum, which has its roots in neo-conservatism. However, in New Zealand, there is less emphasis on neo-conservatism which 'played little, if any, part' (1993: 85) and more attention is given to 'the role of the state and of public administration, informed by particular strands of neo-liberal thought' (1993: 85). Thus, while New Right ideology might be considered a general influencing force here, which was advanced by globalizing tendencies, it must be realized that there are differential effects which are mediated through national (and local) contexts and cultures in what Ball (1993) regards as 'localised complexity'. The way in which a particular influence might be received at the national level can therefore create a significant divergence of policy.

In contrast to the previous case, David (1993) discusses policy convergence between US and UK school systems and illustrates the clear parallels between the countries in the 1980s; the United States and the UK suffered from common economic weaknesses and lacked competitiveness in world markets. Both countries recognized the need for a better-skilled and educated workforce while embracing the neo-liberal tenets of marketization and identifying similar flaws in their school systems, such as weak organizational structures and insufficiently accountable 'trendy' teachers (see Chapter 4). David (1993) also points out that successive US administrations and UK governments acknowledged and addressed these limitations in their education systems in comparable ways through a combination of deregulation on the one hand and greater central prescription on the other. Both governments shared an analogous 'crisis' in education, a similar view of the state's role in improving education and policy solutions which fell under the umbrella of 'choice' and diversity (Edwards and Whitty, 1992). Examples of education policy convergence can be seen in the early 1990s between the magnet schools of the United States and the privately sponsored CTCs in the UK (Walford, 2000). Also there are similarities between the Grant-Maintained Schools in England, schools that opted out of LEA control and finance following the 1988 ERA, and the emergence of the USA charter schools, which followed in the early 1990s (Wohlstetter and Anderson, 1994). Occurrences of transatlantic policy-borrowing and policy-learning are thus clearly illustrated by these examples.

However, the straightforward parallels within education policy between the United States and the UK being presented here can be somewhat misleading; a more comprehensive analysis of this particular case reveals areas of policy divergence. Halpin and Troyna (1995), for example, note that, as in the case of New Zealand, US policies have more of a neo-liberal than neo-conservative emphasis. They maintain the reforms of 1980s in the United States around school choice as well as being a New Right ideal were promoted by the Liberal Left to accentuate parental involvement as well as redress historical educational disadvantage. This is quite different from the UK, where the sway of the political Right essentially brought about a consolidation of fundamental inequalities of educational opportunity and social inequity through its parental choice policies (Gewirtz et al., 1995) (see Chapter 3). Also, neo-conservatism is more apparent in the UK, where successive Conservative governments took steps to prescribe a mandated National Curriculum and weaken the control of LEAs in order to standardize and centralize control over education. Conversely, the control of education in the United States lies at the state level, with local, federal government having much greater involvement in decision-making and very little change is driven from the centre. Thus, there is likely to be diversity between the states in the United States.

A further illustrative case is the introduction by the former New Labour government of Threshold Assessment. This is a form of performance-related pay which was introduced for school teachers in England and Wales in the late 1990s (DfEE, 1999b,c). This form of remuneration restructured the pay scales of teachers in England and Wales as movement through the main pay scale on to an upper pay scale (post-threshold) became dependent upon performance. Thus, there is a much greater emphasis on performativity in schools (Forrester, 2005). Threshold standards to measure effective performance were developed by the management consultants Hay McBer (DfEE, 2000a). These relate to teachers on the main professional grade and formed part of the professional competence framework of National Standards[1] already devised for the teaching profession (TTA, 1997, 1998a,b). Threshold Assessment was eventually embedded into a system of performance management, which was introduced into all maintained schools in England and Wales in 2000 (DfEE, 2000b). Performance management is, in essence, a strategic managerial tool which originates from the private sector, although it has been drawn on by the public sector as an audit mechanism for monitoring and measuring with the aim of improving public services. Since the 1980s governments in the UK and other parts of Westernized world – namely Australia, New Zealand and the United States – have adopted performance management as a mechanism to rectify perceived inadequacies of their public sectors. Performance management was thus presented to teachers in England and Wales as 'the kind of system which is the norm across the public and private sectors' (Blunkett, 1999). There was seemingly no recognition by policy-makers, however, of the limitations of performance management (Forrester, 2011).

Threshold Assessment was introduced by New Labour for a number of reasons, purportedly to 'modernize' the profession (DfEE, 1998a), but also to address problems in the morale, recruitment and retention of teachers. These issues are not unique to the UK, but have been experienced in education systems around the world where significant policy pressure has been directed towards greater accountability of teachers as a means of improving teaching quality and student outcomes. Mahony and others' (2002) comparative study of England and Australia is just one which illustrates the similarities in the nature of these particular 'problems' and policy approaches. Their findings, however, exemplify the different approaches taken by governments citing the 'complex relationships between the Federal Government and the States' (2002: 160) as a fundamental reason for the different policy-making contexts. The confines of the chapter limit a fuller discussion here of the complexities of the English model of performance management, but taking the issue of 'standards' alone provides an enlightening illustration of policy convergence/divergence.

'Effective' teaching has been conceptualized in England and Wales through a set of professional standards. Arguably all of these standards require a great deal of monitoring. Teachers are required to demonstrate that these standards have been met and thus they place a form of control over teachers' work. Mahony and others (2002: 161) found the use of a '"common" language of educational policy' and 'vocabularies of accountability' in their comparative study. So 'standards', for example, is used conventionally in both. The nature of 'standards' in Australia, however, is understood as teachers monitoring themselves for purposes associated with their own personal development needs, hence a completely different emphasis to the way in which 'standards' are comprehended in the United Kingdom. Mahony and others (2002: 162) conclude, 'This is an instance where identical language means very different things. Alternatively language and discourse may proclaim distance from, and indeed rejection of, a particular policy trend whilst implementing very similar procedures under different guises.' Australian participants in Mahony and others' (2002: 162) study explained the 'occupational impossibility' of implementing in their context the English model of performance management and threshold standards. Nevertheless, the permeation of policy ideas of this nature is promulgated often through the activities of major and influential consultancy firms, such as Hay McBer, mentioned above, and also the likes of McKinsey & Company and PricewaterhouseCoopers, who are significant and influential players internationally.

So while Mahony and others' (2002) comparative study provides an indication of some homogeneity, there is also evidence of differentiation; it is not the case that 'one-size-fits-all'. While discussing the Australian case here, it is interesting to note, as an aside, that the grade of Advanced Skills Teacher (AST), which was incorporated into the education system in England and Wales in 1998, originates from Australia. The AST policy was aimed at attracting and retaining excellent teachers in the classroom, as opposed to them leaving the classroom to take on management duties within their school, with a focus on developing classroom expertise. The notion of 'expert teacher' is found elsewhere in the world as well, such as in the status of the Master Teacher (Singapore), Advanced Classroom Expertise Teacher (New Zealand) and Chartered Teacher (Scotland), and this demonstrates how international policies share common policy understandings. O'Neill (1995: 9) contends this is 'the new orthodoxy' that represents a shift in the relationship between politics, government and education. The consequences are, as the above cases illustrate, global similarities and local differences.

A recent example of policy-borrowing can be seen in the creation of Free Schools in England. The idea for Free Schools emanates from the USA Charter Schools and, more emphatically, from a Swedish model known as *friskolor*. Free Schools should not be confused with the freedom-based education based on democratic principles and offered by, for example, the White Lion School in London, Summerhill in Suffolk or the Scotland Road Free School in Liverpool (see Chapter 10). The recently created Free Schools in England was a flagship initiative of the Conservative-Liberal Democrat Coalition, although it is often associated more with the Conservative Party and, in particular, Michael Gove, who championed their introduction. Gove was forthright in exclaiming that to develop its education policies the government would 'shamelessly plunder from – policies that have worked in other high-performing nations' (Gove, 2012). Gove's (2011) aims for the Free Schools programme in England can be discerned as raising attainment, creating additional school places where there were not enough and, if established in socially deprived areas, reducing inequality. The programme embodies the Big Society agenda (see Chapter 3), whereby 'the demand-led character of free school policy will grant a greater role to civil society in the delivery of public services' (Higham, 2014: 137).

Free Schools came into being in England via the 2010 Academies Act and are an extension of the Academies Programme. Free Schools are funded centrally and, unlike their Swedish counterpart, they are 'not-for-profit' schools, and, as such, there is some policy divergence here. The majority of Free Schools in Sweden are profit-making and are private; they belong to chains and are owned and operated by companies (Ball, 2013). They were introduced in the early 1990s as Sweden moved away from a highly centralized system to one where local municipalities could take control of education provision. Inspired by the free market ideals of Milton Friedman, the Swedes introduced a voucher system (see Chapter 5) whereby parents choose the school for their child/children; funding then follows the child/children. Free Schools in England are independent and centrally funded (so they are state schools, not private ones) and thus sit outside the supervision of local authorities. They have autonomy over staff pay and conditions, budgets, curriculum, the school year (term times) and can employ unqualified teachers. They can be proposed; established; and run by groups of parents, teachers, charities, businesses, universities, trusts, religious and voluntary groups and, according to government, can 'set up in response to real demand [i.e. from parents] within a local area for a greater variety of schools' (DfE, 2011e). Once again, it can be seen how policy-makers give propensity to the education market through greater choice and diversity, which is premised on the idea that standards will improve 'through competition amongst schools offering diversity of pedagogical approaches and ethos' (Allen, 2015: R36).

It is too early in the English Free Schools trajectory to determine the effectiveness, popularity or wholesale impact of this high-profile policy-borrowing venture. Nevertheless, there is some merit in examining how Free Schools in Sweden have panned out, particularly in relation to raising attainment, creating additional school places and reducing inequality – which are essentially the aims of the Free Schools' policy for England. First, regarding raising attainment, evidence suggests Free Schools in Sweden are expensive and the learning gains insignificant overall (Wiborg, 2010; Weale, 2015). The director general of the Swedish National

Agency for Education forewarned that Free Schools had 'not led to better results' in Sweden, but their success was linked to the 'better backgrounds' of the pupils who attended (Shepherd, 2010). While the media has reported on their success (Munkhammar, 2007), Sweden's PISA scores have declined in each survey from 2000. The 'plummet' down the tables in all subjects has been more rapid than any other participating country, and has taken Sweden from about average in 2000 to significantly below average by 2012 (Weale, 2015). This has raised questions about the 'political failure' of the education market in Sweden, particularly the involvement of private companies which 'has opened the door for schools more interested in making a profit than providing education' (2015). Free Schools in England are promoted by policy-makers as providing diversification in the education market, which will encourage competition in order to 'improve quality and responsiveness' (Higham, 2014: 137). English Free Schools have received varied Ofsted school inspection reports so far, and many have been graded 'good' or 'outstanding'. Rather ominously, however, some have already been put into special measures, identified as 'inadequate' or 'requires improvement' or forced to close (Garner, 2014; Guardian, 2014). Allen's (2015: R36) analysis of Coalition policy is thus a reminder of the inherent workings of the market, whereby 'Resulting educational disruption through entry and exit of schools from the market should be hailed as a success rather than a cause for concern'. While it is difficult to ascertain the extent to which Free Schools may have influenced Sweden's diminishing PISA scores, they 'have played an indirect role' (Wiborg, quoted in Weale 2015). The market idea and school independence has created a fragmented system and there is speculation that Sweden's central government may take back the running of schools from municipalities (Adams, 2013). The second issue to consider relates to the expansion of provision. Free Schools in England were devised to provide more school places, which were needed due to an increase in the birth rate, which has been rising since 2002, resulting in increases in primary-aged children from 2010. Projected pupil numbers in maintained nursery and primary schools are projected to increase by 9 per cent between 2014 and 2023 (DfE, 2015). In due course, these children will move into secondary schools, where numbers are projected to increase from 2015 (2015). However, a recent critical report noted 'applications for new Free Schools are not emerging from areas of greatest forecast need for more and better school places' (House of Commons 2014: 1), and, additionally, they had attracted fewer pupils than planned and thus had unfilled places. The first twenty-four Free Schools opened in September 2011. By September 2013 there were 174 Free Schools, providing education for approximately 24,000 pupils, but which fell somewhat short of the almost 82,000 places these schools could provide (2014). Under the Coalition 254 Free Schools were opened and the Conservative government is encouraging the development of a further 500, which will create 270,000 school places (Morgan, 2015). There are 800 Free Schools in Sweden, but now their backing seems to be waning. Due to the present condition of education in Sweden, fewer businesses are prepared to open new schools, approval rates are declining and banks are hesitant about lending money (Weale, 2015). The third issue to explore regards the role of Free Schools in reducing inequality, but evidence suggests Free Schools in Sweden increased social segregation and inequality (Wiborg, 2010). Sweden's education minister recently pronounced, 'Instead of breaking up social differences and class differences in the education system, we have a system today that's creating a wider gap between the ones that have and the ones that have not' (Fridolin quoted in Weale, 2015: n.p.). A quantitative study by Green and others (2015) which explores the first three years of Free School intakes in England suggests they are set up in areas where there is less social disadvantage and 'are socially selective within their neighbourhoods'. Their findings acknowledge that few Free Schools exist, have very small cohorts and recruit from 'very dispersed areas' (2015). Nevertheless, they show that the social composition of secondary Free Schools is comparable with the national average; however, in primary Free Schools children enrol with above-average ability. The researchers note 'very substantive differences between the ethnic composition of Free Schools and other schools', but find that little evidence of 'the presence of Free Schools is having an effect on the social composition of intakes to other schools in their neighbourhoods or on segregation in the local authority as a whole'. So, while it may be too early to ascertain their impact, nonetheless, Free Schools exemplify the current policy trajectory towards the privatization of education and self-governing schools.

'Policy networks' and 'policy entrepreneurs'

It has been established in this chapter that countries may observe other educational systems to see 'what works' elsewhere and may sometimes 'borrow' particular aspects of policy and practice either purposefully and intentionally or through their general influence and permeation (Phillips, 2011). However, it is quite difficult to fathom out just how the process of observing or establishing what works in one place and the ultimate decision to borrow policy actually takes place in reality. It is not necessarily a smooth and straightforward transfer of ideas from one place to another, and it invariably involves a network of people who mediate policy in some way. Typically, the people in the network may be disparate and unknown to each other as their involvement and participation in the process may not be explicit or directly connected; they could be operating in different ways and even with a different set of not necessarily connected agendas. Nevertheless, what their involvement brings to the process, along with their unique set of knowledge, experiences, contacts, motivations and so on, could serve to influence the development of policy in a particular way. As such, it is quite tricky to disentangle the kind of activity and uncover the relationships within networks in order to comprehend exactly what is involved in the making of policy. As has been discussed earlier in this chapter, motivations for countries being attracted to the educational approaches and methods of others can differ considerably. What is a most fascinating area to research, but is often a very difficult, almost impossible, endeavour is to try and uncover who is actually involved in the observing and facilitation of policy-borrowing, policy-learning and policy-making and how this actually takes place. So, for example, it might be that, aware of a particularly effective or successful development in education, politicians and/or policy-makers and/or educational practitioners and/or academics make a scheduled international visit elsewhere. This may be with the deliberate intention of witnessing that development in action and to ascertain its suitability as a potential remedy to a particular national policy 'problem'. Or it could be that similar ideas are fermenting at different national levels, but the success of a particular policy in one country provides sufficient evidence for mutual endorsement from ministers or policy-makers in another to implement the policy in their own country. Deeper analysis of these kinds of scenarios uncovers a level of activity that is often invisible and so usually difficult to attribute.

Drawing on the case of the creation of the National College for School Leadership (NCSL)[2] in England, the intention here is to provide a clearer insight into the somewhat murky waters of policy-making, which often obscures its complexities, and reveal ways in which policy might be shaped and enacted. The decision by the former New Labour government to establish the NCSL was initially fuelled by policy-makers' desire to improve school leadership in England. Improving the quality of school leadership was seen by policy-makers in the late 1990s as the solution to a number of 'perceived' problems in education, and, the argument went that, improving the quality of leadership would ultimately raise standards in schools. The prevailing discourse was that 'effective' school leadership could not be left to 'chance', but required regulated training and the meeting of national standards (Gunter and Forrester, 2008a). Evidence for the setting up of a National College came from home and, significantly for purposes of this chapter, from abroad. The Harvard Principal Centre in the United States, for example, was regarded as a model of good practice, and caught the attention of some of those indirectly involved in influencing the decision to create the NCSL. Additionally, the New Labour government sought advice and assistance from particular educational 'experts' based in the United States, Australia and Canada. Gunter and Forrester's (2009: 496) findings illuminate the interplay between 'a range of agents who are actively and variously involved in the development and enactment of policy'. The label of 'agent' is used explicitly to signify a catalytic role involving mediation, facilitation and/or negotiation. Gunter and Forrester (2008b) examined the aims and strategies of New Labour's policy-making specifically in relation to its policies for school leaders and school leadership. They identified a complex set of contributing factors, which ultimately led to the decision to create the NCSL. Interviews with twenty-eight ministers, civil servants, policy advisors and private consultants who were directly involved in the construction and implementation of this decision uncovered a 'school leadership policy network' (Gunter and Forrester, 2008a: 144). Significantly, the research revealed aspects of the policy-making process that are hardly ever discussed or written about. As a means of illustrating an area of activity that is not usually made public, the comments of a consultant are presented below. This particular consultant, who operated internationally, spoke about 'facilitating' the policy-making process. This consultant, arguably an individual carrier of policy, divulged the nature of their 'connecting' and 'networking' activities as a consultant advisor:

> Brokers is the most recent expression around this sort of stuff; boundary riders. I don't think it's a set of roles that has been explored, perhaps as much as it might, but part of the reason is because it's not a set of activities that are always well understood, because by definition, 'success' means that it's less visible, deliberately so. It is highly tactical, so therefore it's of a different order. And, to be at the sharp end of it, it practises some arts that are not ones that people necessarily want to reveal. Right. So it's a funny game to be in. (2008a: 155)

The extract above illustrates the more subtle and enigmatic roles within the processes of policy-making, policy-learning and policy-borrowing. Gunter and Forrester (2008a,b) ascertained the networks and/or constructed networks and interconnections between the various 'policy entrepreneurs' who played a key role in the development and establishment of the NCSL. The activities and contributions of some people involved were sometimes intentional, categorical and forthright; the activities and involvement of others, however, were sometimes more subtle, inadvertent and fortuitous. Nevertheless, the policy entrepreneurs who made up this particular network (nationally and internationally) revealed their 'harmonized dispositions regarding neo-liberal reforms' (Gunter and Forrester, 2009: 354). Their assorted roles and positions, ideas, experiences, strategies and personal connections (i.e. people and organizations who they themselves were connected to nationally and internationally) helped to influence, shape and adapt this policy in a particular way.

Another strand of the same project provides further insight into a particular feature of policy influences and involved interviews with sixty-three academics[3] (Gunter and Forrester, 2008b). Some have been identified as 'experts' by policy-makers and their advice and opinions officially sought by national government, and by international governments in some cases, on issues relating to school leadership as well as a range of other education-related matters. These particular academics are revered by UK policy-makers as 'legitimate knowers' (Gunter and Forrester, 2010:

56) and are invited, periodically or through a secondment, into the Department, the National College or to various Select Committees, for example. Some also engage at the international level, working in an advisory capacity for other governments across the globe and/or with multilateral organizations, notably the OECD, UNESCO and UNICEF. As such, they are in a position to utilize their 'expert' position via a range of advisory activities, which may influence national and international education policies in some way. An academic explained their individual situation:

> I try to position myself as somebody who works within policy and tries to influence it by, at times, offering a critique, but a critique which tries to stay within the environment where you can actually be talking to the people who are making policy and implementing policy. So that's the dangerous collaborating game that I'm involved in, in a way, because inevitably it requires compromises. ... my argument would be that if I took an extreme view of whatever policy it is ... then I know the policy-makers won't even invite me to the discussion. ... Now I think people like myself and others who work with me; by and large we get invited. And then we try to work out how can we influence a thing to achieve the kind of things that we are committed with ... the downside of being inside is that you can collude. And indeed you can be used. ... It's a risky game. (Forrester and Gunter, 2009: 13)

Academic 'experts', thus, may also contribute to the development of policy ideas. As the extract from the academic above demonstrates, there is a game to be played and personal motivations may include utilizing their 'expert' position to affect their core educational purpose(s); they influence education policy via advisory activities in a significant way in order to bring about the kind of changes they believe to be required.

The case of the creation of the NCSL thus serves to illustrate the workings of an intertwined web of international and national influences and individuals, which culminated in the inimitable making and implementation of policy. Significantly, the establishment of the NCSL in England sparked a great deal of interest overseas, with delegations of inquisitive international observers coming over to Nottingham to visit the college. Equally important, policy-makers from around the globe looking for solutions to their own perceived problems in education watched closely to see what was happening in England. The NCSL was established by policy-makers, as a non-departmental public body, in response to, and as an antidote for, a particular set of 'perceived' problems in the English education system. A decade or so on from its creation, the NCSL was promoting on its website its role as a 'unique' college 'dedicated' to the professional development of school leaders and its work as a national and international 'benchmark for excellence in leadership development'. Its website housed a multitude of publications regarding 'up-to-date research on current practice'. Increasingly, the college was acting in a consultancy capacity to advise international governments on strategic approaches to school leadership and thus prominent in influencing the thinking and practice of school leadership globally. In

April 2012 NCSL became an executive agency of the DfE. It was called the National College for Teaching and Leadership in April 2013 following its merger with the Teaching Agency. The resources and research developed by NSCL are now accessible online via The National Archives.

The extent to which international governments utilize and adopt the thinking and practice billowing from the college in their own systems is, of course, likely to vary. As has been illustrated above, any adoption of such ideas will be mediated through individual local contexts and cultures. The case of the college, however, demonstrates how the outcome of one national policy can have far-reaching implications globally. Policy-borrowing and learning is not a straightforward activity, and all kinds of agendas may be at play, which impact and reconcile the making of policy. It is not the case of the 'smooth highway' and an easy transfer of policy from one context to another. For, as Dale (1999: 2) suggests, 'globalization cannot be reduced to the identical imposition of the same policy on all countries'.

The penetrating influences of globalization and global processes discussed at the beginning of this chapter, however, cannot be overlooked, for education policy-learning and borrowing sit within the broader framework of global economic restructuring, global competition, political uncertainties and social change. The chapter has shown how 'globalization' is an inexact term with shifting definitions. It is not a linear, consistent or homogenous process, though it is extremely complex and there are different theories of globalization within the literature. Nevertheless, an appreciation of the effects of globalization enables us to understand more fully education systems and their relationship to society as a whole. Globalization affects national education systems as has been seen from the case illustrations provided; there is an intersection between global politics and the national education policy-making. Henry and others (2008: 58) note:

> The political, cultural and economic configurations of globalization do not deny a space for national policy making – far from it – but they have certainly altered the setting within which national governments establish their policy priorities. They have added new layers to the processes of policy production.

There are global similarities in terms of policy problems and solutions; and so instances of convergence can sometimes be seen. Supranational agencies and international consultancy firms, strongly committed to neo-liberal ideologies and educational priorities, are ardent advocates of the market logic and performance indicators in education. These agencies, along with consultants, academics, experts and researchers, play a significant part in influencing and fuelling a 'global policy paradigm' (Ball, 1999: 199) that legitimates the convergence of economic and education functions in a global context. However, their capacity to enforce policy direction and decisions should not be overestimated, for while there are developments and reforms in education systems, which are connected to the effects of globalization, there are local differences and points of resistance, which lead to divergence. Policy-makers are also operating within similar frames of reference, and so while there may appear to be parallel policies between nations, it is not always the case that one has simply borrowed from the other. Thus, the 'lending' and 'borrowing' of policy, along with the 'teaching of' and 'learning from' policy, can be a very complex process to unravel.

Notes

1   National standards for the teaching profession are in place at entry to the profession (Qualified Teacher Status and Induction), movement through the performance threshold for main scale teachers, and for leadership (advanced skills teacher and head teachers).

2   The National College for School Leadership was opened in Nottingham in 2000. It was set up to provide a range of accredited training opportunities for head teachers and teachers with leadership roles and also identify, fund and promote leadership-related research. The college building cost £28 million (NCSL, 2002). In April 2013, the National College merged with the Teaching Agency to become the National College for Teaching and Leadership.

3   These were mostly professors of education who work, or have previously worked, in various UK universities and through their research and scholarly activities were involved in the creation of knowledge about educational/school leadership.

Further reading

Ball, S. J. (2012) *Global Education Inc.: New Policy Networks and the Neoliberal Imaginary*, Abingdon, Oxon: Routledge.

Burbules, N. and C. Torres, eds (2000) *Globalization and Education: Critical Perspectives*, London: Routledge.

Elliott, G., C. Fourali and S. Issler, eds (2010) *Education and Social Change: Connecting Local and Global Perspectives*, London: Continuum.

Rizvi, F. and B. Lingard (2010) *Globalizing Education Policy*, Abingdon, Oxon: Routledge.

Sheilds, R. (2013) *Globalization and International Education*, London: Bloomsbury Academic.

10

Possibilities for Education Policy

Unravelling policy

The title of this book *Education Policy Unravelled* is an interesting one, for it can be read as signifying several different things simultaneously. One meaning implies that at heart its purpose is to undo, take apart or disassemble education policy in order to reveal important features and characteristics about content and political formation. Another is that, to the best of our ability, we have endeavoured to provide a lens, or a set of theoretical lenses, to make clear the often complex trajectories and interrelationships between policy and practice, illuminate important perspectives and further appreciate the nuances of policy-making over time. A third and equally significant point is that in writing this book we have attempted to separate or disentangle some of the threads that constitute an intricately woven tapestry of themes resting upon broader social, political and economic movements such as neo-liberalism and globalization. In the end, we may have *unravelled* (i.e. come undone) in our attempt to unravel some of the complexities involved in education policy-making, but if we have then it is surely because education policy is constantly evolving, in a continuous flow of change and quickly becoming dated as new initiatives and developments come to the fore.

Futures perspectives

It is thus on the theme of transition and social change that we wish to proceed in this final chapter. Until now, we have dealt with a broad range of substantive issues relating to a variety of policy-making themes, including race, identity and citizenship in the context of education for improvement or control, social justice, primary education, early years, post-compulsory education, the economics of education, inclusive schools and globalization. In each case we have attempted to chart the continuity of policy development along neo-liberal lines, taking an historical perspective and moving towards the current Conservative government, in the process drawing attention to the strong similarities and nuanced disagreements between successive modern governments. The accounts have been largely factual and analytical even if expressed from a keenly critical perspective of policy-making, aiming to challenge the status quo. However, we now wish to take our analysis further, by invoking a futures perspective that allows us to project somewhat speculatively beyond the 'here' and 'now' towards a number of possibilities to develop education policy in the future. Such analysis will not be based upon what some have referred to as 'hard-futures research' (Leaton Gray, 2006), drawing heavily upon the empiricist tradition of quasi-positivist studies and using hard quantitative data to predict accurately and further forecast the outlook for the future. Neither will we be soliciting or otherwise surveying the opinions of policy-making stakeholders to relate our expectations and possibilities for the future of education policy-making and practice. Rather, we intend to be entirely conjectural but also visionary in a way that aligns with what has been termed 'soft-futures research' (2006), where ideas about the future, deriving from empirical data, are often more radical, complex and multiple in nature. In our case, however, 'data' are contained in the discourse of policy texts and discursive practices that ritually impact educational structures, cultures and potential futures. As Leaton Gray (2006: 144) explains,

> The new futures methodology has grown out of a desire to move debate beyond the superficial and obvious … in a new way, taking into account the social environments of the researcher as well as the subject. In the case of educational research, this is very important. Deciding who is privileged in any construction of knowledge allows us to see who is making assumptions about right and wrong … Good citizens are seen to be those who appear to understand why government policy is necessary and who respond by changing themselves in order to implement it, either directly or indirectly. Bad individuals are silenced within this discourse, however. Playing with ideas we might decide that examples of the silences might vary.

In the spirit of seeking new possibilities and opening up the discourse, we may be regarded 'bad' but fully embrace the term in the interest of showing alternative pathways and trajectories for future policy-making. Conceptually, this plays to the idea of 'undoing' perspectives on education policy but in a way that resists simple reconciliation. Ambiguities and tensions abound in the various threads of policy we have identified throughout and are, indeed, important aspects we would wish to retain, or at least avoid ironing out. For us, such tensions convey dissonance and dissensus rather than broad agreement, suggesting further that there can be no philosophical resolution to the question of how best policy can be formed in the context of the areas we have analysed. This means that imaginative leaps of speculative new ideas, while in one sense improbable, and possibly far-fetched, can usefully serve to disturb and dislocate contemporary policy. In this, we produce a more radical critique of the assumptions underpinning its social and political structures and institutional functioning. We turn now to consider the political context in which we rehearse an alternative model of social justice through Amartya Sen's capabilities approach, before considering a range of more radical possibilities for a futures perspective on education policy, drawing on the work of Steiner, Neill, Dewey, Illich and Freire.

Political context

A recurring theme throughout the book is the spectre of neo-liberalism, a modern regime infiltrating education policy at every conceivable level since the early 1970s, gathering momentum during the 1980s, resurfacing through the reign of New Labour and permeating both the former Coalition and current Conservative governments' policy-making. Successive modern governments have placed a premium on the health of the domestic economy and its ability to compete internationally in a fiercely intense global market. Rightly or wrongly, probably since the mid-1970s, following James Callaghan's speech at Ruskin College Oxford, education has been publicly framed as a panacea for the ills of the economy, and further regarded an important mechanism through which competitive advantage is gained as a means to secure future prosperity. However, this has come at a price – the opportunity cost of which is arguably human development. Unfettered instrumentalism has transformed the process of education into a capitalist mode of production, from which *human* commodities emerge through the acquisition and application of human capital. Human capital theory dating back to the mid-1960s (Becker, 1964) conveys the idea that human knowledge and skills rather than physical machinery or technological advancement will provide the necessary competitive edge in a powerful, economically driven knowledge economy. We need only reflect upon Chapter 7 and the current state of higher education to realize that the discourse of widening participation is often 'only concerned with the "desire to participate" and universities' recruitment strategies, rather than addressing the "ability to participate", once at university' (Crozier et al., 2010: 168). Again, this serves to reinforce the primacy of economics in the education policy-making equation, a formula through which various forms of measurement and audited credentials translate ultimately into human capital. However, an important question for us to consider is whether education policy-making should continue along this path or whether instead there is a contrasting vision of 'educational quality' which might otherwise lead to more desirable educational outcomes through 'ethical goal revision' (Walker, M., 2008)?

Social justice revisited

In Chapter 3, for example, we considered the theme of social justice in a variety of forms and different manifestations, including liberal-humanist, market-individualism and social-democratic perspectives. The liberal-humanist and social-democratic perspectives, in particular, convey a notion of justice along egalitarian lines, but still do not challenge the status quo as they variously attempt to find ways of creating policies and interventions to facilitate improved access, or remove barriers and/or produce new opportunities for disadvantaged groups. The purpose of distributive justice is a redistribution of resources or welfare to enhance or equalize opportunity and participation in the 'weak' sense or, alternatively, to equalize outcomes in the 'stronger' sense. What it does not do more fundamentally, however, is question the framework within which improved opportunities or outcomes are established in order to consider 'difference', and the particular freedoms that individuals have reasons to value.

This kind of theorizing has often been applied historically through the primary curriculum, where in Chapter 4 we noted a gradual and progressive centralization and colonization of primary education from the early 1970s onwards. In a climate of unprecedented reform, notions of social justice still prevailed but the introduction of a more disciplined structure to the curriculum, more heavily prescribed teaching styles and classroom pedagogy and a more clearly defined notion of pupil progress monitored through standardized assessment conspired to reduce choice all round. The National Curriculum was the centrepiece of the ERA (1988), which imposed, in turn, a severe restriction on what could be taught in schools and, more crucially, provided a definitive view on what counts as knowledge. As suggested in Chapter 2, the focus of the revised curriculum post-2014 raises questions about the legitimation of core/essential knowledge. As examined in Chapter 5, the creation of a curriculum for the EYFS, while dovetailing awkwardly with the primary curriculum, engenders 'school readiness' and accentuates the notion of 'schoolification' of the early years. In the spirit of a futures perspective, we now ask what early years and primary education might look like if such bureaucratically inspired and centrally driven restrictions were lifted, and if the voice of the younger generation was heard rather than muted, and their ideas usefully acted upon. Our starting point for this debate is the work of the economist and political philosopher Amartya Sen.

Sen's perspective on social justice is markedly different from all others, for his concept of equality of capability, articulated through a 'capabilities' approach to social justice, is based on the notion of opportunity freedoms, which place emphasis on the 'functionings' of individuals to 'be' and 'do': 'to choose the lives they have reasons to value. It is this actual freedom that is represented by the person's "capability" to achieve various alternative combinations of functionings' (Sen, 1992: 81). Put simply, this means that individuals are to be regarded as 'ends' in themselves, rather than as 'means' to other social and political ends, as noted, for example in Chapter 6 on post-compulsory education, where vocational education's overt policy aim is economic growth. This represents an interesting political shift because if individuals are to live not just free from constraint but with the possibility of acting upon real choices (what Berlin [1969] would call 'positive liberty'), then policy and process in education are likely to necessitate some reconfiguration and 'ethical goal revision' (Walker, M., 2008). In this revised context, then, educational processes would be required to countenance an evaluation of the conditions that individuals need in order to thrive and further enable their potential to be realized.

Five alternative philosophies

The suggestion for early years and primary education is to dispense with the model of a formal National Curriculum in order to adopt a more nuanced and progressive approach to education in children's formative years. The Steiner model ([1907] 1996) offers an alternative ideology, encouraging a unity of the mind, body and soul, and which is free from the shackles of the state and imposition of a centrally prescribed curriculum. However, even with such apparent extended freedoms (from constraint) there are significant limitations imposed through the particular requirements of a spiritual dimension. Accordingly, Steiner is neither child-centred nor freedom-based, but instead imposes a discipline through a structured curriculum and daily routine or rhythm related to the teaching of spirituality. In this crucial respect it parts company with the concept of a capabilities approach as advocated by Sen.

A different alternative model in the recent history of contemporary education, and one which departs radically from mainstream policy, is the democratic philosophy and practice of a school in Suffolk, Summerhill. Founded by A. S. Neill in 1924, Summerhill School focuses on securing the emotions of young people and their contentment both at school and across the life course. As Neill (1968: 20, 99) explains,

> We set out to make a school in which we should allow children to be themselves. In order to do this we had to renounce all discipline, all direction, all suggestion, all moral training, all religious instruction ... If the emotions are permitted to be really free, the intellect will look after itself.

We believe the democratic model of Summerhill has a great deal in common with Sen's capabilities approach, not least the emphasis placed upon individuals having particular freedoms to orient themselves around the things they have reasons to value. This offers the potential for what Neill refers to as 'inner contentment' and personal fulfilment. Moreover, the democratic ethos of Summerhill is a fundamental element of institutional and cultural life within the school, as exemplified through the 'Meeting' which takes place three or possibly four times per week and is held mainly in order 'to scrutinise breaches of the democratically agreed Laws' (Garratt and Piper, 2011: 77). In this, pupil voice is more than a rhetorical device; it is an essential characteristic of life within the school. However, since 'Summerhill School operates as a closed community' (2011: 78), we suggest that while in one sense it provides a propitious example of positive liberty it does little to bridge the gap between the individual and the social, young people and their local communities. It is our contention that the future of education policy should not be concerned exclusively with individual learning but should also nurture an ethical social disposition, as part of the ambit of living within an inclusive learning society.

To this end, we call upon a third example and the work of John Dewey ([1916] 2007) in *Democracy and Education*. For Dewey, school and community are not separate entities but rather different sides of the same coin of democracy, insofar as a democratic school is regarded the best preparation for a democratic society. Dewey also suggests that personal growth does not occur from what is already there but rather through a gradual expansion of experience according to the social and cultural environment into which young people are socialized. This means that learning amounts to more than a facile gathering of facts or simple acquisition of propositional knowledge; it is rather more concerned with experience and philosophical enquiry which provides important edification for ideas, meanings and values that allows the possibility for young people to develop socially and educationally. So, while 'thinking is as much an individual matter as is the digestion of food' ([1916] 2007: 223), such activity is socially and culturally embedded, for 'when the social factor is absent, learning becomes a carrying over of some presented material into a purely individual consciousness' ([1916] 2007: 222). Importantly, Dewey considers that the relegation of social interests to a traditionally academic curriculum is likely to produce a 'rupture of social continuity' ([1916] 2007: 238) and further forge a separation of 'practical and intellectual activity, man and nature, individuality and association, culture and vocation', culminating in the separation of 'knowing and doing, theory and practice, between mind as the end and spirit of action and the body as its organ and means' ([1916] 2007: 246). While the social dimension of education is undoubtedly important for Dewey, much like Sen his conception of learning is that it be structured around the interests of young people, through what he calls the 'instrument of effective self-direction' or learning by *doing*. This determination to avoid blueprints in learning does not, however, eclipse the crucial role of the teacher in the educational process, in helping children link their interests to sustained intellectual development and educative experiences. For us, a point of contention is what can be seen to count here as an educative experience and to what extent teachers may become involved in the process of determining what counts as knowledge – that is, what is considered legitimate and, alternatively, what is not.

Going still further, a fourth alternative example, which provides a more radical means to address the problem of closed communities and teacher indoctrination, is advanced through the work of Ivan Illich (1971). In his book *Deschooling Society* Illich assembles a compelling critique of the corrupting impact of institutions (i.e. schools) on young people, in particular their tendency to institutionalize myths about society. One such widely propagated 'myth' is that the 'imagination is "schooled" to accept service in place of value' (Illich, 1971: 9). As he elaborates further:

> Equal educational opportunity is ... both a desirable and a feasible goal, but to equate this with obligatory schooling is to confuse salvation with the Church. School has become the world religion of a modernized proletariat, and makes futile promises of salvation to the poor of the technological age ... neither learning nor justice is promoted by schooling because educators insist on packaging instruction with certification. (1971: 10–11)

This critique resonates strongly against the perspective presented in Chapters 4–8, in which we conveyed the impact of the neo-liberal regime upon contemporary policy and politics, and neat alignment with instrumental education and training. For Illich, the concept of learning is often confused and conflated with teaching, which carries with it ulterior motives and purposes. A relatively recent example of this is the development of the so-called 'free school' movement, which should not be confused with iconic historical examples like Summerhill or the Scotland Road Free School in Liverpool or White Lion School in London, which are/were affirmed on democratic principles and freedom-based education of a libertarian ilk. Rather, the new political movement of Free Schools in England, a programme which since its start-up in 2011 is estimated to have cost the DfE £1.1 billion by March 2014 (House of Commons, 2014), is reported by some as flattering to deceive. As Benn (2011) argues:

> Few among this first wave are truly parent-promoted projects, and nor are they likely to benefit the most deprived in our society. Instead this is an odd, hybrid movement that incorporates failing independent schools, diverse faith groups, and charitable educational groups ... the final irony may be that parents flood back to local schools as

the increasingly unattractive values of niche marketing, social snobbery and religious interests begin to take hold. Broad-based secular comprehensives that draw in families across the class, faith and ethnic spectrum, entirely free of private control, could hold a new appeal.

This resonates strongly with Illich's point that if we can deinstitutionalize education, then we may, in turn, be able to deinstitutionalize society and so dispel myths surrounding the neo-liberal agenda, in particular the trend to impose private interests and agendas (see, for example, Beckett, 2007) upon the educational needs of young people and/or the accumulation of qualifications in pursuit of human capital. Interestingly, Illich's philosophy offers the possibility of reinventing learning in ways that respect the capability freedoms of individuals (vis-a-vis Sen), but which also embraces a social policy dimension in connecting people through 'peer matching' and communication/learning networks, that is, where people list the skills they wish to acquire (what Illich calls 'skill exchanges') and find a match to work with, and learn from others in a collaborative fashion. A further dimension to Illich's book proffers that institutionalized education is a luxury good and that public funding should not be used to finance state education. While the current state system is some way off reaching this conclusion, the future of higher education in England is lurching ever nearer to this outcome. Annual student fees of up to £9,000 were reported to be the third highest in the developed world according to an OECD study of thirty-four countries (Vasagar and Shepherd, 2011), and the government's contribution to higher education in England was some two percentage points lower than the OECD average of 5.9 per cent of GDP (gross domestic product). This is serious in terms of the implications for social justice, and the fact that tuition fees are variable, some might say radically different, across the UK (see Chapters 1 and 7) raises a further question of equity in the process. Aside from the fact, this may well encourage young people to seek higher education elsewhere in Europe, in countries/ institutions where there are no fees, and thus become 'tuition tourists'. The global career and education network QS[1] provides a world-ranking list of universities. Tuition fees can be compared and the most recent ranking (2015/16) shows many of the top 200 universities globally have tuition fees of less than £9,000, the maximum threshold in the UK. The statutory tuition fees are €1,951 (approximately £1,412) in the Netherlands, and universities offer many undergraduate degree courses in English, such as the University of Amsterdam, ranked 55, and Utrecht University, ranked 94. There are numerous other attractively priced alternatives across Europe in Scandinavia, Switzerland and France, which offer competitively priced undergraduate programmes for students who, in each case, are able to speak the native language. Such alternatives outside the UK serve to underscore just how expensive HE has become in the UK, and in England more especially. Government policies thus can have major implications for individuals, institutions and nations. The fact remains there is a discernible ratcheting-up of fees and reduction in public funding of higher education in England, which is, arguably, limiting the capabilities of disadvantaged students while privileging those from more affluent backgrounds.

Thus, while we agree with the spirit of Illich's former point on deinstitutionalizing state education for appropriate normative reasons, we must part company with his argument that formal education is a luxury good, to be enjoyed (by default) only by a privileged minority, on important ethical grounds. Indeed, a further problem in the process of deinstitutionalizing education is that it has the potential to encourage prejudice and fanaticism among networks of like-minded individuals, to the detriment of the interests of other people and communities within society. Consider, for example, the thorny problem of citizenship education as noted in Chapter 2 and the historical absence of critical discourses around 'race' and ethnicity in education policy and practice at all levels engagement. To address this shortfall, we suggest education requires a different trajectory which might offer a more discerning critical pedagogy.

One such model can be found in the work of political philosopher Paulo Freire ([1970] 1993) and his seminal book *Pedagogy of the Oppressed*. For Freire, the project of education is not so much to encourage 'social continuity' as with Dewey, but instead a reconstruction of education through social responsibility and the development of critical thinking relating to the conditions of society. In this transformatory project, teachers and students work together to question dominant practices and ideologies so that education always involves social relations and is always essentially a political act. Freire suggests that education can be liberating only if it helps us understand the world we live in:

> the oppressed ... must perceive the reality of oppression not as a closed world from which there is no exit, but as a limiting situation which they can transform. ([1970] 1993: 31)

In Chapter 2 we discussed the problem of successive policies for citizenship education which had served to erase discourses of 'race' and ethnicity through what some critical race theorists (Gillborn, 2009) call a 'naturalized', 'sanitized' or 'white-washed' version of history and 'majoritarian' conception of 'Britishness'. A more critical orientation, however, would allow the absent presence of 'race' in citizenship discourses to be challenged through a process of 'conscientization' (raising critical awareness in order to promote change) and purposeful 'dialogue' between teachers and students in a reciprocal relationship of co-intentionality. As Freire ([1970] 1993: 53) notes, 'education must begin with the solution of the teacher-student contradiction ... both are simultaneously teachers *and* students'. This would serve to address the problem widely reported in the research literature that many teachers are reluctant to engage with issues of 'race' and 'racism' and so avoid them completely. This would also address the reported problem that far-right political groups, such as the English Defence League, are beginning to fill a vacuum left by mainstream politics and political parties (Meikle, 2011), many of whom are failing to win the hearts and minds of young people in local communities. Through a form of Freirean 'praxis', it is possible to envisage how adults and young people might be brought closer together inter-generationally in order to challenge and subvert traditional hierarchies and further engender greater equity in education, starting with the cultural experiences of young people or their community cultural wealth (Yosso, 2005), as a means to challenge prejudice and potentially harmful extremism.

An additional feature of Freirean praxis is the critique of education as 'banking', that is, the accumulation of facts and information as a political device to obscure critical consciousness and thus preserve the status quo. Revisiting the theme of early years and primary education, for example, it is possible to imagine in this context how the process of learning to read can be taken well beyond the teaching of synthetic phonics, to incorporate a process of political literacy, so that becoming literate is not just learning to read but developing greater political awareness of the world around us – that is, learning to 'read' the world. This futures perspective, we contend, is apt to nurture not only a more critical disposition in young people but a more socially just approach to education through enhanced recognition of the internal capabilities of young people (the capacity to realize individual potential) (Nussbaum, 2000).

In a different context we believe that Freirean philosophy may be usefully applied to the instrumental and potentially exploitative situation developing in post-compulsory education. Earlier in Chapter 6, we noted the popular belief in the ability of school-based education or work-based training to provide the engine for economic growth, and argued that unfettered instrumentalism had created a focus upon human capital and, with this, a preoccupation with 'academic functionings' (or credentials) at the expense of capabilities (personal freedoms). While Sen (1999: xi) is correct to point out that 'the freedom of agency that we individually have is inescapably qualified and constrained by the social, political and economic opportunities that are available to us', or in educational terms that 'individuals only have choices … to the extent that prevailing structures – of curriculum, pedagogy, and assessment of learning' (Garratt, 2011: 217) – are sensitive to 'difference' and the effect of 'social arrangements and social relations upon individual lives' (Walker and Unterhalter, 2007: 10), we believe that Freirean praxis may provide a useful antidote to the hegemony of neo-liberal policy and politics. Thus, rather than vocational education and training setting out to prepare young people for their role in the world of work (and capitalist mode of production), we would encourage the development of improved political literacy in the sense of helping less privileged communities recognize the conditions of their oppression, as concealed, for example, in the rhetoric of David Cameron's political speech concerning 'real qualifications' (privileging 'functionings' rather than 'capabilities') at the beginning of Chapter 6.

In our aim to open up the discourse around education policy, anticipating a different and more liberated future, we have invoked several useful perspectives and philosophical trajectories, drawing on the work of Steiner, Neill, Dewey, Illich and Freire. In the spirit of a 'soft-futures' approach, which resists stepping 'outside of the discourse in order to find objectivity' (Leaton Gray, 2006: 146) and which refuses to position ideas in a hierarchy, we prefer to accept and live with complexity and multiplicity. This is reflected in the overlaps (imbrications) and spaces in between (liminality of) the philosophical perspectives considered above, each of which reveal significant possibilities for the future direction of education policy, but none that are definitive or all-encompassing. In our consideration of the future, we note the ambivalence and uncertainty that is characteristic of the contradictions and confusions at the heart of policy reform. Our methodological response to the issues raised throughout this book is to propose a more optimistic construction of ideas from diverse sources (i.e. bricolage) and philosophical possibilities, taking us beyond the current constraints of neo-liberal policy to a more democratic future. Here, critical involvement rather than implicit resolution might usefully create the intellectual conditions to enable individual capabilities to flourish. However, ultimately only deliberative ethical goal revision is likely to achieve a radical shift in the axis of education policy towards a more socially just and democratic future.

Note

1   See http://www.topuniversities.com/university-rankings.

References

Adams, R. (2013), 'Swedish Results Fall Abruptly as Free School Revolution Falters', *The Guardian*, 3 December. Available online: http://www.theguardian.com/world/2013/dec/03/swedish-results-fall-free-schools-pisa-oecd (accessed 7 March 2015).

Adler, M. E., A. J. Petch and J. W. Tweedie (1989), *Parental Choice and Educational Policy*, Edinburgh: Edinburgh University Press.

Ainley, P. (2013), 'Education and the Reconstitution of Social Class in England', *Research in Post-Compulsory Education*, 18(1–2): 46–60.

Ainscow, M. (2016), *Struggles for Equity in Education: The Selected Works of Mel Ainscow*, Abingdon, Oxon: Routledge.

Ainscow, M., A. Dyson, S. Goldrick and M. West (2011), *Developing Equitable Education Systems*, Abingdon, Oxon: Routledge.

Alexander, R.J. (1984), *Primary Teaching*, London: Holt, Rinehart & Winston.

Alexander, R. J. ed. (2009), *Children, Their World, Their Education: Final Report and Recommendations of the Cambridge Primary Review*, Abingdon: Routledge.

Alexander, R.J. (2010), 'Implications of the Cambridge Primary Review for Primary Initial Teacher Education'. *The Cambridge Primary Review and Initial Teacher Education*, Universities' Council for the Education of Teachers (UCET), and National Primary Teacher Education Council (NaPTEC): Manchester, 26 March.

Alexander, R., J. Rose and C. Woodhead (1992), *Curriculum, Organisation and Classroom Practice in Primary Schools: A Discussion Paper*, London: HMSO.

Allen, R. (2015), 'Education Policy', *National Institute Economic Review*, 231: R36–R43.

Angus, L. (1994), 'Sociological Analysis and Education Management: The Social Context of the Self Managing School', *British Journal of Sociology of Education*, 15(1): 79–91.

Apple, M. W. (1990), *Ideology and Curriculum*, 2nd edn, London: Routledge.

Apple, M. W. (1999), 'The Absent Presence of Race in Educational Reform', *Race Ethnicity and Education*, 2(1): 9–16.

Armstrong, D. (1998), 'Changing Faces, Changing Places: Policy Routes to Inclusion', in P. Clough (ed.), *Managing Inclusive Education: From Policy to Experience*, 31–47, London: Paul Chapman Publishing.

Arnot, M., M. David and G. Weiner (1999), *Closing the Gender Gap – Postwar Education and Social Change*, Cambridge: Polity Press.

Avis, J. (2014), 'Austerity and Modernisation, One Nation Labour – Localism, the Economy and Vocational Education and Training in England', *Journal for Critical Education Policy Studies*, 12(2): 225–254.

Baldock, P. (2011), *Developing Early Childhood Services. Past, Present and Future*, Maidenhead, Berks: Open University Press.

Ball, S. J. (1990), *Politics and Policy Making in Education – Exploration in Policy Sociology*, London: Routledge.

Ball, S. J. (1993), 'What Is Policy? Texts, Trajectories and Toolboxes', *Discourse*, 13(20): 10–17.

Ball, S. J. (1999), 'Labour, Learning and the Economy: A "Policy Sociology" Perspective', *Cambridge Journal of Education*, 29(2): 195–206.

Ball, S. J. (2007), *Education plc – Understanding Private Sector Participation in Public Sector Education*, London: Routledge.

Ball, S. J. (2013), *The Education Debate*, 2nd edn, Bristol: Policy Press.

Ball, S. J. and C. Vincent (2005), 'The "Childcare Champion"? New Labour, Social Justice and the Childcare Market', *British Educational Research Journal*, 31(5): 557–570.

Ball, S. J., R. Bowe and S. Gewirtz (1995), 'Circuits of Schooling: A Sociological Exploration of Parental Choice of School in Social Class Contexts', *Sociological Review*, 43(1): 52–78.

Bangs, J., J. MacBeath and M. Galton (2010), *Reinventing Schools, Reforming Teaching: From Political Visions to Classroom Reality*, Abingdon, Oxon: Routledge.

Barber, M. (1992), *Education and the Teacher Unions*, London: Cassell.

Barker, M. (1981), *The New Racism*, London: Junction Books.

Barr, N. (2004), 'Higher Education Funding', *Oxford Review of Economic Policy*, 20(2): 264–283.

Basford, J. and C. Bath (2014), 'Playing the Assessment Game: An English Early Childhood Education Perspective', *Early Years*, 34(2): 119–132.

Bassey, M. and 99 UK academics (2013), 'Letters: "Gove Will Bury Pupils in Facts and Rules"', *The Independent*, 20 March. Available online: http://www.independent.co.uk/voices/letters/letters-gove-will-bury-pupils-in-facts-and-rules-8540741.html (accessed 25 March 2013).

Bates, E. A. and L. K. Kaye (2014), '"I'd be Expecting Caviar in Lectures": The Impact of the New Fee Regime on Undergraduate Students' Expectations of Higher Education', *Higher Education*, 67(5): 655–673.

Batho, G. (1990), *Political Issues in Education*, London: Cassell.

BBC (2006), 'Blair Wants Another 200 Academies', *BBC News*, 30 November. Available online: http://news.bbc.co.uk/1/hi/education/6157435.stm (accessed 28 May 2012).

BBC (2008), 'British Citizenship Tests Planned', *BBC News*, 20 February. Available online: http://news.bbc.co.uk/1/hi/uk_politics/7253933.stm (accessed 31 August 2008).

BBC (2012), 'Students March in London Protest, Education and Family', *BBC News*, 21 November. Available online: http://www.bbc.co.uk/news/education-20412792 (accessed 28 May 2015).

Beck, U. (2000a), 'The Cosmopolitan Perspective: Sociology of the Second Age of Modernity', *British Journal of Sociology*, 51(1): 79–105.

Beck, U. (2000b), *What Is Globalization?* Cambridge: Polity Press.

Beck, U. (2006), *Cosmopolitan Vision*, Cambridge: Polity Press.

Becker, G. (1964), *Human Capital*, Chicago: University of Chicago Press.

Becker, G. (1993), *Human Capital*, 3rd edn, Chicago: University of Chicago Press.

Beckett, F. (2007), *The Great City Academy Fraud*, London: Continuum.

Benn, M. (2011), 'The Real Cost of "Free" Schools Will Be Paid by the Poorest', *The Guardian*, 8 September. Available online: www.guardian.co.uk/commentisfree/2011/sep/08/cost-free-schools-paid-by-poorest (accessed 23 September 2011).

Bennett, N. (1976), *Teaching Styles and Pupil Progress*, London: Open Books.

Bennett, N. (1992), 'Beyond Ruskin: Recent Conceptions of Children's Learning and Implications for Primary School Practice', in M. Williams, R. Daugherty and F. Banks (eds), *Continuing the Education Debate*, 65–73, London: Cassell.

Berlin, I. (1969), *Four Essays on Liberty*, Oxford: Oxford University Press.

Bernstein, B. (1968), 'Education Cannot Compensate for Society', *New Society*, 387: 334–337.

Bew, P. (2011), *Independent Review of Key Stage 2 Testing, Assessment and Accountability, Final Report*, June, London: HMSO.

Bhattacharya, B. (2013), 'Academy Schools in England', *Childhood Education*, 89(2): 94–98.

BIS (Department for Business Innovation and Skills) (2011), *Higher Education: Students at the Heart of the System* (Cm. 8122), London: HMSO.

Blair, T. (1996), *New Britain – My Vision of a Young Country*, London: Fourth Estate Ltd.

Blair, T. (1998), *The Government's Annual Report 1997–98*, London: The Stationery Office.

Blunkett, D. (1998), 'Cash for Competence', *Times Educational Supplement*, 24 July. www.tes.co.uk.

Blunkett, D. (1999), *New Teachers' Pay Arrangements Will Cut through Bureaucracy*, Association of Teachers and Lecturers' Annual Conference, Harrogate, 30 March, DfEE Press Release, 139/99.

Blyth, W. A. L. (1965), *English Primary Education (Part 2)*, London: Routledge, Kegan Paul.

Board of Education (1905), *Reports on Children Under Five in Public Elementary Schools, by Women Inspectors* (Cd 2726), London: HMSO.

Board of Education (1908), *Report of the Consultative Committee upon the School Attendance of Children below the Age of Five* (Cd. 4259), London: HM Stationery Office. Available online: http://www.educationengland.org.uk/documents/acland1908/acland08.html#204 (accessed 27 July 2015).

Board of Education (1931), *Report of the Consultative Committee on the Primary School. Report (The Hadow Report)*, London: HMSO.

Board of Education (1933), *Report of the Consultative Committee on Infant and Nursery Schools* (The Hadow Report), London: HMSO.

Boden, R. and M. Nedeva (2010), 'Employing Discourse: Universities and Graduate "Employability"', *Journal of Education Policy*, 25(1): 37–54.

Boffey, D. (2011), 'Willetts in Secret Talks with Banks on Funding of Student Loans', *The Observer*, 26 June: 6.

Boliver, V. (2013), How Fair Is Access to More Prestigious UK Universities? *The British Journal of Sociology*, 64: 344–364.

Boronski, T. and N. Hassan (2015), *Sociology of Education*. London: Sage.

Bourdieu, P. and J. C. Passeron (1990), *Reproduction in Education, Society and Culture*, 2nd edn, London: Sage.

Boyd, D. and N. Hirst, eds (2015), *Understanding Early Years Education across the UK: Comparing Practice in England, Northern Ireland, Scotland and Wales*, London: Routledge.

Boyles, D., T. Carusi and D. Attick (2009), 'Historical and Critical Interpretations of Social Justice', in W. Ayers, T. Quinn and D. Stovall (eds), *Handbook of Social Justice in Education*, 30–42, Abingdon, Oxon: Routledge.

Bradbury, A. (2014), 'Early Childhood Assessment: Observation, Teacher "Knowledge" and the Production of Attainment Data in Early Years Settings', *Comparative Education*, 50(3): 322–339.

Braithwaite, R. J. (1992), 'School Choice as a Means of Attaining Excellence in Education', *Cambridge Journal of Education*, 22(1): 43–53.

Brown, G. (2004), 'The Golden Thread that Runs Throughout History', *The Guardian*, 8 July. Available online: www.guardian.co.uk/politics/2004/jul/08/britishidentity. economy/print (accessed 23 July 2009).

Brown, G. (2006), 'Who Do We Want to Be? The Future of Britishness', Speech presented to the Fabian New Year Conference, January 14, Imperial College, London.

Brown, P. and H. Lauder (1992), 'Education, Economy and Society: An Introduction to a New Agenda', in P. Brown and H. Lauder (eds), *Education for Economic Survival: From Fordism to Post-fordism? London: Routledge*.

Brown, P. and H. Lauder (1996), 'Education, Globalization and Economic Development', *Journal of Education Policy*, 11(1): 1–25.

Brown, P., A. Hesketh and S. Williams (2003), 'Employability in a Knowledge-driven Economy', *Journal of Education and Work*, 16(2): 107–126.

Browne, J. (2010), *Securing a Sustainable Future for Higher Education – An Independent Review of Higher Education Funding and Student Finance (The Browne Report)*, London: Department for Business, Innovations and Skills.

Brundrett, M. (2015), 'Policy on the Primary Curriculum since 2010: The Demise of the Expert View', *London Review of Education*, 13(2): 49–59.

Bryman, A. (2004), *The Disneyization of Society*, London: Sage.

Burbules, N. C. and C. A. Torres (2000), 'Globalisation and Education: An Introduction', in N. C. Burbules and C. A. Torres (eds), *Globalisation and Education: Critical Perspectives*, London: Routledge.

Butterfield, S. (1995), *Educational Objectives and National Assessment*, Buckingham: Open University Press.

Cabinet Office (1999), *Modernising Government (Cm. 4310)*, London: The Stationery Office.

Cabinet Office (2010), *The Coalition: Our Programme for Government*, London: Cabinet Office.

Cabinet Office (2011), *Building the Big Society*, London: Cabinet Office.

CACE (Central Advisory Council for Education) (1967), *Children and Their Primary Schools: A Report* (The Plowden Report), London: HMSO.

Callaghan, J. (1976), 'Towards a National Debate', The Great Debate: 25 years on, *Education Guardian*, 15 October 2001. Available online: http://www.theguardian.com/education/thegreatdebate/0,9857,564054,00.html (accessed 25 May 2015).

Callender, C. (2014), 'Student Numbers and Funding: Does Robbins Add Up?' *Higher Education Quarterly*, 68: 164–186.

Callender, C. and P. Scott (2014), 'Conclusions', in C. Callender and P. Scott (eds), *Browne and Beyond. Modernizing English Higher Education*, 206–218, London: Bedford Way Papers, Institute of Education Press.

Callinicos, A. (2010), *Bonfire of Illusions – The Twin Crises of the Liberal World*, Cambridge: Policy Press.

Cameron, D. (2013), 'Prime Minister: Apprenticeships Are Central to Rebuilding Economy', 11 March. Available online: https://www.gov.uk/government/news/prime-minister-apprenticeships-are-central-to-rebuilding-economy (accessed 4 August 2015).

Cameron, D. (2015), 'The Two-Speed Society Stops Right Here: This Is One Nation', *The Sunday Times*, 24 May: 20.

Campbell, J. (1993), 'The Broad and Balanced Curriculum in Primary Schools. Some Limitations on Reform', *The Curriculum Journal*, 4(2): 215–229.

Campbell, J. (2001), 'The Colonisation of the Primary Curriculum', in R. Phillips and J. Furlong (eds), *Education Reform and the State – Twenty-five Years of Politics, Policy and Practice*, 31–44, London: RoutledgeFalmer.

Campbell, R. J. and S. R. St. J. Neill (1994), *Primary Teachers at Work*, London: Routledge.

Campbell-Barr, V. and M. Nygård (2014), 'Losing Sight of the Child? Human Capital Theory and Its Role for Early Childhood Education and Care Policies in Finland and England since the Mid-1990s', *Contemporary Issues in Early Childhood*, 15(4): 346–359.

Capling, A., M. Considine and M. Crozier (1998), *Australian Politics in the Global Era*, Melbourne: Addison-Wesley.

Carr, W. (1991), 'Education for Citizenship', *British Journal of Educational Studies*, 39(2): 373–385.

Carroll, S. and G. Walford (1997), 'Parents' Responses to the School Quasi-market', *Research Papers in Education*, 12(1): 3–26.

Castells, M. (1997), *The Power of Identity: The Information Age: Economy, Society and Culture (Vol. 1)*, Oxford: Blackwell.

Castells, M. (2000), *End of Millennium*, 2nd edn, Oxford: Blackwell.

CBI (Confederation of British Industry) (1989), *Towards a Skills Revolution*, London: CBI.

CBI (Confederation of British Industry) (1993), *Routes for Success – Careership: A Strategy for All 16–19 Year Old Learners*, London: CBI.

Cerny, P. (1997), 'Paradoxes of the Competition State: The Dynamics of Political Globalization', *Government and Opposition*, 32(2): 251–274.

Chapman, C. and H. M. Gunter, eds (2009), *Radical Reforms.Perspectives on an Era of Educational Change*, Abingdon, Oxon: Routledge.

Chapman, L. and J. West-Burnham (2010), *Education for Social Justice – Achieving Wellbeing for All*, London: Continuum.

CHE (Committee of Higher Education, Robbins Committee) (1963), Higher Education: Report (Cmnd. 2154), London: HMSO.

Cheng, J. H. S. and H. W. Marsh (2010), 'National Student Survey: Are Differences between Universities and Courses Reliable and Meaningful?', *Oxford Review of Education*, 36(6): 693–712.

Chitty, C. (1989), *Towards a New Education System: The Victory of the New Right?* London: Falmer Press.

Chitty, C. (2009), *Education Policy in Britain*, 2nd edn, Cambridge: Polity Press.

Chrostowska, M. (2015), 'An Examination of Teachers' Professional Autonomy in a Primary Academy School'. Paper presented to the British Educational Research Association (BERA) Annual Conference, Queen's University, Belfast, Northern Ireland, 15–17 September.

Clarke, J. and J. Newman (1997), *The Managerial State – Power, Politics and Ideology in the Remaking of Social Welfare*, London: Sage.

Clemitshaw, G. and L. Jerome (2009), 'Can Citizenship Education Promote Democracy and Britishness? A Survey of Trainee Teachers' Attitudes on the Purposes of Citizenship Education', *CitizED Report*. Available online: www.citized.info/pdf/commarticles/Citized%20Britishness%20Professional%20Report%20FINAL%20May09.doc (accessed 23 July 2009).

Coard, B. (1971), *How the West Indian Child Is Made ESN in the British School System*, London: New Beacon Books.

Coates, S. (2015), 'More Free Childcare Will Force Nurseries to Increase Prices', *The Times*, 1 June: 5.

Coffield, F. (1999), 'Breaking the Consensus: Lifelong learning as Social Control', *British Educational Research Journal*, 25(4): 479–499.

Collins, N. (2011), 'Student Protests: Key Dates for 2011', *The Telegraph*, 5 January. Available online: http://www.telegraph.co.uk/education/educationnews/8240181/Student-protests-key-dates-for-2011.html (accessed 25 May 2015).

Conservative Party (2010), *Invitation to Join the Government of Britain. The Conservative Party Manifesto 2010*, Uckfield, East Sussex: Pureprint Group.

Conservative Party (2015), 'The Conservative Party Manifesto 2015'. Available online: https://www.conservatives.com/manifesto (accessed 3 June 2015).

Considine, M. (1994), *Public Policy: A Critical Approach*, Melbourne. Australia: Macmillan Education.

Coughlan, S. (2010) 'Students Face Tuition Fees Rising to £9,000', *BBC News Education and Family*, 3 November. Available online: http://www.bbc.co.uk/news/education-11677862 (accessed 12 May 2011).

Coughlan, S. (2013), 'UK Makes No Progress in Pisa Tests', *BBC News*, 3 December. Available online: http://www.bbc.co.uk/news/education-25187998 (accessed 4 August 2015).

Coughlan, S. (2015), 'AC Grayling Says End "Closed Shop" for New Universities', *BBC News*, 27 October. Available online: http://www.bbc.co.uk/news/education-34638283 (accessed 27 October 2015).

Coughlan, S. (2016), 'Baseline Tests dropped as Progress Measure', *BBC News*, 7 April. Available online: http://www.bbc.co.uk/news/education-35989662 (accessed 7 April 2016).

Coulby, D. (1989a), 'From Educational Partnership to Central Control', in L. Bash and D. Coulby (eds), *The Education Reform Act – Competition and Control*, London: Cassell Educational Ltd.

Coulby, D. (1989b), 'The National Curriculum', in L. Bash and D. Coulby (eds), *The Education Reform Act – Competition and Control*, London: Cassell Educational Ltd.

Cox, C. B. and A. E. Dyson, eds (1969a), *Black Paper 1, Fight for Education, March*, London: Critical Quarterly Society.

Cox, C. B. and A. E. Dyson, eds (1969b), *Black Paper 2, The Crisis in Education, October*, London: Critical Quarterly Society.

Cox, C. B. and A. E. Dyson, eds (1970), *Black Paper 3, Goodbye Mr. Short, November*, London: Critical Quarterly Society.

Cox, C. B. and R. Boyson, eds (1975), *Black Paper 4, The Fight for Education*, London: Dent.

Cox, C. B. and R. Boyson, eds (1977), *Black Paper 5, Black Paper 1977, March*, London: Maurice Temple Smith.

Crick, B. (2000), *Essays on Citizenship*, London: Continuum.

Crozier, G., D. Reay and C. Clayton (2010), 'The Socio-cultural and Learning Experiences of Working-Class Students in Higher Education', in M. David (ed.), *Improving Learning by Widening Participation in Higher Education*, 62–74, London: Routledge.

Cunningham, P. (1988), *Curriculum Change in the Primary School since 1945 – Dissemination of the Progressive Ideal*, London: The Falmer Press.

Curriculum and Assessment Authority for Wales (1996), *Desirable Outcomes for Children's Learning before Compulsory School Age*, Cardiff: Curriculum and Assessment Authority for Wales.

Curtis, S. J. (1967), *History of Education in Great Britain*, 6th edn, London: University Tutorial Press.

Dadds, M. (1993), 'The Changing Face of Topic Work in the Primary Curriculum', *The Curriculum Journal*, 4(2): 253–267.

Dale, R. (1999), 'Specifying Globalization Effects on National Policy: A Focus on the Mechanisms', *Journal of Education Policy*, 14(1): 1–17.

Dale, R. and J. Ozga (1993), 'Two Hemispheres – Both New Right? 1980's Education Reform in New Zealand and England and Wales', in R. Lingard, J. Knight and P. Porter (eds), *Schooling Reform in Hard Times*, Lewis: Falmer Press.

Daniels, H., V. Hey, D. Leonard and M. Smith (1995), 'Gendered Practice in Special Educational Needs', in L. Dawtrey, J. Holland and M. Hammer with S. Sheldon (eds), *Equality and Inequality in Education Policy*, 204–218, Clevedon, Avon: The Open University.

David, M. E. (1980), *The State, the Family and Education*, London: Routledge and Kegan Paul.

David, M. E. (1993), *Parents, Gender and Education Reform*, Cambridge: Polity Press.

David, M. E. ed. (2010), *Improving Learning by Widening Participation in Higher Education*, London: Routledge.

David, T. (1998), 'Learning Properly? Young Children and Desirable Outcomes', *Early Years: An International Research Journal*, 18(2): 61–65.

DCSF (Department for Children, Schools and Families) (2009), *Independent Review of the Primary Curriculum: Final Report*, Nottingham: DCSF Publications.

Dearing, R. (1993), *The National Curriculum and Its Assessment: Interim Report*, York and London: NCC/SEAC.

Dearing, R. (1996a), *Review of Qualifications for 16–19 Year Olds*, Hayes, Middlesex: SCAA.

Dearing, R. (1996b), *Report of the National Committee of Inquiry into Higher Education*, London: DfEE Publications.

DE (Department of Employment) (1988), *Training for Employment*, London: HMSO.

DE/DES (Department of Employment/Department of Education and Science) (1986), *Working Together – Education and Training*, London: HMSO.

Deem, R. (2004), 'Sociology and the Sociology of Higher Education – A Missed Call or a Disconnection?' *International Studies in the Sociology of Education*, 14(1): 21–45.

Delanty, G. (2008), 'Academic Identities and Institutional Change', in R. Barnett and R. Di Napoli (eds), *Changing Identities in Higher Education – Voicing Perspectives*, London: Routledge, 124–133.

DENI (Department of Education in Northern Ireland) (1997), *Curricular Guidance for Pre-School Education*, Belfast: Northern Ireland Council for the Curriculum, Examinations and Assessment.

DES (Department of Education and Science) (1972), *Education: A Framework for Expansion* (Cm. 5174), London: HMSO.

DES (Department of Education and Science) (1973), *Nursery Education*, Circular 2/73, London: HMSO.

DES (Department of Education and Science) (1977), *Education in Schools: A Consultative Document* (Cmnd. 6869), London: HMSO.

DES (Department of Education and Science) (1978a), *Primary Education in England: A Survey by HMI*, London: HMSO.

DES (Department of Education and Science) (1978b), *Special Educational Needs. Report of the Committee of Enquiry into the Education of Handicapped Children and Young People* (Cmnd. 7212), London: HMSO.

DES (Department of Education and Science) (1981), *The School Curriculum*, London: HMSO.

DES (Department of Education and Science) (1984), *Parental Influence at School: A New Framework for School Government in England and Wales, Green Paper* (Cmnd. 9242), London: HMSO.

DES (Department of Education and Science) (1985a), *The Curriculum from 5–16: Curriculum Matters 2*, London: HMSO.

DES (Department of Education and Science) (1985b), *The Development of Higher Education into the 1990s*, London: HMSO.

DES (Department of Education and Science) (1987a), *Primary Staffing Survey*, London: HMSO.

DES (Department of Education and Science) (1987b), *Higher Education: Meeting the Challenge* (Cm. 114), London: HMSO.

DES (Department of Education and Science) (1987c) *The National Curriculum 5-16: A Consultative Document*, London: HMSO.

DES (Department of Education and Science) (1988), *Advancing A-levels, Report of the Committee Chaired by Professor Higginson*, London: HMSO.

DES (Department of Education and Science) (1991a), *Education and Training for the 21st Century*, London: HMSO.

DES (Department of Education and Science) (1991b), *Higher Education: A New Framework* (Cm. 1541), London: HMSO.

DFE (Department for Education) (1992a), *Choice and Diversity and New Framework for Schools*, London: DfE.

DFE (Department for Education) (1992b), *Special Educational Needs: Access to the System*, London: DfE.

DfE (Department for Education) (1994), *Code of Practice on the Identification and Assessment of Children with Special Educational Needs*, London: DfE.

DfE (Department for Education) (2010a), *The Importance of Teaching. The Schools White Paper* (Cm.7980), London: TSO.

DfE (Department for Education) (2011a), *Positive for Youth – Young People's Involvement in Decision Making, Discussion Paper*, London: DfE.

DfE (Department for Education) (2011b), Timetable for the National Curriculum Review. Available online: www.education.gov.uk/schools/teachingandlearning/curriculum/nationalcurriculum/a0073092/timetable-for-the-national-curriculum-review (accessed 12 April 2011).

DfE (Department for Education) (2011c), *The Framework for the National Curriculum. A Report by the Expert Panel for the National Curriculum Review*, London: DfE.

DfE (Department for Education) (2011d), *Support and Aspiration: A New Approach to Special Educational Needs and Disability: A Consultation*, Cm 8027, London: TSO.

DfE (Department for Education) (2011e), 'What Are Free Schools?' Available online: http://webarchive.nationalarchives.gov.uk/20130123124929/http://www.education.gov.uk/schools/leadership/typesofschools/freeschools/b0061428/free-schools/what (accessed 16 September 2015).

DfE (Department for Education) (2013a), *The National Curriculum in England. Key Stages 1 and 2 Framework Document*. Reference: DFE-00178-2013, September. London: DfE.

DfE (Department for Education) (2013b), *More Great Childcare. Raising Quality and Giving Parents More Choice*, London: DfE.

DfE (Department for Education) (2014a), *Statutory Framework for the Early Years Foundation Stage. Setting the Standards for Learning, Development and Care for Children from Birth to Five. Effective September 2014*, London: DfE.

DfE (Department for Education) (2014b), *Reforming Assessment and Accountability for Primary Schools: Government Response to Consultation on Primary School Assessment and Accountability*, London: DfE.

DfE (Department for Education) (2014c), Children and Families Act. Available online: http://www.legislation.gov.uk/ukpga/2014/6/contents/enacted (accessed 4 August 2015).

DfE (Department for Education) (2015), *Statistical First Release, School Workforce in England: November 2014* SFR 21/2015, London: DfE.

DfE/DH (Department for Education/Department of Health) (2011a), *Families in the Foundation Years*, London: DfE.

DfE/DH (Department for Education/Department of Health) (2011b), *Supporting Families in the Foundation Years*, London: DfE.

DfEE (Department for Education and Employment) (1997a), *Excellence in Schools* (Cm. 3681), London: Stationery Office.

DfEE (Department for Education and Employment) (1997b), *Excellence in Cities*, London: DfEE.

DfEE (Department for Education and Employment) (1997c), *Qualifying for Success: A Consultation Paper on the Future of Post-16 Qualifications*, London: Crown Copyright.

DfEE (Department for Education and Employment) (1997d), *Excellence for All Children. Meeting Special Educational Needs* (Cm. 3785), London: Stationery Office.

DfEE (Department for Education and Employment) (1998a), *Teachers: Meeting the Challenge of Change*, London: The Stationery Office.

DfEE (Department for Education and Employment) (1998b), *National Literacy Strategy Framework for Teaching*, London: DfEE.

DfEE (Department for Education and Employment) (1998c), *National Numeracy Framework*, London: DfEE.

DfEE (Department for Education and Employment) (1998d) *Meeting the Childcare Challenge: A Framework and Consultation Document*, London: HMSO.

DfEE (Department for Education and Employment) (1998e), *The Learning Age: A Renaissance for a New Britain*, London: HMSO.

DfEE (Department for Education and Employment) (1998f), *Higher Education for the 21st Century – Response to the Dearing Report*, London: DfEE.

DfEE (Department for Education and Employment) (1998f), *Meeting Special Educational Needs: A Programme of Action*, London: DfEE.

DfEE (Department for Education and Employment) (1999a), *Learning to Succeed: A New Framework for Post-16 Learning*, London: DfEE Publications.

DfEE (Department for Education and Employment) (1999b), *Teachers: Meeting the Challenge of Change – Technical Consultation Document on Pay and Performance Management*, London: DfEE Publications Centre.

DfEE (Department for Education and Employment) (1999c), *Performance Management Framework for Teachers: Consultation Document*, London: DfEE Publications.

DfEE (Department for Education and Employment) (2000a), *A Model of Teacher Effectiveness. Report by Hay McBer to the Department for Education and Employment*, London: The Stationery Office.

DfEE (Department for Education and Employment) (2000b), *Performance Management in Schools. Performance Management Framework (Guidance. Teachers and Staffing) (Ref: DfEE 0051/2000)*, London: DfEE Publications.

DfE/ED/WO (Department for Education/Employment Department/Welsh Office) (1991), *Education and Training for the 21st Century*, London: HMSO.

DfES (Department for Education and Skills) (2002), *Birth to Three Matters*, London: DfES.

DfES (Department for Education and Skills) (2003a), *Excellence and Enjoyment. A Strategy for Primary Schools*, London: DfES.

DfES (Department for Education and Skills) (2003b), *Foundation Stage Profile Arrangements*, London: DfES.

DfES (Department for Education and Skills) (2003c), *Full Day Care. National Standards for Under 8s Day Care and Childminding*, London: DfES.

DfES (Department for Education and Skills) (2003d), *The Future of Higher Education*, London: HMSO.

DfES (Department for Education and Skills) (2004a), *Every Child Matters: Change for Children*, London: HMSO.

DfES (Department for Education and Skills) (2004b), *Removing the Barriers to Achievement. The Government's Strategy for SEN*, Nottingham: DfES Publications.

DfES (Department for Education and Skills) (2005), *14–19 Education and Skills*, London: DfES.

DfES (Department for Education and Skills) (2007a), *Curriculum Review: Diversity and Citizenship (Ajegbo Report)*, London: DfES.

DfES (Department for Education and Skills) (2007b), *Pedagogy and Personalisation*, Ref.00126, London: DfES.

DfES/DTI/DWP (Department for Education and Skills, Department of Trade and Industry and Department for Work and Pensions) (2003), *21st Century Skills Realising Our Potential: Individuals, Employers, Nation*, London: DfES/DTI/DWP.

Dewey, J. ([1916] 2007), *Democracy and Education*, Teddington, Middlesex: Echo Library.

DH/HO (Department of Health, Home Office) (2003), *The Victoria Climbié Inquiry, Report of an Inquiry by Lord Laming* (Cm. 5730), Norwich: TSO.

Docking, J. (2000), 'What Is the Solution? An Overview of National Policies for Schools, 1979–99', in J. Docking (ed.), *New Labour's Policies for Schools. Raising the Standard*, 21–42, London: David Fulton Publishers.

Driver, S. (2008), 'New Labour and Social Policy', in M. Beech and S. Lee (eds), *Ten Years of New Labour*, Basingstoke, Hampshire: Palgrave Macmillan.

Driver, S. and L. Martell (1998), *New Labour – Politics after Thatcherism*, Cambridge: Polity Press.

DTI (Department of Trade and Industry) (1995), *Competitiveness: Forging Ahead*, London: HMSO.

DTI (Department of Trade and Industry) (1998), *Our Competitive Future: Building the Knowledge Driven Economy* (Cm. 4176), London: The Stationery Office.

Dyson, A., P. Farrell, K. Kerr and N. Mearns (2009), '"Swing, Swing Together": Multi-agency Work in the New Children's Services', in C. Chapman and H. M. Gunter (eds), *Radical Reforms. Perspectives on an Era of Educational Change*, 155–168, Abingdon, Oxon: Routledge.

Earl, L. M., N. Watson, B. Levin, K. Leithwood, M. Fullan and N. Torrance (2003), *Watching and Learning 3: Final Report of the External Evaluation of England's National Literacy and Numeracy Strategies*, Nottingham: DfES Publications.

Education Act (1996), *Education Act*, London: The Stationery Office Ltd. Available online: http://www.legislation.gov.uk/ukpga/1996/56/section/312 (accessed 12 October 2012).

Edwards, T. and G. Whitty (1992), 'Parental Choice and Educational Reform in Britain and the United States', *British Journal of Educational Studies*, 40(2): 101–117.

Eggins, H., ed. (2003), *Globalisation and Reform in Higher Education*, Buckingham: Open University Press.

Eggleston, J. (1977), *The Sociology of the School Curriculum*, London: Routledge and Kegan Paul.

Ellison, M. (2014), *The Stephen Lawrence Independent Review. Possible Corruption and the Role of Undercover Policing in the Stephen Lawrence Case. Summary of Findings*, London: House of Commons.

Ertl, H. and S. Wright (2008), 'Reviewing the Literature on the Student Learning Experience in Higher Education', *London Review of Education*, 6(3): 195–210.

Exley, S. and S. J. Ball (2011), 'Something Old, Something New: Understanding Conservative Education Policy', in H. Bochel (ed.), *The Conservative Party and Social Policy*, 97–117, Cambridge: Policy Press.

Fairclough, N. (2000), *New Labour, New Language*, London: Routledge.

Faulks, K. (2006), 'Education for Citizenship in England's Secondary Schools: A Critique of Current Principles and Practice', *Journal of Education Policy*, 21(1): 59–74.

Ferlie, E., L. Ashburner, L. Fitzgerald and A. Pettigrew (1996), *The New Public Management in Action*, Oxford: Oxford University Press.

FEU (Further Education Unit) (1979), *A Basis for Skills*, London: FEU.

Finegold, D. (1993), 'The Emerging Post-16 System: Analysis and Critique', in W. Richardson, J. Woolhouse and D. Finegold (eds), *The Reform of Post 16 Education and Training in England and Wales*, Harlow: Longman.

Finegold, D., E. Keep, D. Miliband, D. Raffe, K. Spours and M. Young (1990), *A British Baccalaureate: Overcoming Division between Education and Training*, London: Institute for Public Policy Research.

Flude, M. and M. Hammer, eds (1990), *The Education Reform Act, 1988 – Its Origins and Implications*, London: Falmer Press.

Flynn, N. (1999), 'Modernising British Government', *Parliamentary Affairs*, 52(4): 582–597.

Forrester, G. (2000), 'Professional Autonomy versus Managerial Control: The Experience of Teachers in an English Primary School', *International Studies in Sociology of Education*, 10(2): 133–151.

Forrester, G. (2005), 'All in a Day's Work: Primary Teachers "Performing" and "Caring"', *Gender and Education*, 17(3): 271–287.

Forrester, G. (2011), 'Performance Management in Education: Milestone or Millstone?' *Management in Education*, 25(1): 5–9.

Forrester, G. and H. M. Gunter (2009), 'The Academic Work, Identities and Cultures of Education Leadership Researchers in the UK'. Paper presented to the American Educational Research Association (AERA), Annual Meeting, San Diego, USA, 13–17 April.

Foskett, N., D. Roberts and F. Maringe (2006), 'Changing Fee Regimes and Their Impact on Student Attitudes to Higher Education', *Report of a Higher Education Academy Funded Research Project 2005–2006*. Southampton: University of Southampton.

Available online: http://hca.ltsn.ac.uk/assets/documents/research/changing_fees_regimes_full_report.pdf (accessed 7 March 2011).

Foucault, M. (1980), 'Truth and Power', in C. Gordon (ed.), *Power/Knowledge: Selected Interviews and Other Writings 1972–1977*, Brighton: Harvester, 109–133.

Foucault, M. (1988), 'Sexuality, Morality and the Law', in Kritzman, L.D. (ed.), *Michel Foucault: Politics, Philosophy, Culture. Interviews and Other Writings*, New York: Routledge, 271–285.

Foucault, M. (2002), *Michel Foucault – Power Volume 3 – the Essential Works of Foucault 1954–1984*, J. D. Faubion (ed.), London: Penguin.

Freeden, M. (2003), *Ideology – A Very Short Introduction*, Oxford: Oxford University Press.

Freire, P. ([1970] 1993), *Pedagogy of the Oppressed*, revised edn, London: Penguin.

Fuller, A. and S. Heath (2010), 'Educational Decision-Making, Social Networks and the New Widening Participation', in M. David (ed.), *Improving Learning by Widening Participation in Higher Education*, 132–146, London: Routledge.

Gallagher, A. (2009), 'David Cameron Sets Out His Vision for "Big Society"', *The Guardian*, 10 November. Available online: www.guardian.co.uk/politics/video/2009/nov/10/david-cameron-hugo-young-lecture?intcmp=239 (accessed 15 June 2011).

Galton, M. and J. MacBeath (2008), *Teachers under Pressure*, London: Sage.

Galton, M., B. Simon and P. Croll (1980), *Inside the Primary Classroom*, London: Routledge and Kegan Paul.

Gamble, A. (1988), *The Free Economy and the Strong State*, London: Macmillan.

Gamble, A. (2009), *The Spectre at the Feast – Capitalist Crisis and the Politics of Recession*, Basingstoke: Palgrave Macmillan.

Garner, R. (2014), 'Troubled Islamic Free School in Derby to Close Its Secondary School', *The Independent*, 7 February. Available online: http://www.independent.co.uk/news/education/schools/troubled-derby-free-school-to-close-its-secondary-school-9115056.html (accessed 7 March 2015).

Garratt, D. (2011), 'Reflections on Learning: Widening Capability and the Student Experience', *Cambridge Journal of Education*, 41(2): 211–225.

Garratt, D. and L. Hammersley-Fletcher (2009), 'Academic Identities in Flux: Ambivalent Articulations in a Post-1992 University', *Power and Education*, 1(3): 307–318.

Garratt, D. and H. Piper (2008a), *Citizenship Education, Identity and Nationhood – Contradictions in Practice?* London: Continuum.

Garratt, D. and H. Piper (2008b), 'Citizenship Education in England and Wales: Theoretical Critique and Practical Considerations', *Teachers and Teaching: Theory and Practice*, 14(5–6): 481–496.

Garratt, D. and H. Piper (2010), 'Heterotopian Cosmopolitan Citizenship Education?' *Education, Citizenship and Social Justice*, 5(2): 43–55.

Garratt, D. and H. Piper (2011), 'Citizenship Education and Philosophical Enquiry: Putting Thinking Back into Practice', *Education, Citizenship and Social Justice*, 7(1): 71–84.

Gewirtz, S. (1998), 'Conceptualizing Social Justice: Mapping the Territory', *Journal of Education Policy*, 13(4): 469–484.

Gewirtz, S. (2002), *The Managerial School. Post-Welfarism and Social Justice in Education*, London: Routledge.

Gewirtz, S., S. Ball and R. Bowe (1994), 'Parents, Privilege and the Education Market-place', *Research Papers in Education*, 9(1): 3–29.

Gewirtz, S., S. Ball and R. Bowe (1995), *Markets, Choice and Equity in Education.* Buckingham: Open University Press.

Giddens, A. (1987), *Social Theory and Modern Sociology*, Cambridge: Polity.

Giddens, A. (1990), *The Consequences of Modernity*, Cambridge: Polity Press.

Giddens, A. (1994), *Beyond Left and Right: The Future of Radical Politics*, Cambridge: Polity Press.

Giddens, A. (1998), *The Third Way: The Renewal of Social Democracy*, Cambridge: Polity Press.

Giddens, A. (2000), *The Third Way and Its Critics*, Cambridge: Polity Press.

Gillborn, D. (1998), 'Racism, Selection, Poverty and Parents: New Labour, Old Problems?' *Journal of Education Policy*, 13(6): 717–735.

Gillborn, D. (2005), 'Education Policy as an Act of White Supremacy: Whiteness, Critical Race Theory and Education Reform', *Education Policy*, 20: 485–505.

Gillborn, D. (2009), 'Education Policy as an Act of White Supremacy', in E. Taylor, D. Gillborn and G. Ladson-Billings (eds), *Foundations of Critical Race Theory in Education*, 51–69, London: Routledge.

Gillborn, D. and D. Youdell (2000), *Rationing Education – Policy, Practice, Reform and Equity*, Buckingham: Open University Press.

Gilpin, R. (1987), *The Political Economy of International Relations*, Princeton, NJ: Princeton University Press.

Gilroy, R. (1987), *There Ain't No Black in the Union Jack*, London: Hutchinson.

Gilroy, R. (2004), *After Empire: Melancholia or Convivial Culture*, Oxfordshire: Routledge.

Gorard, S. (2014), 'The Link between Academies in England, Pupil Outcomes and Local Patterns of Socio-economic Segregation between Schools', *Research Papers in Education*, 29(3): 268–284.

Gove, M. (2009), Speech: 'Failing Schools need New Leadership', 7 October. Available online: http://conservative-speeches.sayit.mysociety.org/speech/601288 (accessed 20 September 2015).

Gove, M. (2011), Michael Gove's Speech to the Policy Exchange on Free Schools. 20 June. Available online: https://www.gov.uk/government/speeches/michael-goves-speech-to-the-policy-exchange-on-free-schools (accessed 16 September 2015).

Gove, M. (2012), Michael Gove to the Education World Forum. Education for Economic Success. Speech. 11 January. Available online: https://www.gov.uk/government/speeches/michael-gove-to-the-education-world-forum (accessed 15 April 2014).

Gove, M. (2013), 'Curriculum, Exam and Accountability Reform. Oral Statement to Parliament', 7 February. Available online: https://www.gov.uk/government/speeches/curriculum-exam-and-accountability-reform (accessed 14 July 2015).

Grace, G. (1987), 'Teachers and the State in Britain: A Changing Relation', in M. Lawn and G. Grace (eds), *Teachers: The Culture and Politics of Work*, Lewes: Falmer Press.

Green, A. (1990), *Education and State Formation: The Rise of Education Systems in England, France and the USA*, Basingstoke: Palgrave.

Green, A. (1997), 'Core Skills, General Education and Unification in Post-16 Education', in A. Hodgson and K. Spours (eds), *Dearing and Beyond: 14–19 Qualifications, Frameworks and Systems*, London: Kogan Page.

Green, F., R. Allen and A. Jenkins (2015), 'Are English Free Schools Socially Selective? A Quantitative Analysis', *British Educational Research Journal*, First Published Online 13 MAY: DOI: 10.1002/berj.3190.

Grek, S. (2009), 'Governing by Numbers: The PISA "Effect" in Europe', *Journal of Educational Policy*, 24(1): 23–37.

Guardian (2014), Free School to Be Put in Special Measures by Ofsted, *The Guardian*, 11 March. Available online: http://www.theguardian.com/education/2014/mar/11/free-school-ies-breckland-suffolk-special-measures-ofsted (accessed 10 October 2014).

Gunter, H. M., ed. (2011), *The State and Education Policy: The Academies Programme*, London: Continuum.

Gunter, H. M. and G. Forrester (2008a), 'New Labour and School Leadership 1997–2007', *British Journal of Educational Studies*, 56(2): 144–162.

Gunter, H. M. and G. Forrester (2008b), Knowledge Production in Educational Leadership (KPEL), Project. Final Report to the ESRC. RES-000-23–1192.

Gunter, H. M. and G. Forrester (2009), 'Institutionalised Governance: The Case of the National College for School Leadership', *International Journal of Public Administration*, 32: 349–369.

Gunter, H. M. and G. Forrester (2010), 'New Labour and the Logic of Practice in Educational Reform', *Critical Studies in Education*, 51(1): 55–69.

Hall, D. and C. Raffo (2009), 'New Labour and Breaking the Education and Poverty Link: A Conceptual Account of Its Educational Policies', in C. Chapman and H. M. Gunter (eds), *Radical Reforms – Perspectives on an Era of Educational Change*, 155–168, Abingdon, Oxen: Routledge.

Halpin, D. and B. Troyna (1995), 'The Politics of Education Policy Borrowing', *Comparative Education*, 31(3): 303–310.

Hand, M. and J. Pearce (2009), 'Patriotism in British Schools: Principles, Practices and Press Hysteria', *Educational Philosophy and Theory*, 41(4): 453–465.

Hansard (1870), *Hansard's Parliamentary Debates (Third Series: Vol. CC. 16 March to 29 April 1870, Second Volume of the Session)*, London: Cornelius Buck.

Hansard (1993), 'Family Support' (HC Deb 06 December, Vol. 234 CC. 1–3). Available online: http://hansard.millbanksystems.com/commons/1993/dec/06/family-support (accessed 25 Aug 2015).

Harris, A. and C. Chapman (2004), 'Towards Differentiated Improvement for Schools in Challenging Circumstances', *British Journal of Educational Studies*, 52(4): 417–431.

Hartley, D. (2003), 'New Economy, New Pedagogy?' *Oxford Review of Education*, 29(1): 81–94.

Harvey, D. (1990), *The Condition of Postmodernity: An Enquiry into the Conditions of Cultural Change*, Oxford: Blackwell.

Harvey, D. (1993), 'Class Relations, Social Justice and the Politics of Difference', in J. Squires (ed.), *Principled Positions: Postmodernism and the Rediscovery of Value*, 85–120, London: Lawrence and Wishart.

Harvey, D. (2010), *The Enigma of Capital and the Crises of Capitalism*, Cambridge: Polity Press.

Hatcher, R. (2011), 'The Conservative-Liberal Democrat Coalition Government's "Free Schools" in England', *Educational Review*, 63(4): 485–503.

Held, D., A. McGrew, D. Goldblatt and J. Perraton (1999), *Global Transformations*, Cambridge: Polity Press.

Helle, L. and K. Klemelä (2010), 'Like a Rolling Stone? Recent Trends in Finnish Upper Secondary Education', in D. S. Beckett (ed.), *Secondary Education in the 21st Century*, New York: Nova Science Publishers, Inc.

Henkel, M. (2000), *Academic Identities and Policy Change in Higher Education*, London: Jessica Kingsley.

Henry, M., B. Lingard, F. Rizvi and S. Taylor (2008), *The OECD, Globalisation and Education Policy*, Bingley, UK: Emerald Group Publishing Ltd.

High Fliers Research (2015), *The Graduate Market in 2015*, London: High Fliers Research Ltd.

Higham, R. (2014), 'Free Schools in the Big Society: The Motivations, Aims and Demography of Free School Proposers', *Journal of Education Policy*, 29(1): 122–139.

Higher Education Funding Council for England (HEFCE) (2004), *Widening Participation and Fairer Access Research Strategy*, Bristol: HEFCE.

HM Government (1994) *White Paper – Competitiveness: Helping Business to Win*. London: HMSO.

HM Government (2013), *More Affordable Childcare*. DFE-00025-2013, London: DfE

HM Treasury (2003), *Every Child Matters* (Cm. 5860), Norwich: TSO.

HM Treasury (2004), *2004 Spending Review. New Public Spending Plans 2005–2008* (Cm 6237), Norwich: The Stationery Office.

Hodgson, A. and K. Spours (1997), 'From the 1991 White Paper to the Dearing Report: A Conceptual and Historical Framework for the 1990s', in A. Hodgson and K. Spours (eds), *Dearing and Beyond 14–19 Qualifications, Frameworks and Systems*, London: Kogan Page, 4–24.

Hodgson, A. and K. Spours (1999), *New Labour's Educational Agenda. Issues and Policies for Education and Training from 14+*, London: Kogan Page.

Hodgson, A. and K. Spours (2002), 'Key Skills for All? The Key Skills Qualification and Curriculum 2000', *Journal of Education Policy*, 17(1): 29–47.

Hodgson, A. and K. Spours (2006), 'An Analytical Framework for Policy Engagement: The Contested Case of 14–19 Reform in England', *Journal of Education Policy*, 21(6): 679–696.

Hodkinson, A. (2015), *Key Issues in Special Educational Needs and Inclusion*, London: Sage.

Hodkinson, P. and A. Sparkes (1995), 'Markets and Vouchers: The Inadequacy of Individualist Policies for Vocational Education and Training in England and Wales', *Journal of Education Policy*, 10(2): 189–207.

Hoffman, J. (2004), *Citizenship beyond the State*, London: Sage.

Home Office (2001a), '*Community Cohesion': A Report of the Independent Review Team (Cantle Report)*, London: Home Office.

Home Office (2001b), *The Report of the Ministerial Group on Public Order and Community Cohesion (Denham Report)*, London: Home Office.

Home Office (2002), *Secure Borders, Safe Haven: Integration with Diversity in Modern Britain*, London: Home Office.

Home Office (2005), *Life in the United Kingdom: A Journey to Citizenship*, London: TSO.

Hood, C. (1995), 'Contemporary Public Management: A New Global Paradigm?' *Public Policy and Administration*, 10(2): 104–117.

House of Commons (1986), *Achievement in Primary Schools: Third Report from the Education, Science and Arts Committee Session 1985–86*, Vol. 1, London: HMSO.

House of Commons (2011), *The Big Society*, HC902-1, London: TSO.

House of Commons (2014), *Committee of Public Accounts. Establishing Free Schools. Fifty-sixth Report of Session 2013–14*, HC941, London: The Stationery Office Limited.

Hurst, G. (2015), 'Future Tense for Tories as Return of the Grammar Reopens Wounds', *The Times*, 15 October: 8–9.

Hurst, P. (1981), 'Aid and Educational Development: Rhetoric and Reality', *Comparative Education*, 17(2): 117–125.

Illich, I. (1971), *Deschooling Society*, London: Calder and Boyers.

Illich, I. and E. Verne (1976), *Imprisoned in the Global Classroom*, London: Writers and Readers Publishing Cooperative.

Independent (2013), '85 Applicants – or more – per Graduate Job', *The Independent*, 10 July. Available online: http://www.independent.co.uk/student/news/85-applicants-or-more-per-graduate-job-8699943.html (accessed 7 March 2015).

James, M. (2012), 'For the Record' – Some (Lesser-Known) Factual Background to the Work of the Expert Panel for the National Curriculum Review in England 2010–2012. 11 June. Available online: www.bera.ac.uk (accessed 16 September 2015).

Jarvis, P. (2000), 'The Changing University: Meeting a Need and Needing to Change', *Higher Education Quarterly*, 54(1): 43–67.

Jerome, L. (2009), 'New Labour, New Citizens: Citizenship Education as the Creation of "Model" Citizens', Paper presented at Liverpool John Moores University, in the 'Working with Young People and Children' Seminar Series, 24 April, in Liverpool.

Jessop, B. (2002), *The Future of the Capitalist State*, Cambridge: Polity Press.

Johnson, N. (1990), *Reconstructing the Welfare State. A Decade of Change 1980–1990*, London: Harvester Wheatsheaf.

Johnson, P. (2004), 'Education Policy in England', *Oxford Review of Economic Policy*, 20(2): 173–197.

Johnson, R. and D. Steinberg (2004), 'Distinctiveness and Difference within New Labour', in D. Steinberg and R. Johnson (eds), *Blairism and the War of Persuasion*, London: Lawrence & Wishart.

Jones, G. E. (1992), 'Education in Wales: A Different "Great Debate"?', in M. Williams, R. Daugherty and F. Banks (eds), *Continuing the Education Debate*, London: Cassell.

Jones, K. (1991), *The Making of Social Policy in Britain: 1830–1990*, London: The Athlone Press.

Jones, K. (2003), *Education in Britain: 1944 to the Present*, Cambridge: Polity Press.

Jones, N. (1999), *Sultans of Spin*, London: Victor Gollancz.

Jones, P. W. (1988), *International Policies for Third World Education: UNESCO, Literacy and Development*, London and New York: Routledge.

Jupp, V. (2006), 'Documents and Critical Research', in R. Sapsford and V. Jupp (eds), *Data Collection and Analysis* 2nd edn, London: Sage Publications Ltd, 272–290.

Keating, A., A. Green and J. G. Janmaat (2015), 'Young Adults and Politics Today: Disengaged and Disaffected or Engaged and Enraged? The Latest Findings from the Citizenship Education Longitudinal Study (CELS). *LLAKES Research Brief*. UCL Institute of Education. Available online: http://www.llakes.ac.uk/sites/llakes.ac.uk/files/LLAKES%20young%20people%20and%20politics%20briefing%20paper.pdf (accessed 16 September 2015).

Keay, D. (1987), 'Aids, Education and the Year 2000!' *Women's Own*, 31 October: 8–10.

Keddie, A. (2014), 'It's like Spiderman … with Great Power Comes Great Responsibility': School Autonomy, School Context and the Audit Culture, *School Leadership & Management*, 34(5): 502–517.

Keep, E. (2005), 'Reflections on the Curious Absence of Employers, Labour Market Incentives and Labour Market Regulation in English 14–19 Policy: First Signs of a Change in Direction?' *Journal of Education Policy*, 20(5): 533–553.

Keep, E. and K. Mayhew (2004), 'The Economic and Distributional Implications of Current Policies on Higher Education', *Oxford Review of Economic Policy*, 20(2): 298–314.

King, D. S. (1987), *The New Right: Politics, Markets and Citizenship*, London: Macmillan.

Kingdon, Z. and J. Gourd, eds (2013), *Early Years Policy: The Impact on Practice*, Abingdon, Oxon: Routledge.

Kiwan, D. (2008), *Education for Inclusive Citizenship*, London: Routledge.

Kymlicka, W. (1995), *Multicultural Citizenship*, Oxford: Oxford University Press.

Kymlicka, W. (2002), *Contemporary Political Philosophy*, Oxford: Oxford University Press.

Lauder, H., P. Brown, J. A. Dillabough and A. H. Halsey, eds (2006), *Education, Globalization and Social Change*, Oxford: Oxford University Press.

Lawton, D. (1980), *The Politics of the School Curriculum*, London: Routledge and Kegan Paul.

Leaton Gray, S. (2006), *Teachers under Siege*, Stoke-on-Trent: Trentham Books.

Legge, K. (1995), *Human Resource Management – Rhetorics and Realities*, Basingstoke: Macmillan Business.

Le Grand, J. (1998), 'The Third Way Begins with CORA', *New Statesman*, 6 March: 26–27.

Le Grand, J. and W. Bartlett, eds (1997), *Quasi-Markets and Social Policy*, London: Macmillan.

Leitch, S. (2006), *Prosperity for All in the Global Economy – World Class Skills. Final Report of the Leitch Review of Skills*, London: HMSO/HM Treasury.

Leonard, P. (1997), *Postmodern Welfare: Reconstructing an Emancipatory Project*, London: Sage.

Letch, R. (2000), 'Special Educational Need and Inclusion', in J. Docking (ed.), *New Labour's Policies for Schools. Raising the Standard?* 105–118, London: David Fulton Publishers.

Levacic, R. (1995), *Local Management of Schools: Analysis and Practice*, Milton Keynes: Open University Press.

Levitas, R. (1998), *The Inclusive Society? Social Exclusion and New Labour*, Basingstoke: Palgrave.

Lewis, J. (2011), 'From Sure Start to Children's Centres: An Analysis of Policy Change in English Early Years Programmes', *Journal of Social Policy*, 40(1): 71–88.

Lewis, P., J. Vasagar, R. Williams and M. Taylor (2010), 'Student Protest over Fees Turns Violent', *The Guardian*, 10 November. Available online: http://www.theguardian.com/education/2010/nov/10/student-protest-fees-violen t (accessed 28 May 2015).

Lloyd, E. (2015), 'Early Childhood Education and Care Policy in England under the Coalition Government', *London Review of Education*, 13(2): 144–156.

Londinium (2008), 'MPs Demand Tighter Immigration Controls', *The London Echo – Politics News for London*, 22 October. Available online: www.londonecho.com/20081022363/mps-demand-tighter-immigration-controls.html (accessed 18 August 2009).

Lowe, R. (1993), *The Welfare State in Britain since 1945*, Basingstoke: Macmillan.

Lumby, J. and D. Muijs (2014), 'Corrupt Language, Corrupt Thought: The White Paper "The Importance of Teaching"', *British Educational Research Journal*, 40(3): 523–538.

Lupton, R. and S. Thomson (2015a), 'The Coalition's Record on Schools: Policy, Spending and Outcomes 2010–2015', *Social Policy in a Cold Climate Series, Working Paper 13*, January, London: Centre for Analysis of Social Exclusion, LSE.

Lupton, R. and S. Thomson (2015b), 'Socio-economic Inequalities in English Schooling under the Coalition Government 2010–15', *London Review of Education*, 13(2): 1–17.

Lupton, R., L. Unwin and S. Thomson (2015), 'The Coalition's Record on Further and Higher Education and Skills: Policy, Spending and Outcomes 2010–2015', *Social Policy in a Cold Climate Series, Working Paper 14*, January, London: Centre for Analysis of Social Exclusion, LSE.

McGillivray, G. (2007), 'England', in M. M. Clark and T. Waller (eds), *Early Childhood Education and Care: Policy and Practice*, 19–50, London: Sage.

McGrew, A. (1992), 'A Global Society?' in S. Hall, D. Held and T. McGrew (eds), *Modernity and Its Futures*, 61–102, Cambridge: Polity Press.

Maguire, M. (1996), 'In the Prime of Their Lives? Older Women in Higher Education', in L. Morley and V. Walsh (eds), *Breaking Boundaries: Women in Higher Education*, London: Taylor & Francis Ltd, 24–36.

Mahony, P., I. Hextall and I. Menter (2002), 'Threshold Assessment: Another Peculiarity of the English or More McDonaldisation?' *International Studies in Sociology of Education*, 12(2): 145–168.

Malik, S. and A. McGettigan (2014), 'Thousands of "Fake" Students at UK's New Higher Education Colleges', *The Guardian*, 2 December. Available online: http://www.theguardian.com/education/2014/dec/02/students-private-higher-education-colleges-taxpayer-subsidy-benefits-nao-loans (accessed 28 May 2015).

Mason, D. (2000), *Race and Ethnicity in Modern Britain*, Oxford: Oxford University Press.

Mason, D. (2006), 'Ethnicity', in G. Payne (ed.), *Social Divisions*, 102–130, Basingstoke: Palgrave.

Mathers, S., H. Ranns, A. Karemaker, A. Moody, K. Sylva, J. Graham and I. Siraj-Blatchford (2011), *Evaluation of the Graduate Leader Fund Final Report*, Research Report DFE-RR144, London: DfE.

Maylor, U., B. Read, H. Mendick, A. Ross and N. Rollock (2007), *Diversity and Citizenship in the Curriculum: Research Review (Brief No RB819)*, London: DfES.

Meikle, J. (2011), 'English Defence League Filling Vacuum Left by Mainstream Parties, Says Report', *The Guardian*, 22 September. Available online: www.guardian.co.uk/world/2011/sep/22/far-right-doorstep-hearts-minds (accessed 23 September 2011).

Melhuish, E., J. Belsky and J. Barnes (2010), 'Evaluation and Value of Sure Start', *Arch Dis Child*, 95(3), 159–161.

Meyer, H. and A. Benavot, eds (2013), *PISA, Power and Policy: The Emergence of Global Educational Governance*, Oxford: Symposium Books.

Miles, R. (1993), *Racism after Race Relations*, London: Routledge.

Miliband, D. (2006), 'Choice and Voice in Personalised Learning', in Centre for Educational Research and Innovation (ed.), *Personalised Education*, Paris, France: OECD. Available online: www.oecd.org/dataoecd/50/41/41175554.pdf (accessed 20 May 2011).

Miller, D. (1999), *Principles of Social Justice*, Cambridge, MA: Cambridge University Press.

Miller, D. (2000), *Citizenship and National Identity*, Cambridge: Polity Press.

Mirza, H. S. (2007), 'Understanding the Multicultural Malaise'. Available online: www.multiverse.ac.uk/attachments/335aecf3-a096–438d-a121–608e86a8d2a5.pdf (accessed 8 September 2009).

Modood, T. (2007), *Multiculturalism*, Cambridge: Polity.

MoE (Ministry of Education) (1959), *15 to 18: Report of the Central Advisory Council for Education – England* (Vol. 1), London: HMSO.

Moore, R. (1984), 'Schooling and the World of Work', in I. Bates, J. Clarke, P. Cohen, D. Finn, R. Moore and P. Willis (eds), *Schooling for the Dole*, London: Macmillan, 65–103.

Moorse, L. (2015), 'Citizenship in the National Curriculum', in L. Geron (ed.), *Learning to Teach Citizenship in the Secondary School: A Companion to School Experience*, 3rd edn, 30–52, Abingdon, Oxon: Routledge.

Morgan, N. (2015), Press Release: 'Free Schools Drive Social Justice', 22 May. Available online: https://www.gov.uk/government/news/free-schools-drive-social-justice-nicky-morgan (accessed 16 September 2015).

Morley, L. (2003), *Quality and Power in Higher Education*, Maidenhead: Open University Press.

Moser Report (1999), *Improving Literacy and Numeracy: A Fresh Start*, London: DfES.

Moss, P. (2014), 'Early Childhood Policy in England 1997–2013: Anatomy of a Missed Opportunity', *International Journal of Early Years Education*, 22(4): 346–358.

Moss, P. and H. Penn (1996), *Transforming Nursery Education*, London: Paul Chapman Publishing Ltd.

Mulholland, H. and J. Vasagar (2011), 'Willetts Forced on to Back Foot over Premium Rate University Places', *The Guardian*, 10 May. Available online: www.guardian.co.uk/education/2011/may/10/plan-rich-pay-extra-university-places-entrech-privilege (accessed 15 May 2011).

Mullard, C. (1973), *Black Britain*, London: Allen and Unwin.

Mundy, K. (1998), 'Educational Multilateralism and World (Dis)order', *Comparative Education Review*, 42(4): 448–478.

Munkhammar, J. (2007), 'How Choice Has Transformed Education in Sweden', *The Telegraph*, 25 May. Available online: http://www.telegraph.co.uk/news/1435386/How-choice-has-transformed-education-in-Sweden.html (accessed 10 October 2011).

Murray, R. (1989), 'Fordism and Post-Fordism', in S. Hall and M. Jacques (eds), *New Times: The Changing Face of Politics in the 1990s*, 38–53, London: Lawrence Wishart.

National College for School Leadership (NCSL) (2002), *Prime Minister Performs Official NCSL Opening*, NCSL Press Release, 25 October.

NCC (National Curriculum Council) (1990), *Curriculum Guidance 8 – Education for Citizenship*, York: NCC.

Neill, A. S. (1968), *Summerhill*, Harmondsworth: Penguin Books.

Norman, J. and J. Ganesh (2006), *Compassionate Conservatism. What It Is. Why We Need It*, London: Policy Exchange.

Norwich, B. (1994), 'Differentiation: From the Perspective of Resolving Tensions between Basic Social Values and Assumptions about Individual Differences', *Curriculum Studies*, 2(3), 289–308.

Nozick, R. (1974), *Anarchy, State and Utopia*, Oxford: Wiley-Blackwell.

Nussbaum, M. (2000), *Women and Human Development: The Capabilities Approach*, Cambridge: Cambridge University Press.

Nutbrown, C. (2012), *Foundations for Quality – The Independent Review of Early Education and Childcare Qualifications*, Final Report (Nutbrown Review), London: DfE.

Nutbrown, C. (2013), *Shaking the Foundations of Quality? Why 'Childcare' Policy Must Not Lead to Poor Quality Early Education and Care*, Sheffield: The University of Sheffield.

O'Neill, M. (1995), 'Introduction', in D. S. G. Carter and M. H. O'Neill (eds), *International Perspectives on Educational Reform and Policy Implementation*, 1–10, London: RoutledgeFalmer.

Oates, T. (2011), 'Could do Better: Using International Comparisons to Refine the National Curriculum in England', *The Curriculum Journal*, 22(2): 121–150.

Ofsted (Office for Standards in Education) (2004), *Special Educational Needs and Disability: Towards Inclusive Schools*, London: Ofsted.

Ofsted (Office for Standards in Education) (2005), *Primary National Strategy. An Evaluation of Its Impact in Primary Schools 2004/05*. Ref. HMI 2396, London: Ofsted.

Ofsted (Office for Standards in Education, Children's Services and Skills) (2015), *Apprenticeships: Developing Skills for Future Prosperity*, Reference no: 150129, Manchester: Ofsted.

Olssen, M. (2004), 'From the Crick Report to the Parekh Report: Multiculturalism, Cultural Difference and Democracy – the Re-visioning of Citizenship Education', *British Journal of Sociology of Education*, 25(2): 179–192.

Organisation for Economic Cooperation and Development (OECD) (2004), *Policy Brief: Lifelong Learning*, Paris: OECD.

Organisation for Economic Cooperation and Development (OECD) (2014), *PISA 2012 Results in Focus. What 15-Year-Olds Know and What They Can Do with What They Know*, Paris: OECD.

Osler, A. (2008), 'Citizenship Education and Ajegbo Report: Re-Imagining a Cosmopolitan Nation', *London Review of Education*, 6(1): 11–25.

Osler, A. (2009), 'Patriotism, Multiculturalism and Belonging: Political Discourse and the Teaching of History', *Educational Review*, 61(1): 85–100.

Osler, A. and H. Starkey (2001), 'Citizenship, Human Rights and Cultural Diversity', in A. Osler (ed.), *Citizenship and Democracy in Schools: Diversity, Identity and Equality*, 19–32, Stoke-on-Trent: Trentham.

Osler, A. and H. Starkey (2005), *Changing Citizenship – Democracy and Inclusion in Education*. Maidenhead, Berks: Open University Press.

Ozga, J. (1995), 'Deskilling a Profession: Professionalism, Deprofessionalism and the New Managerialism', in H. Busher and R. Saran (eds), *Managing Teachers as Professionals in Schools*, London: Kogan Page.

Ozga, J. (2000), *Policy Research in Educational Settings – Contested Terrain*, Buckingham: Open University Press.

Palaiologou, I. (2010), 'Policy Context in England and the Implementation of the Early Years Foundation Stage', in I. Palaiologou (ed.) *The Early Years Foundation Stage. Theory and Practice*, London: Sage.

Pantazis, C. and S. Pemberton (2009), 'From the "Old" to the "New" Suspect Community – Examining the Impacts of Recent Counter-terrorist Legislation', *The British Journal of Criminology*, 49: 646–666.

Paton, G. (2011), 'Graduate Gloom as 83 Students Apply for Every Vacancy', *The Telegraph*, 28 June. Available online: www.telegraph.co.uk/education/8602101/Graduate-gloom-as-83-students-apply-for-every-vacancy.html (accessed 28 June 2011).

Patterson, S. (1963), *Dark Strangers: A Study of West Indians in London*, Harmondsworth: Penguin.

Phillips, A. (1997), 'From Inequality to Difference: A Severe Case of Displacement', *New Left Review*, 224: 143–153.

Phillips, D. (2011), *The German Example. English Interest in Educational Provision in Germany since 1800*, London: Continuum.

Phillips, R. and J. Furlong, eds (2001), *Education, Reform and the State – Twenty-five Years of Politics, Policy and Practice*, London: RoutledgeFalmer.

Piore, D. and Sabel, C. (1984), *The Second Industrial Divide*, New York: Basic Books.

Pollard, A., ed. (1996), *Readings for Reflective Teaching in the Primary School*, London: Cassell.

Pollard, A., P. Broadfoot, P. Croll, M. Osborn and D. Abbott (1994), *Changing English Primary Schools? The Impact of the Education Reform Act at Key Stage 1*, London: Cassell.

Pollitt, C. (1993), *Managerialism and the Public Services: Cuts or Cultural Change in the 1990s?* 2nd edn, Oxford: Blackwell Business.

Prime Minister's Office (2015), Queen's Speech 2015. Press Office, Prime Minister's Office, London, 27 May. Available online: https://www.gov.uk/government/uploads/system/uploads/attachment_data/file/430149/QS_lobby_pack_FINAL_NEW_2.pdf (accessed 3 June 2015).

Pring, R. (1986), 'Privatisation of Education', in R. Rogers (ed.), *Education and Social Class*, Lewes: Falmer Press, 65–82.

Pring, R. (1992), 'Liberal Education and Vocational Preparation', in M. Williams, R. Daugherty and F. Banks (eds), *Continuing the Education Debate*, London: Cassell, 54–64.

Pring, R. (2004), *Philosophy of Education*, London: Continuum.

Pring, R. (2005), 'Labour Government Policy 14–19', *Oxford Review of Education*, 31(1): 71–85.

Prison Reform Trust (2011), 'Build the Big Society Behind Bars', *Prison Reform Trust Online*, 16 May. Available online: www.prisonreformtrust.org.uk/PressPolicy/News/vw/1/ItemID/129 (accessed 27 May 2011).

Pykett, J. (2007), 'Making Citizens Governable? The Crick Report as Governmental Technology', *Journal of Education Policy*, 22(3): 301–319.

Pyper, D. (2015), *Flexible Working*. Briefing Paper, Number 01086, London: House of Commons.

QCA (Qualifications and Curriculum Authority) (1998a), *Education for Citizenship and the Teaching of Democracy in Schools (Crick Report)*, London: QCA.

QCA (Qualifications and Curriculum Authority) (1999a), *Citizenship*, London: QCA.

QCA (Qualifications and Curriculum Authority) (1999b), *The Review of the Desirable Outcomes for Children's Learning on Entering Compulsory Education*, London: QCA.

QCA (Qualifications and Curriculum Authority) (1999c), *Early Learning Goals*, London: QCA.

QCA (Qualifications and Curriculum Authority) (2000), *Curriculum Guidance for the Foundation Stage*, London: QCA.

QCA (Qualifications and Curriculum Authority) (2001), *Planning for Learning in the Foundation Stage*, London: QCA.

QCA (Qualifications and Curriculum Authority) (2008), *The Early Years Foundation Stage Profile Handbook*, London: Qualifications and Curriculum Authority.

Raffe, D., C. Howieson, K. Spours and M. Young (1998), 'The Unification of Post-compulsory Education: Towards a Conceptual Framework', *British Journal of Educational Studies*, 46(2): 169–187.

Rafferty, F. and N. Barnard (1998), 'Blair Warns Teachers Not to Resist Reforms', *Times Educational Supplement*, 2 October: 8.

Randall, V. (2000), *The Politics of Child Daycare in Britain*, Oxford: Oxford University Press.

Ranson, S. (1993), 'Markets or Democracy for Education', *British Journal of Educational Studies*, 41(4): 333–352.

Ranson, S. (1994), *Towards a Learning Society*, London: Continuum.

Rawls, J. (1999), *A Theory of Justice*, 2nd edn, Oxford: Oxford University Press.

Rentoul, J. (1990), 'Individualism', in R. Jowell, S. Witherspoon and L. Brook (eds), *British Social Attitudes – The Seventh Report*, Aldershot: Gower.

Resnik, J. (2006), 'International Organizations, the "Education-economic Growth" Black Box and the Development of World Education Culture', *Comparative Education Review*, 50(2): 173–195.

Rex, J. and R. Moore (1967), *Race Community and Conflict*, London: Oxford University Press.

Reynolds, D. (1986), *School Effectiveness*, London: Falmer Press.

Richards, C. (1999), *Primary Education – At a Hinge of History?* London: Falmer Press.

Richardson, H. (2011), 'Many Children's Centres "Under Threat of Closure"', *BBC News*, 14 January. Available online: http://www.bbc.co.uk/news/education-12182994 (accessed 27 July 2015).

Ritzer, G. F. (2008), *The McDonaldization of Society 5*, Thousand Oaks, CA: Pine Forge Press.

Rizvi, F. (2000), 'International Education and the Production of Global Imagination', in N. C. Burbules and C. A. Torres (eds), *Globalisation and Education: Critical Perspectives*, 205–225, London: Routledge.

Rizvi, F. (2004), 'Debating Globalization and Education after September 11', *Comparative Education*, 40(2): 157–171.

Rizvi, F. (2009), 'International Perspectives on Social Justice and Education', in W. Ayers, T. Quinn and D. Stovall (eds), *Handbook of Social Justice in Education*, 91–94, Abingdon, Oxon: Routledge.

Roberts-Holmes, G. (2012), '"It's the Bread and Butter of Our Practice": Experiencing the Early Years Foundation Stage', *International Journal of Early Years Education*, 20(1): 30–42.

Roberts-Holmes, G. (2015), 'The "Datafication" of Early Years Pedagogy: "If the Teaching is good, the Data should be good and if there's Bad Teaching, there is Bad Data"', *Journal of Education Policy*, 30(3): 302–315.

Robertson, R. (1992), *Globalization: Social Theory and Global Culture*, London: Sage.

Robertson, R. (1995), 'Glocalization: Time-Space and Homogeneity-Heterogeneity', in M. Featherstone, S. Lash and R. Robertson (eds), *Global Modernities*, 25–44, London: Sage.

Robertson, R. (2005), 'Re-imagining and Re-scripting the Future of Education: Global Knowledge Economy Discourses and the Challenge to Education Systems', *Comparative Education*, 41(2): 151–170.

Robins, Lord (1963) *Higher Education, Report of the Committee on Higher Education*, Cmnd 2154, London: HMSO.

Roche, J. and S. A. Tucker (2007), 'Every Child Matters: "Tinkering" or "Reforming" – An Analysis of the Development of the Children Act (2004) from an Educational Perspective', *Education 3-13: International Journal of Primary, Elementary and Early Years Education*, 35(3): 213–223.

Rose, J. (2006), *Independent Review of the Teaching of Early Reading, Final Report*, Nottingham: DfES Publications.

Rosenau, J., ed. (1992), *Governance without Government: Order and Change in World Politics*, Cambridge: Cambridge University Press.

Rosenau, J. and J. P. Singh, eds (2002), *Information Technologies and Global Politics: The Changing Scope of Power and Governance*, Albany, NY: State University of New York Press.

Rothenberg, L. (2003), 'The Three Tensions of Globalisation', *Issues in Global Education*, 175: 3–6.

Rowan, P. (1997), 'From One Extreme to the Other', *TES Magazine*, 25 April. Available online: www.tes.co.uk/article.aspx?storycode=47075 (accessed 21 April 2011).

Rowley, E. (2010), 'UK's Total Debt Forecast to Hit £10 Trillion by 2015', *The Telegraph*, 9 November. Available online: www.telegraph.co.uk/finance/economics/8118467/UKs-total-debt-forecast-to-hit-10-trillion-by-2015.html (accessed 24 June 2011).

Rumbold Report (1990), *Starting with Quality. The Report of the Committee of Inquiry into the Quality of the Educational Experience Offered to Three and Four Year Olds*, London: Her Majesty's Stationery Office.

Sabur, R. (2013), 'Student Protests: A Day of Action in London', *The Telegraph*, 11 December. Available online: http://www.telegraph.co.uk/education/universityeducation/student-life/10511957/Student-protests-a-day-of-action-in-London.html (accessed 28 May 2015).

Sahlberg, P. (2013), 'The PISA 2012 Scores Show the Failure of "Market Based" Education Reform', *The Guardian*, 8 December. Available online: http://www.theguardian.com/commentisfree/2013/dec/08/pisa-education-test-scores-meaning (accessed 7 March 2015).

SCAA (School Curriculum and Assessment Authority) (1996), *Nursery Education: Desirable Outcomes for Children's Learning on Entering Compulsory Education*, London: DfEE/SCAA.

Scott, P. (2011), 'The White Paper Is a Mess. It Does Not Do What It Says on the Tin', *Education Guardian*, 5 July: 2.

Scott, P. (2014), 'The Coalition Government's Reform of Higher Education: Policy Formation and Political Process', in C. Callender and P. Scott (eds), *Browne and Beyond. Modernizing English Higher Education*, 32–56, London: Bedford Way Papers, Institute of Education Press.

Scottish Office (1997), *A Curriculum Framework for Children in Their Pre-School Year*, Edinburgh: The Scottish Office.

Scottish Office (1998), *Meeting the Childcare Challenge – A Childcare Strategy for Scotland* Cm 3958, London: The Stationery Office.

Scruton, R. (1980), *The Meaning of Conservatism*, Harmondsworth: Penguin.

Sellgren, K. (2013), For-profit College Gains Full University Status, *BBC News*, 8 August. Available online: http://www.bbc.co.uk/news/education-23605046 (accessed 28 May 2015).

Sen, A. (1992), *Inequality Re-examined*, Oxford: Oxford University Press.

Sen, A. (1999), *Development as Freedom*, Oxford: Oxford University Press.

Shepherd, J. (2009), 'Tories Pledge to Make Schools "Engines of Social Change"', *The Guardian*, 6 November. Available online: www.guardian.co.uk/politics/2009/nov/06/tories-michael-gove-education (accessed 1 June 2011).

Shepherd, J. (2010), 'Swedish-Style "Free Schools Won't Improve Standards"', *The Guardian*, 9 February. Available online: http://www.theguardian.com/education/2010/feb/09/swedish-style-schools-wont-raise-standards (accessed 10 October 2012).

Shepherd, J. (2011), 'Private University BPP Launches Bid to Run 10 Publicly Funded Counterparts', *The Guardian*, 21 June. Available online: www.guardian.co.uk/education/2011/jun/21/bpp-private-bid-run-public-universities (accessed 28 June 2011).

Silver, H. (1990), *Education, Change and the Policy Process*, London: The Falmer Press.

Simmons, R. (2013), '"Sorry to Have Kept You Waiting So Long, Mr Macfarlane": Further Education after the Coalition', in M. Allen and P. Ainley (eds), *Education Beyond the Coalition: Reclaiming the Agenda*, 82–105, London: Radicaled Books.

Simon, B. (1967), *Education and the Labour Movement 1870–1920*, London: Lawrence and Wishart.

Simon, B. (1991), *Education and the Social Order – British Education since 1944*, London: Lawrence and Wishart.

Smithers, A. (2015), 'The Coalition and Society (II): Education', in A. Seldon and M. Finn (eds), *The Coalition Effect, 2010–2015*, 257–289, Cambridge: Cambridge University Press.

Smithers, R. (2002), 'Government Fails to Meet Targets for 11-year-olds', *The Guardian*, 27 September. Available online: www.guardian.co.uk/politics/2002/sep/27/uk.schools?INTCMP=SRCH (accessed 7 March 2011).

Sparrow, A. (2011), 'Cameron Attacks "State Multiculturalism"', *The Guardian*, 26 February. Available online: www.guardian.co.uk/politics/2008/feb/26/conservatives.race (accessed 3 March 2011).

Speaker's Commission on Citizenship (1990), *Encouraging Citizenship: Report of the Commission on Citizenship*, London: HMSO.

Spear, C. E. (1999), 'The Changing Pressures on Primary Schools', in C. Chitty and J. Dunford (eds), *State Schools – New Labour and the Conservative Legacy*, London: Woburn Press.

Spours, K. (1995), *Issues of Post-16 Participation, Attainment and Progression, Working Paper No 17, Post-16*, Education Centre, London: London University Institute of Education.

Spours, K. (1997), 'GNVQs and the Future of Broad Vocational Qualifications', in A. Hodgson and K. Spours (eds), *Dearing and Beyond 14–19 Qualifications, Frameworks and Systems*, London: Kogan Page, 57–74.

Staggs, L. (2012), 'The Rhetoric and Reality of a National Strategy for Early Education and Assessment', in L. Miller and D. Hevey (eds), *Policy Issues in the Early Years*, 139–153, London: Sage.

Steiner, R. ([1907] 1996), *The Education of the Child*, London: Steiner Books.

Stewart, W. (2012), '"Financial Malpractice Rife in Schools", says Council', *TES Magazine*, 31 August. Available online: https://www.tes.com/article.aspx?storycode=6287760 (accessed 12 October 2012).

Stewart, W. and H. Ward (2012), 'Experts Wanted to Quit Curriculum Panel over "Prescriptive" Proposals'. *Times Educational Supplement*, 22 June. Available online: https://www.tes.com/article.aspx?storycode=6257908 (accessed 16 September 2015).

Stiglitz, J. (2002), *Globalization and Its Discontents*, London: Penguin Books.

Straw, J. (2007), 'We Need a British Story – Nationality Should Not Require Individuals to Give up Distinctive Cultural Attributes', *The Sunday Times*, 29 April. Available online: www.timesonline.co.uk/tol/comment/columnists/guest_contributors/article1720 (accessed 23 July 2009).

Stronach, I. (1988), 'Vocationalism and Economic Recovery: The Case against Witchcraft', in S. Brown and R. Wake (eds), *Education in Transition*, Edinburgh: Scottish Council for Research in Education, 55–70.

Sullivan, M. (1992), *The Politics of Social Policy*, Hemel Hempstead: Harvester Wheatsheaf.

Sullivan, M. (1994), *Modern Social Policy*, Hemel Hempstead: Harvester Wheatsheaf.

Sylva, K. (1994), 'The Impact of Early Learning on Children's Later Development', in C. Ball (ed.), *Start Right: The Importance of Early Learning* (Appendix C), London: Royal Society for the Encouragement of Arts, Manufactures and Commerce, 84–96.

Sylva, K., E. Melhuish, P. Sammons, I. Siraj-Blatchford and B. Taggart (2004), *Technical Paper 12. The Final Report: Effective Pre-School Education*, London: The Institute of Education.

Tan, J. and S. Gopinathan (2000), 'Education Reform in Singapore: Towards Greater Creativity and Innovation?' *NIRA Review*, 7(3): 5–10.

Taylor, C. (1992), *Multiculturalism and 'The Politics of Recognition'*, Princeton: Princeton University Press.

Taylor, E. (2009), 'The Foundations of Critical Race Theory in Education: An Introduction', in E. Taylor, D. Gillborn and G. Ladson-Billings (eds), *Foundations of Critical Race Theory in Education*, 1–13, London: Routledge.

Taylor, M. (2014), 'Student Protest over Tuition Fees Ends in Scuffles with Police', *The Guardian*, 19 November. Available online: http://www.theguardian.com/education/2014/nov/19/student-protest-tuition-fees-scuffles-police (accessed 28 May 2015).

Teacher Training Agency (TTA) (1997), *Standards for the Award of Qualified Teacher Status*, London: Teacher Training Agency.

Teacher Training Agency (TTA) (1998a), *National Standards for SENCOs, Subject Leaders and Headteachers*, London: Teacher Training Agency.

Teacher Training Agency (TTA) (1998b), *National Standards for Headteachers*, London: Teacher Training Agency.

Teather, S. (2011), 'Families in the Foundation Years Education Written Statement – Made on 18th July'. Available online: http://www.theyworkforyou.com/wms/?id=2011-07-18a.72WS.0 (accessed 27 July 2015).

Telegraph (2005), 'Warnock U-turn on Special Schools', *The Telegraph*, 9 June. Available online: http://www.telegraph.co.uk/news/uknews/1491679/Warnock-U-turn-on-special-schools.html (accessed 25 May 2015).

Telegraph (2011), 'David Cameron Says Reform of Education Is the Only Way to Tackle Record Youth Unemployment', *The Telegraph*, 14 April. Available online: www.telegraph.co.uk/finance/economics/8447318/David-Cameron-says-reform-of-education-is-the-only-way-to-tackle-record-youth-unemployment.html (accessed 14 April 2011).

Temple, P. (2014), 'Aspects of UK Private Education', in C. Callender and P. Scott (eds), *Browne and Beyond. Modernizing English Higher Education*, 159–172, London: Bedford Way Papers, Institute of Education Press.

Temple, P. (2015), 'What has the Coalition Government Done for Higher Education?' *London Review of Education*, 13(2): 174–178.

Thrupp, M. and S. Tomlinson (2005), 'Introduction: Education Policy, Social Justice and "Complex Hope"', *British Educational Research Journal*, 31(5): 549–556.

Tickell, C. (2011), *The Early Years: Foundations for Life, Health and Learning. An Independent Report on the Early Years Foundation Stage to Her Majesty's Government*, London: DfE.

Toffler, A. (1990), *Powershift*, New York: Bantam.

Tomlinson, J. (1993), *The Control of Education*, London: Cassell.

Tomlinson, S. (2005), Education in a Post-Welfare Society, 2nd edn, Maidenhead, Berks: Open University Press.

Tomlinson, S. (2008), *Race and Education – Policy and Politics in Britain*, Maidenhead: Open University Press.

Trowler, P. (2003), *Education Policy*, 2nd edn, London: Routledge.

Troyna, B. (1993), *Racism and Education*, Buckingham: Open University Press.

TSO (The Stationery Office) (2002), *Nationality, Immigration and Asylum Act 2002*, London: TSO.

UCAS Analysis and Research (2015a), *Interim Assessment of UCAS Acceptances by Intended Entry Year, Country of Provider and Qualifications Held. (2015 Cycle, 4 Weeks after A Level Results)*: 24 September, Cheltenham, Gloucestershire: UCAS.

UCAS Analysis and Research (2015b) *UK Application Rates by Country, Region, Constituency, Sex, Age and Background. (2015 Cycle, January Deadline)*: 30 January, Cheltenham, Gloucestershire: UCAS.

UNESCO (United Nations Educational, Scientific and Cultural Organization) (1994), *The Salamanca Statement and Framework for Action*, Paris: UNESCO.

UNICEF (The United Nations Children's Fund) (1989), *United Nations Convention on the Rights of the Child*, London: UNICEF UK.

Vasagar, J. and Shepherd, J. (2011) 'UK Tuition Fees are Third Highest in Developed World, say OECD', *The Guardian*, 13 September. Available online: http://www.guardian.co.uk/education/2011/sep/13/uk-young-people-education-oecd (accessed 23 September 2011).

Walford, G. (2000), 'From City Technology Colleges to Sponsored Grant-Maintained Schools', *Oxford Review of Education*, 26(2): 145–158.

Walker, E. (2008), 'Are Degrees Worth the Paper They're Printed On?' *The Independent Higher*, 8 September. Available online: www.independent.co.uk/news/education/higher/are-degrees-worth-the-paper-theyre-printed-on-922410.html (accessed 15 April 2011).

Walker, M. (2008), 'Widening Participation; Widening Capability', *London Review of Education*, 6(3): 267–279.

Walker, M. and E. Unterhalter (2007), 'The Capability Approach: It's Potential for Work in Education', in M. Walker and E. Unterhalter (eds), *Amartya Sen's Capability Approach and Social Justice in Education*, 1–8, Basingstoke, Hampshire: Palgrave Macmillan.

Wallerstein, I. (2011), *Historical Capitalism with Capitalist Civilisation*, 3rd edn, London: Verso.

Warnock, M. (2010), 'Special Educational Needs: A New Look', in L. Terzi (ed.), *Special Educational Needs: A New Look*, 11–45, London: Bloomsbury Academic.

Watkins, K. and P. Fowler (2003), *Rigged Rules and Double Standards*, Oxford: Oxfam.

Watson, C. W. (2000), *Multiculturalism*, Buckingham: Open University Press.

Watson, D. (2014), 'Leading the British University Today: Your Fate in Whose Hands?' in C. Callender and P. Scott (eds), *Browne and Beyond. Modernizing English Higher Education*, 194–205, London: Bedford Way Papers, Institute of Education Press.

Weale, S. (2015), "It's a Political Failure": How Sweden's Celebrated Schools System Fell into Crisis", *The Guardian*, 10 June. Available online: http://www.theguardian.com/world/2015/jun/10/sweden-schools-crisis-political-failure-education (accessed 11 June 2015).

Webb, R. (1993), 'The National Curriculum and the Changing Nature of Topic Work', *The Curriculum Journal*, 4(2): 239–251.

Webb, R. and G. Vulliamy (1996), 'A Deluge of Directives: Conflict between Collegiality and Managerialism in the Post-ERA Primary School', *British Educational Research Journal*, 22(4): 441–458.

Webster, P. and J. O'Leary (1999), 'Teacher "Excuse Culture" Attacked by Blair', *The Times*, 21 October: 1.

Webster, R. and P. Blatchford (2015), 'Worlds Apart? The Nature and Quality of the Educational Experiences of Pupils with a Statement for Special Educational Needs in Mainstream Primary Schools', *British Educational Research Journal*, 41(2): 324–342.

Wedell, K. (1988), 'Special Educational Needs and the Education Reform Act', *FORUM*, 31(1): 19–21.

West, A. (2006), 'School Choice, Equity and Social Justice: The Case for More Control', *British Journal of Educational Studies*, 54(1): 15–33.

West, A. (2015), 'Education Policy and Governance in England under the Coalition Government (2010–15): Academies, the Pupil Premium, and Free Early Education', *London Review of Education*, 13(2): 21–36.

White, J. (1982), *The Aims of Education Restated*, London: Routledge.

Whitty, G. (1990), 'The New Right and the National Curriculum: State Control or Market Forces?', in M. Flude and M. Hammer (eds), *The Education Reform Act, 1988: Its Origins and Implications*, London: The Falmer Press, 21–36.

Whitty, G. (2001), 'Education, Social Class and Exclusion', *Journal of Education Policy*, 16(4): 287–295.

Whitty, G. (2014), 'Recent Developments in Teacher Training and Their Consequences for the "University Project" in Education', *Oxford Review of Education*, 40(4): 466–481.

Wiborg, S. (2010), 'Learning Lessons from the Swedish Model', *FORUM*, 52(3): 279–284.

Wilby, P. (2013), 'Don't Let Dubious Pisa League Tables Dictate How We Educate Our Children, *The Guardian*, 1 December. Available online: http://www.theguardian.com/commentisfree/2013/dec/01/dont-let-pisa-league-tables-dictate-schooling (accessed 4 August 2015).

Wilkinson, J. R. (1999), 'Pre-school Education in UK', in D. Matheson and I. Grosvenor (eds), *An Introduction to the Study of Education*, 42–58, London: David Fulton Publishers.

Willetts, D. (2013), 'David Willetts: Our Privately Funded University Revolution',
    The Telegraph, 24 July. Available online: http://www.telegraph.co.uk/education/
    universityeducation/10198076/David-Willetts-our-privately-funded-university-
    revolution.html (accessed 28 May 2015).

Williams, F. (1989), *Social Policy: A Critical Introduction*, Cambridge: Polity Press.

Williams, L. (2009), 'Globalisation of Education Policy: Its Effects on Developing
    Countries', in J. Zajda and V. Rust (eds), *Globalisation, Policy and Comparative
    Research – Discourses of Globalisation*, 77–92, London: Springer.

Williams, M., R. Daugherty and F. Banks, eds (1992), *Continuing the Education Debate*,
    London: Cassell.

Willms, J. D. and E. H. Echols (1992), 'Alert and Inert Clients: The Scottish Experience
    of Parental Choice of Schools', *Economics of Education Review*, 11(4): 339–350.

Wohlstetter, P. and L. Anderson (1994), 'What Can US Charter Schools Learn from
    England's Grant-maintained Schools?' *Phi Delta Kappan*, 75(February): 486–491.

Wolf, A. (2002), *Does Education Matter? Myths about Education and Economic Growth*,
    London: Penguin.

Wolf, A. (2004), 'Education and Economic Performance: Simplistic Theories and their
    Policy Consequences', *Oxford Review of Economic Policy*, 20(2): 315–333.

Wolf, A. (2007), 'Round and Round the Houses: The Leitch Review of Skills', *Local
    Economic*, 22(2): 111–117.

Wolf, A. (2011), *Review of Vocational Education – The Wolf Report*, London: DFE.

Wolf, A. (2015), *Heading for the Precipice: Can Further and Higher Education Funding
    Policies Be Sustained?* London: The Policy Institute at King's.

Wolf, A., A. Jenkins and A. Vignoles (2006), 'Certifying the Workforce: Economic
    Imperative or Failed Social Policy?' *Journal of Education Policy*, 21(5): 535–565.

Wolff, J. (2008), 'Social Justice and Public Policy: A View from Political Philosophy', in
    G. Craig, D. Gordon and T. Burchardt (eds), *Social Justice and Public Policy: Seeking
    Fairness in Diverse Societies*, 17–32, Bristol: Policy Press.

Woodhead, C. (2002), *Class War: The State of British Education*, London: Little, Brown
    & Company.

Woolcock, N. (2015), 'Boys Are Trading in University for an Apprenticeship', *The Times*,
    15 August: 13.

Working Group on 14–19 Reform (2004), *14–19 Curriculum and Qualifications Reform:
    Final Report of the Working Group*, London: DfES.

World Education Forum (2000), *The Dakar Framework for Action. Education for All:
    Meeting Our Collective Commitments*, Paris: UNESCO.

Wyse, D. and U. Goswami (2008), 'Synthetic Phonics and the Teaching of Reading',
    British Educational Research Journal, 34(6): 691–710.

Wyse, D., E. McCreery and H. Torrance (2008), *The Trajectory and Impact of National
    Reform: Curriculum and Assessment in English Primary Schools (Primary Review
    Research Survey 3/2)*, Cambridge: University of Cambridge Faculty of Education.

Yeatman, A. (1994), *Postmodern Revisionings of the Political*, New York: Routledge.

Yorke, M. (2009), 'Student Experience' Surveys: Some Methodological Considerations
    and an Empirical Investigation', *Assessment & Evaluation in Higher Education*, 34(6):
    721–739.

Yosso, T. (2005), 'Whose Culture Has Capital? A Critical Race Theory Discussion of Community Cultural Wealth', *Race, Ethnicity and Education*, 8(1): 69–91.

Young, I. M. (1990), *Justice and the Politics of Difference*, Princeton, NJ: Princeton University Press.

Young, I. M. (2004), 'The Ideal of Community and the Politics of Difference', in C. Farrelly (ed.), *Contemporary Political Theory*, 195–204, London: Sage.

Young, M. (1993), 'A Curriculum for the 21st Century? Towards a New Basis for Overcoming Academic/Vocational Divisions', *British Journal of Educational Studies*, XXXXI(3): 203–222.

Young, M. (1997), 'The Dearing Review of 16–19 Qualifications: A Step towards a Unified System?' in A. Hodgson and K. Spours (eds), *Dearing and Beyond: 14–19 Qualifications, Frameworks and Systems*, 25–39, London: Kogan Page.

Young, M. and T. Leney (1997), 'From A-levels to an Advanced Level Curriculum of the Future', in A. Hodgson and K. Spours (eds), *Dearing and Beyond 14–19 Qualifications, Frameworks and Systems*, 40–56, London: Kogan Page.

Zifcak, S. (1994), *New Managerialism: Administrative Reforms in Whitehall and Canberra*, Buckingham: Open University Press.

Index

Note: Locators with letter 'n' refer to notes.